Helen Franks is an a............ lished several books on health, the family, ageing and social issues, and has also contributed many articles on similar topics to newspapers and magazines.

Jacky Fleming is a best-selling cartoonist. Her books, *Be a Bloody Train Driver*, *Never Give Up*, *Falling in Love*, and *Dear Katie* are published by Penguin.

Also by Helen Franks

Prime Time
Goodbye Tarzan
Remarriage
Mummy Doesn't Live Here Any More
Bone Boosters *(with Diana Moran)*
Getting Older Slowly

HIDDEN FEARS

Self help for anxiety and phobias

Helen Franks

HEADLINE

Copyright © 1996 Helen Franks
Cartoons Copyright © 1996 Jacky Fleming

The right of Helen Franks to be identified as the Author of
the Work has been asserted by her in accordance with the
Copyright, Designs and Patents Act 1988.

First published in 1996
by HEADLINE BOOK PUBLISHING

10 9 8 7 6 5 4 3 2 1

All rights reserved. No part of this publication may be
reproduced, stored in a retrieval system, or transmitted,
in any form or by any means, without the prior written
permission of the publisher, nor be otherwise circulated
in any form of binding or cover other than that in which
it is published and without a similar condition being
imposed on the subsequent purchaser.

ISBN 0 7472 5345 5

Typeset by
Letterpart Limited, Reigate, Surrey

Printed and bound in Great Britain by
Cox & Wyman Ltd, Reading, Berks

HEADLINE BOOK PUBLISHING
A division of Hodder Headline PLC
338 Euston Road
London NW1 3BH

Contents

INTRODUCTION If You Have a Hidden Fear . . .   1

SECTION 1 What's Really Going On   5

1. How You Feel About Your Fears   7
2. How Fears Start and How They Grow   13

SECTION 2 The Basic De-Stress Programme   21

3. Ways to Overcome Panic Attacks   23
4. Getting Off the Anxiety Treadmill   31
5. Relaxation Really Works   35
6. Do-It-Yourself Massage   41
7. Give Yourself Positive Thinking Power   47
8. Exposing Yourself to the Fear   51
9. The Alternative Way – Herbal and Homeopathic   57

SECTION 3 Finding Freedom: Best Ways to Tackle Specific Fears   65

10. Getting Out of the House   67
11. Feeling Hemmed In   73
12. When You Suffer from Social Fears   79
13. Fear of Flying   91
14. Who's Afraid of the Big, Fast Motorway?   99
15. Insects, Animals and Objectionable Objects   103
16. Anything Medical   109

17.	Body Functions	117
18.	Obsessions and Compulsions	123
19.	Sexual Troubles	131
20.	After the Event – Post-Traumatic Stress	137

SECTION 4 Getting Help from Others — 141

21.	Making Connections: the Self-Help Group	143
22.	What Friends and Relations Can Do	147
23.	Professional Help	153
24.	Keeping up the Good Work	169

| Contacts and Addresses | 173 |
| Index | 177 |

If You Have a Hidden Fear...
...this is a book for you.

We all have fears which may, to other people, seem unjustified. A fear may be small or big, a minor anxiety, an everyday worry or a major aversion which is usually known as a phobia. If that fear, of whatever proportion, is something we feel we have to hide or is 'too silly' to talk about, one thing is sure – it hurts in some way.

The hurt comes from the fear itself, of course, and also the sense of shame or embarrassment or inadequacy that often goes with it. It's very hard to admit fear about things that other people do all the time or take for granted as harmless – such as eating out in restaurants, or going to a party, or travelling on public transport, or seeing spiders, or ambulances or some other unthreatening object or situation.

That's one part of the hurt. The other part comes from the uncomfortable sensations we have when we expose ourselves to whatever frightens us. Those uncomfortable sensations are panic. The mind goes blank, the heart beats faster, you feel faint or sick or trembly and weak. A big part of the fear is that you may think you will die or will lose control. You may be embarrassed and tongue-tied, or just plain terrified.

Fears can also turn into obsessions. This happens when some intense anxiety impels you to repeat certain activities as a reassurance that your world will not turn upside down.

Hidden fears can, at the least, spoil enjoyment and spontaneity, or at their worst seriously curtail ordinary activities. The first line of defence is to avoid things that cause unpleasant reactions, and even to avoid thinking about situations that have in the past been unpleasant or painful. This can work up to a point. You can avoid travelling by air if you hate flying, or make sure you use the stairs if you panic in a lift. The nuisance isn't that great. But small fears can grow if you keep up this avoidance game. They can end up dominating every activity, so the person who fears using a particular form of transport or encountering spiders may gradually withdraw from the outside world, perhaps in due course opting to stay at home in a comparatively danger-free environment.

That's the worst scenario. For most of us, living with an untold fear is an irritant we could do without. And yet, we don't have to live with it. There are a number of techniques that teach how we can distance ourselves from that fear and how we can learn to understand and control it. If you are reading these words now, you are on the path to liberation.

In the following pages you will find simple-to-follow techniques to make fears more manageable, and in time to eliminate them altogether. The techniques are effective for minor, occasional fears and social embarrassment, as well as for the more dominating or specific phobias. Some have been developed and recommended by psychologists to be used on a do-it-yourself basis. Others are adapted from the many different stress-relieving programmes used by alternative practitioners.

You will find many different kinds of fears explored in detail, and the techniques adapted to each type. There are special tips and suggestions to help you plan your programme in the best possible way and adapt them to different situations. There are case histories (the names have been changed), and there's advice to friends and relations to help them understand what's going on and how they can do the right things.

No single method will suit all people. A combination of some of the different self-help methods plus some professional help may be the best answer, so at the end of this book there is a comprehensive section on professional help available, and a list of useful contacts.

Always, with self help, there is the question of commitment. The programme that you follow must be taken seriously. Otherwise there is little point in doing it. You will have to give time and thought and effort to your fear and your new ways of coping with it. If you do the rewards will be great.

If You Have a Hidden Fear . . .

READ THIS BOOK AND YOU COULD CHANGE YOUR LIFE

oh no - I HATE change, it makes me panic

SECTION 1

What's Really Going On

CHAPTER 1

How You Feel About Your Fears

Beverly works in public relations. She's on the phone all day talking to clients, yet her friends complain that she never rings them. Beverly says she's often too tired in the evenings, but the truth is that picking up the phone just for a chat brings out unsettling feelings of insecurity and uncertainty in her. So she avoids doing it.

Brian is a successful architect. When he shows people his house, they admire the pale wood floors and concealed low-level lighting. He doesn't tell them that they have a hidden purpose. Brian is afraid of spiders and has designed his home lighting so that he can spot them easily.

Alan gets into a panic driving on motorways, and so always takes the 'scenic' routes. Ruth is terrified of dogs and tells everyone that she is allergic to them. Roy for a long time refused invitations as he became very anxious eating out in unfamiliar places. Hazel couldn't go into supermarkets on her own and let her family think she was too exhausted to shop. John has a secret fear of getting cancer.

These are normal, average people living otherwise normal, average lives. They hold down responsible jobs, bring up families, see their friends. They are you and me, and they – or many of them – have some hidden fear or worry or anxiety that they have to accommodate in their lives.

We all know when a fear is justified. If a serious illness is diagnosed, it is perfectly reasonable to be fearful of the future. Should we be exposed to some physical threat such as a fire, a fierce animal or a man brandishing a gun, we know how it would be to feel a proper sense of fear, and our instinct is to escape. But the anxiety brought on by the kinds of fears described here is not due to anything life-threatening. Even a fear of illness is less to do with the likelihood of contracting a disease and more to do with the *idea* of it.

Many fears, if you don't happen to share them, can seem ridiculously over the top. Irrational and intense fears can indeed verge on the absurd (rhubarb, buttons, false hair and Velcro are some of the more unusual phobias recorded). This makes it hard for people to talk about their fears, and it makes it difficult for friends or relatives to understand them.

Hidden fears are uncomfortable to live with, and bringing them out into the open is an important step towards eliminating them.

Here are the first words that will take you on the road to recovery:

YOU ARE NOT UNIQUE OR ALONE IN YOUR FEAR

A Liverpool psychoanalyst, Michael Whitenburgh, claims that 80 per cent of the population suffers from some form of phobia or hidden fear. Others put the figure at about 70 per cent. The fears do not seriously disrupt most people's lives. Only a small minority, about two or three in a thousand, go to the extreme lengths of self-imposed isolation to avoid their fear.

Nevertheless, most of us don't want to be stuck with a hidden fear, no matter how adept we become at organising our lives around it. So the first step to beating it is to know it, and you do that by asking yourself a seemingly simple question: *what exactly are you afraid of?*

This question is not always easy to answer. Ruth, who avoids dogs, got herself into such a state that she wasn't able to go out of the house, nowhere beyond the front door. Earlier, before the fear grew to such proportions, she could go down the street, but not to the park; or she could walk down certain streets but not others. Then she stopped going out altogether. 'I couldn't be sure that there'd be no dogs along the street,' she says. In time, she 'forgot' that she was frightened of dogs because the focus of her fear became the street outside her front door. She came to believe that she was agoraphobic, fearful of going to unfamiliar places, and joined a self-help group on the basis that this was her main problem. It took her several weeks for the penny to drop: if she overcame her fear of dogs, she wouldn't have to worry about going out.

John was in a state of continual anxiety because every physical twinge or pain made him think he had cancer. When he finally confessed to his doctor, they both agreed that John was suffering from a phobia – but in time, John began to realise that the diagnosis was not so clear. His father had died of cancer when John was a teenager, and now, in his thirties, John was experiencing fears which also brought back old, painful memories. He'd had a poor relationship with his father. His girlfriend had recently left him. He came to the conclusion that his problem was not solely related to phobia. He was also depressed, and needed treatment to help with this before he could deal with anything else.

It is not always possible to get to the bottom of a fear when you first begin to look it in the face, and 'complications' may be revealed as you get stronger and more confident, but it is useful to know that this may happen and to be prepared for a change of focus, regarding it as part of increased understanding. You may want to change your approach. You may have a cluster of fears – ranging round different kinds of social situations, or a mixture of fears that are seemingly unrelated. If you are not sure which you should focus on, the next chapter and later sections in this book dealing with specific fears may help you to clarify your priorities. If necessary write them down in order of importance. If you still feel uncertain or confused, then you may benefit from professional help.

Now let's see how you feel about your fears ...

- ★ Foolish
- ★ Ashamed
- ★ Inadequate
- ★ Crazy

- ★ Secretive
- ★ Self-conscious
- ★ Embarrassed
- ★ Misunderstood
- ★ Angry
- ★ Unloved
- ★ Isolated
- ★ Neglected
- ★ Attacked

These are just some of the words people use to describe how they feel about their fears and anxieties. You may have others – write them down, if you can, and tick the ones above that have meaning for you. This may be quite difficult to do, like making your secret thoughts public. But you are only making them public to yourself, and once you have acknowledged what you feel, you are on the way to gaining greater detachment.

What do other people think?
It's bad enough feeling vulnerable. It's even worse suspecting that if other people knew about your fears they'd only ridicule or dismiss them, or perhaps think you are unstable or disturbed. That's what makes it difficult to share fears – imagining what other people might be thinking. But hiding a fear makes it even harder to live with. Things can get out of proportion. You can end up feeling misunderstood or isolated or angry with the world at large.

Most people don't actually ridicule others to their faces, and are unlikely to do so behind their backs even if the fears seem strange. They might, it is true, criticise and misunderstand and be rather curious, but we risk that all the time as a consequence of most of our actions anyway. After all, don't you comment upon and criticise the actions and ideas of friends, even when you are basically in sympathy with them?

There are some people you would not trust, others for whom the knowledge would be inappropriate; but having chosen the people you can confide in, if you explain as simply and honestly as possible, and if you show that you have a problem and that you want to be rid of it, you are far more likely to be understood than you are when you try to disguise the problem. You may come to realise that your sense of isolation is self-imposed.

I'll see you up there — I need the exercise

but it's fifteen floors

The stigma surrounding phobias and anxiety certainly exists. The thought of being labelled 'mad' or 'insane' is humiliating and depressing. It is possible that even the most sympathetic relatives and friends can become exasperated at times, but these possible attitudes of others are often far less potent than self-blame. Here are two thoughts to remember:

YOU ARE LIKELY TO BE FAR MORE CRITICAL OF YOURSELF THAN OTHER PEOPLE ARE OF YOU

WHAT OTHER PEOPLE THINK OF YOU IS FAR LESS IMPORTANT THAN WHAT YOU THINK ABOUT YOURSELF

Why should we be so self-critical? One way of putting it is that we carry a fantasy about ourselves as being perfect. When we don't live up to this, we may hate ourselves and fear censure from others (and maybe hate them too). That's why we don't like making mistakes, and hate being criticised or having our mistakes exposed. It's why we don't like to lose in arguments or show our ignorance, and it's why sometimes we get an inflated sense of superiority when we are the winners of the argument.

Being tolerant towards our own 'inadequacies' helps take the sting out of them. Self-tolerance stops us being swept by a sense of shame or helplessness. Once we feel more comfortable with ourselves it becomes easier to talk more openly about our fears, and the terrible secret isn't so terrible (or secret) any more.

CHAPTER 2

How Fears Start and How They Grow

Nowadays, psychiatrists are not overly taken with the idea that intense fears in adults are always based on something nasty that happened to them in childhood. Since many people are mildly scared of spiders or flying or heights or any slightly unfamiliar situation, they take the view that there may be no special 'cause' that triggers a more severe fear, but that some people react more strongly than others.

Which people and why? Why, for instance, should Beverly, the woman in PR, need to avoid phoning friends, or Brian, the architect, go to such lengths to detect spiders?

The truth is that no one really knows. Some people just are more vulnerable to certain kinds of fears than others. There's some evidence to suggest that a genetic predisposition, in some cases, is the cause of the fear. Obsessive Compulsive Disorders, such as following endless rituals to promote cleanliness, may be inherited, but there are no fixed rules. Tidy, highly organised people are more likely than others to develop specific phobias such as a fear of spiders. Emotional, very sensitive, self-conscious people are more vulnerable to 'social' fears like using the telephone or going to unfamiliar restaurants. A single event in adult life or a series of life stresses can trigger a specific phobia.

Childhood is a normal time for intense fears. Some children become frightened of animals or insects, usually from about the age of two or three, but by eleven most have grown out of their fear. However, nervous, imaginative children who experience a typical childhood fear – of large dogs, perhaps, or 'creepy crawlies' or being in the dark – may carry their fear into adulthood, not necessarily because of a single bad experience but because of a kind of habit that has built up.

Alison, in her thirties, had a fear of balloons that went back to childhood. She remembers going to children's parties and hating the loud noise when they popped. She began to dread parties and as she grew up her dislike of loud noise spread to fireworks, and anything that made a sudden, unexpected bang. She could not recall any single, frightening incident during her childhood, though she remembers being a rather shy and timid child who was smaller than average and may have transferred her fear of larger, more outgoing children on to balloons.

Sometimes, parents transmit their own fears to their children. Being frightened of flying or eating in restaurants may have been picked up in childhood from nervous parents with a social fear who may have tried to reassure their children but nevertheless revealed their unease in a variety of subtle ways.

The changing fears and concerns in society at large also have an effect on children's fears. When over 1,000 seven to twelve-year-olds were interviewed in 1995 and compared with children twenty years earlier, it emerged that there is a fashion in fears. In 1975, these were the top fears in order of precedence:

★ Watching horror films
★ Being alone at night
★ Spiders
★ Bad dreams
★ People saying 'boo' suddenly
★ Ghost and murder stories
★ Dentists
★ Rats and mice
★ The dark
★ Being alone in the house

In 1995, the top ten were:

★ War
★ The dark

How Fears Start and How They Grow

- ★ Killing animals
- ★ Bullying
- ★ Bombs
- ★ Dying and being killed
- ★ Guns
- ★ Losing a parent or member of family
- ★ Spiders
- ★ Wild or fierce animals

Dentists have become more user-friendly, but fear of aggression and violence reflects the current ills and preoccupations of society, not least as portrayed in the media. Children can pick up these trends from films, television, comics.

Divorce and the break-up of families have become a normal part of children's experiences, incidents over which they have no control.

For adults, other threats lurk. The modern world is fast and often impersonal, dominated by technology. Fears about using telephones, flying, travelling in trains, entering lifts or driving on motorways have replaced older fears of the supernatural that haunted our ancestors.

Bullying is a common reason behind school phobia, but agoraphobia, fear of open spaces, is often linked with school phobia too. Fear of leaving home is an important factor here. Hidden anxieties about being abandoned by parents, or fear for a mother's safety (whether the mother is truly at risk or not) are typical reasons found for children not wanting to go to school. Again, the high incidence of divorce feeds into these fears.

Agoraphobia, one of the most common fears in women, can reveal a relationship of over-dependence, with the fearful, insecure child now grown into a housebound wife, and her over-protective husband sometimes unaware that he is encouraging her fear of going out of the house alone. Feminism, with its emphasis on women's assertiveness, can feed into this situation, creating a greater sense of failure in the stay-at-home wife and an unacknowledged sense of relief in a traditionally-minded husband.

In childhood or adulthood, severe fears can sometimes grow out of a single incident, and when they do, they are called Post-Traumatic Stress Disorders. A train crash, a fire, a car accident, a mugging can leave people feeling nervous, anxious and depressed for months and years afterwards. Debbie was assistant manager in a bank when she experienced a hold-up by a masked gunman. 'For months afterwards I kept finding the memory of the incident flashing into my mind. When I went into the bank, the images were so strong that I went to pieces. I couldn't work for months. I was knocked sideways about it because I've never before been one to over-react. I've always seen myself as a pretty tough person, but I've been told that this post-traumatic stress can hit you all the harder when you're like me. It has made me much more sympathetic about other people's fears.'

Check out your responses

Maybe you already know how your fear started and how it grew. If not, it may help to try to define it. Fears are usually broken down into different types. There are the social fears which involve being with or interacting with other people; the 'space' fears which include agoraphobia ('agora' is Greek for the market place), flying, going in lifts or trains; the physical fears, including illnesses and others connected with the body, and then there are the specific, singular fears like an abhorrence of spiders or dogs or roses or buttons. Here are some questions to help you define your fears.

Social fears

★ Do you blush easily?
★ Do you feel people are looking at you in public?
★ Do you fear you might do something silly or shocking in public?
★ Do you feel that people disapprove of you or reject you?
★ In a group, when other people talk together, do you feel ignored?
★ If people are laughing or whispering together do you feel they are talking about you?
★ Do you dislike the telephone and prefer to talk to people face to face because you need to be reassured by their visual feedback?

People who are quick to respond and are sometimes very intuitive can feel insecure in groups, especially when the other people present are not known to them. They may detect certain nuances in the responses of others – an implied slight, a shrug of disapproval, a yawn of possible boredom – and they immediately feel snubbed or criticised and then hurt and then unable to participate. Some rely heavily on visual feedback for approval or acceptance, and without this feedback may feel unsure and vulnerable. Beverly could operate on the telephone at work because she knew she was offering a service and was confident that she could deliver. In her social life, she felt less secure and felt she couldn't be certain that her calls were welcomed.

Social fears often begin in adolescence when the more confident unwittingly overwhelm the more retiring who fear they will say something foolish and then blush and remain tongue-tied. These shy people may begin to refuse invitations, get invited less anyway, and fail to learn social skills through the normal rough and tumble of teenage life. Shyness can then develop into a serious social fear.

'Space' fears

★ Do you feel exposed in public?
★ Do you fear you may panic and lose control in public?
★ Do you only feel secure and safe in small, confined places?
★ Do you feel lost in large spaces?
★ Do you hate having to leave things to often anonymous 'experts'?
★ Do you distrust the safety checks made by lift engineers, mechanics, etc?
★ Do you feel trapped in small spaces?

Space fears reflect a kind of inability to let go. Outside the familiar safety of home, life becomes unpredictable and strange places increase the sense of vulnerability. For some people, this means that it is difficult to relax and have trust in other people, especially those who are in charge. No wonder that flying makes many people feel a bit scared and quite a few people feel very scared. There is the unnatural experience of not being on the ground, and the need to put one's trust in that cheery disembodied voice that tells you unnerving things like how high you are. There is the confined space and the lack of autonomy. (Though we're not on to 'cures' yet, it is cheering to know that thousands of people have successfully overcome their fear of flying.)

Over-dependence can be a feature of agoraphobia as mentioned earlier, but another problem is the fear of showing panic and making a fool of oneself in public. The anxiety this raises is at the root of most social and space fears.

Physical fears

★ Do you have a secret fear that something is wrong with you?
★ Do you begin to worry whenever you have a minor symptom, like a sore throat or a spot on your hand?
★ Do other people's illnesses trigger ideas that you suffer from them too?
★ Do you fear going to the doctor in case he or she finds something you hadn't detected?
★ Do you feel reassured when you go to the doctor, but then begin to have doubts a few weeks later?

Today, newspapers and magazines carry so many features on common and rare illnesses, plus details of their symptoms, that anyone with a scrap of imagination will find something in some of them to worry about. Fear about health and well-being is part of the modern condition, but for some people it's more than that – it becomes a fairly constant background concern, never far from their consciousness. This may have been with them from childhood, picked up from anxious parents worrying about every twinge or symptom in their children. They themselves may have grown up with a sickly member of their family or may have learned that being ill was a way to gain attention. Experience of a frightening disease in someone close can trigger personal anxieties. A friend may have contracted a serious illness, and triggered memories in adolescence or adulthood which stick in the mind forever.

There may be ways to avoid spiders or travelling in lifts or planes, but there is no way to avoid the worry of possible illness. From background concern, it can develop into an obsession such as a need to avoid dirt or blood or other potentially contagious agents. It can spread to many bodily symptoms and physical ailments, creating that condition we call hypochondria, which one dictionary defines as 'exaggerated or obsessive anxiety about one's health; mistaken belief that one is ill'.

Specific fears
Many of the pointers above may apply to people who suffer from a single, intense fear. Specific fears are most easily identifiable as a phobia, a persistent or irrational fear or loathing. And as mentioned earlier the kinds of people who have such phobias may be neat, methodical types who naturally try to keep their lives under strong control. They may even derive a sense of comfort and order from finding ways to avoid their focus of fear – spiders or roses, or whatever.

Avoiding fears is of course one perfectly reasonable way of dealing with them. But are the tactics involved taking too big a bite out of your life? If so, it would make sense to get rid of them, and oddly enough, specific fears, no matter how bizarre, can be dealt with quite quickly and simply through self-help techniques.

How much of an avoider are you?
We can all be very adept at protecting ourselves from unpleasant things as we go through life. And quite right too. Who wants to be a masochist? Too much self-protection, however, not only stops us from growing, it prevents us from having a lot of fun.

If you, reading this, are beginning to wonder whether to bother to go for a 'cure' or to stay with your particular fear after all, then answer the following questions and consider just how much you do or do not confine yourself.

★ Does your fear get in the way of your personal relationships – causing perhaps arguments with a partner or close relative?

★ Does it stop you from making new friends?
★ Does it stop you from going out or going to certain places you would really like to go to?
★ Does it make you avoid watching films or reading certain books or switching on the television for fear of encountering a 'threatening' image of, say, a spider or other object?
★ Does it stop you from speaking easily to other people?
★ Does it mean you have to have secrets?
★ Does it make you feel lonely?
★ Does it make you feel tired and physically exhausted or depressed?

If you answer yes to a lot of the above questions (and you can add others that reveal the self-limiting effect of your avoidance), then refuel your optimism.

YOU CAN GET YOUR FEAR UNDER CONTROL.

SECTION 2

The Basic De-Stress Programme

CHAPTER 3

Ways to Overcome Panic Attacks

By now you will have realised that millions of other people have hidden fears, so you are not alone. You know that shame can play a major part in keeping your fear secret, and that you may go to some lengths to hide it. Indeed, shame is a major reason why you might want to hide it. You realise that the energy you put into avoiding your fear stops you from enjoying certain things in life even though you can, on the outside, carry on a fairly normal existence.

Before you can look your fears in the face, you need to understand the most basic and in some ways the most simple aspect of them – the panic attack. We'll go back to Brian, the architect, and his fear of spiders:

'What do I feel if I see a spider? Panic, blind panic. My mind simply goes to pieces. The fear makes me feel physically uncomfortable. My heart starts to pound. I know I'm breathing quickly, I even get a tightness in the chest.'

And Alison, with her fear of balloons and loud noises:

'My stomach churns. I break out into a sweat. My legs start to tremble. I can't think straight. And I am ashamed of this lack of control.'

Roy, who once hated going to restaurants, describes the way his fear hit him:

'One thing I dreaded was that my hand would shake when I picked up a knife and fork. For some reason, it was always my left hand. I would feel more in control using a fork in my right hand, I suppose because I am right-handed. I guess the trembling was hardly noticeable, but I still would do anything to hide my nervousness.'

These three kinds of fears may be very different, but the reactions they cause are closely related: breathlessness, trembling, sweating, stomach churning, going to pieces mentally, fear of losing control. They are all descriptions of panic. (Others are dizziness, numbness or tingling in hands or fingers, hot and cold flushes, dreamlike sensations or a sense of unreality.) Powerlessness and terror are also aspects of panic, which may trigger the most frightening aspect of all: the fear that you will not recover from these sensations and that you will, in fact, die.

Avoidance of anything that triggers such intense physical and mental sensations may make immediate sense, but in the long run it can be a kind of trap. Avoidance is not only physical, it's mental. You want to shut your mind to the whole thing. For some people, it means they are unprepared for the next encounter. They have no defences to fall back on and are likely to go to pieces again on any subsequent encounter. The majority of people who panic settle for this hit and miss approach, and it can work for much of the time. But several recurrences of panic attack can leave some people so scared that they will not go out of the house or will refuse all social invitations. The panics may need less and less exposure to trigger them, and finally they require almost no trigger at all, becoming like a background hum in a person's consciousness. This kind of response is often the meaning behind that statistic of two or three per thousand of the population who are seriously phobic and live in self-imposed isolation.

There is one obvious truth about all the above symptoms, no matter how stressful and upsetting they are.

PANIC IN THE FACE OF IRRATIONAL FEARS IS NEITHER PHYSICALLY NOR MENTALLY DANGEROUS

Obvious, but worth remembering. A panic attack is really a rush of adrenaline, the hormone that gives us the energy to defend ourselves in real danger. It can last for several minutes and the memory of it can be very painful, but there is no real danger, you are not going to die and you are not going insane.

Why are some people especially vulnerable to panic attacks?

The answer is another of those 'don't knows'. Panic attacks have been found to run in families, but plenty of sufferers have no family history of the problem. There's a theory that just as some people's systems go into overdrive when they encounter house-mites or certain foods – in other words they get an allergy reaction – so others, when exposed to certain things, bring on the adrenaline 'alarm system' of mental and physical mechanisms known as a panic attack. Since what you often feel when you're afraid is panic, it's worthwhile for the moment to put aside the fears themselves and look at ways to control that panic and even make your adrenaline work for you.

Think of it this way. The alarm system is activated by the surge of adrenaline. That burst of energy is overwhelming, it spirals out of your control. So your challenge is to tame the beast, make it work to your command. There are several different ways in which you can do this.

THE BEST ANTI-PANIC MEASURES

Control your breathing
When you are anxious, your breathing is likely to get either fast and shallow or you start taking deep, panting breaths. This is a result of the adrenaline boost your body gives out to help protect you in an emergency. Since we're talking here about inappropriate adrenaline boosts, you don't want to go into either shallow or deep breathing mode. Take the following steps to 're-educate' your responses.

1. *Watch your breathing.*
Next time you feel panic building up, try to be aware of the way you are breathing. When you do anything that seems at all difficult or produces even a small degree of anxiety, again note the way you are breathing. You will probably find it is shallow and faster, and you may even feel as if you are suffocating or choking. For some people the opposite happens, and they take too many deep breaths, which may leave them feeling faint or dizzy or experiencing tingling in the

limbs. You don't have to do anything about the breathing yet. Just take note. This may be difficult to do when you are in the middle of emotional feelings. All the same just try. Perhaps on the second or third attempt you will see what's happening.

2. *Lie down and listen.*
A simple exercise can help you develop new breathing habits and responses. Wear unconstricting clothes and lie down on a carpet or on a bed if you prefer. Have a shallow pillow under your head. Place your hands lightly on your chest with fingertips just touching. Close your eyes and just lie there listening to your breathing and noting the very small and gentle rise and fall under your fingertips. If your mind wanders, which is quite likely, just return to the exercise. You may notice that you are breathing in quite a shallow way, or alternatively, that you breathe heavily, so experiment a little. Try breathing from the abdomen and note to yourself how that feels. Put your hands on your abdomen and feel your body rise and fall. Then try to breathe from the top of your lungs and observe the difference. Do this once a day till you find you can recognise your breathing pattern and are ready to go on to the next stage.

3. *Teach yourself to breathe differently.*
Lie down as above, and allow a few moments to observe your natural breathing. Now, begin to take in a deep breath. First feel your abdomen expand, then your diaphragm. You can move your hands lightly down to your diaphragm to feel the expansion. Gradually let the intake of air rise up into your chest. When you feel totally expanded – remember you are doing this very slowly, with nothing forced – just hold on to the breath for a second. Then gradually let the air out, letting it go naturally, watching how your body sinks. You should take longer breathing out than you did breathing in, and don't force anything. Pause again when all the breath is released. Repeat the whole exercise twice more. Then relax and return to normal breathing before getting up.

Try this once a day, repeating the process three times. If you find yourself feeling tense during the day, give yourself another session.

You may find it difficult at first, with the inhaling capacity quite short and jerky or the exhaling fluttery, but you will quickly gain the necessary control. Just carry on practising and remember it doesn't matter if you get it wrong. Always return to normal breathing and relax before getting up.

4. *Use your new breathing technique.*
Whenever you feel tense, start to calm your breathing, bringing it back to an even pace that you should recognise as feeling 'right' after your re-education exercises above. You will find you can do this without lying down. It is a new skill that you can draw upon at will. Before you do anything challenging or threatening or frightening, whether it is picking up the telephone, going out to a restaurant, getting into a car or lift, or aiming to confront some specific phobia, remember your new breathing technique and use it.

5. *Feeling breathless?*
If you can't catch your breath or feel you could suffocate, try taking in one, long deep breath, holding for as long as you can – say sixty seconds – before breathing out slowly. It gives your body no option but to slow down, and will help reinforce more even breathing.

6. *Too many deep breaths?*
Try breathing into a paper bag. If anxiety causes deep breathing and physical discomfort, the problem is likely to be shortage of carbon dioxide. The trick, of holding a paper bag over your mouth and breathing into it, is that you inhale the carbon dioxide that you have just breathed out. Doing this could produce funny looks in public, so try a less conspicuous, though slightly less efficient version: put both hands over your nose, with the fingertips on the bridge of your nose and the base of your hands on or under your chin, and breathe into that to reabsorb the trapped air.

The 'floating' approach
Facing physical symptoms and feelings and letting them go is another technique to reduce fears and panic. The method favoured by Doctor Claire Weekes in her work, *Self Help for Your Nerves*, is

based on this recognition and acceptance. You do the following exercises when the feelings of panic arise:

1. *Put your symptoms into words.*
Describe what you are feeling by saying out loud what the physical symptoms are. You might say: 'My heart is pounding,' or 'My stomach is churning,' or 'My hands are trembling,' or 'My palms are sweating.' If you are in public, obviously you won't want to do any such thing, but you can still say the words to yourself. Later write them down. They will seem quite trivial and insignificant, even silly perhaps – but you know that anyway, and they are certainly not silly to you. Such acknowledgements can be soothing. They lend detachment, clear the mind and give time to relax – and help make the change to calmer breathing.

2. *Don't be impatient.*
Recognising symptoms doesn't mean they will immediately go away. Observing and accepting are part of the technique. The initial aim is to learn to live with these sensations, to the point when they carry on with the minimum of your attention. This means that you are being tolerant about the things your body and mind are doing to you and are reducing the tension surrounding them.

3. *Let go, don't force yourself.*
Claire Weekes calls this 'floating'. Before making yourself do something difficult, like going into a restaurant or picking up a telephone, you make yourself imagine that you are 'floating' through the door or up to the difficult object. As you float, let any threatening or fearful thoughts float out of your head. If picking up a knife and fork makes your hand tremble, allow the tension to float away, allow the knife and fork to float to your mouth. The beauty of this technique is that it takes away resistance; you bypass the struggle. You relax instead of tensing up.

4. *Don't be discouraged.*
You may well relapse, forget or get your timing wrong. Let your disappointment and possible resentment float too. Resentment?

Ways to Overcome Panic Attacks

Are you SURE this is what the book said?

Well, if someone suggests something (even someone from the printed page) and you go to all that effort to follow the instructions, and then the thing fails, you may well feel let down, and then it can be easier to blame someone else. Don't blame anyone! It's non-productive. You can choose instead to be patient and start again.

In time, the acceptance of symptoms will reduce them. Your heart will eventually stop racing, your hands stop trembling. Believe in this, not in the negative feelings.

CHAPTER 4

Getting Off the Anxiety Treadmill

Do you spend days beforehand worrying because you are going to a party, will be travelling by train or walking to the supermarket or doing whatever you do that brings out the scare factor in you? Do you think you might panic, and understandably dread the idea?

If there's a yes to the above, then you are no stranger to anxiety. Just as there are times when there is good reason to feel fear, so there are times when it is useful to feel anxiety. If you don't have a degree of anxiety about an impending exam, you probably won't be sufficiently prepared for it. If you have no sense of urgency, you will probably be late for appointments and be slow in your reactions. Actors, public speakers, musicians who don't have a touch of stagefright before a performance won't be sufficiently charged to give their best.

However, anxiety that dominates and becomes a nagging worry, or is a runner-up to an irrational panic attack, has nothing but a negative effect on performance. Anxiety before going to the dentist or doctor can produce sleepless nights and unnecessary stress so that you are tense on arrival. Over-anxiety about keeping appointments or being late, fear of missing a train for instance, makes a bad start to the day. Muscular aches and pains, fatigue, stomach cramps, indigestion, lack of concentration, impatience and irritability are typical spin-offs arising out of feelings of anxiety and dread.

The habit of anxiety, like the habit of panic attacks, can become a way of life unless you recognise it and decide to do something about it.

Are you a Woody Allen Character (WAC)?

You know the kind. He (and also she) is an expert at *worrying*. When the WAC invites friends home for a meal, a series of unwanted doubts come floating irresistibly to mind . . .

'If I invite them and they say yes, do they really want to come?'
'Maybe they won't like the other people I've asked.'
'Will they be offended if I serve meat?'
'Will they be offended if I ring and ask them about this?'

And then, after the event . . .

'They seemed to enjoy themselves, but were they just pretending?'
'They ate everything, but were they just being polite?'

And so on . . .

Perhaps the description makes you smile, or does it make you wince? The WAC sample describes a socially anxious person who does not trust his judgement, lacks confidence, has unrealistically high standards which he cannot meet and is burdened with a desire to please at all costs.

No wonder we smile. The whole thing is over the top. We also wince because many of us recognise some truth in the caricature. It's very common to be prone to unnecessary doubt or anxiety.

How to break the pattern

Recognising that you have the pattern is the first step to breaking it. Trying to find out the cause may be the next, though reasons may be impossible to pinpoint – and even if you do, you may be left high and dry with the knowledge but no clear way to deal with it. You might find a cause that can be dealt with in a practical way. For instance, anxiety around the time of a menstrual period is common enough, and due to hormonal imbalance which can be treated medically; but if reasons for your anxiety elude you or leave you without an obvious way forward, go for the more straightforward tactics:

Getting Off the Anxiety Treadmill

★ *Accept the feelings*. They are just something you have, the way other people have specific conditions like asthma or diabetes.

★ *Accept the symptoms* – the aches and pains or disturbed sleep. You won't die of them even if they are, for the moment, uncomfortable.

★ *If you suspect the trigger is hormonal*, keep a menstrual chart for two or three months, marking days of periods and days when you feel more anxious, keyed up or emotional. Plan a less challenging schedule on those days in future or try a suitable premenstrual remedy available from chemists.

★ *If several things worry you*, make a list and break them down into small, single tasks or items.

★ *Concentrate on one item at a time*. Take the difficulties in the order you may encounter them, or in order of urgency or importance. Tackle them step-by-step, firmly returning to the present if you find your mind is racing ahead.

★ *Remind yourself that each task is manageable*, and keep a sense of proportion.

★ *Keep to a set routine* or timetable; leave yourself plenty of time to get to appointments.

★ *Prepare yourself methodically and slowly* for whatever task it is that worries you. Carry it out slowly too.

★ *Eat balanced, regular meals*. No 'grazing' and nothing on the run. A frenetic lifestyle only leads to greater anxiety.

★ *Avoid caffeine in tea and coffee*. Keep alcohol for social occasions, not as a means to relax in private.

★ *Use the even breathing technique* described on page 26 whenever you feel tension rising.

★ *Take daily exercise*. Even twenty minutes brisk walking can create a change of mood and use pent-up energy.

★ *Don't bottle up your feelings*, but don't take them out on other people either. Go and kick a football or punch a cushion instead. Yell as much as you can (or dare) as you do it.

★ *Give yourself an hour's worry time a day* if you must, whittling down the time gradually if you can.

★ *Don't be hard on yourself*. You can forgive yourself for your own weaknesses or the aspects of your behaviour that you feel don't come up to scratch. Self-forgiveness is a much better preparation for change than self-blame and guilt can ever be.

★ *Tell someone you trust* how you feel, even if you do it in a jokey, WAC way. You'll realise you're not such a freak after all, and will be warmed by a sympathetic response.

★ *Use relaxation techniques*, a major contribution to anxiety control. The next chapter shows how.

CHAPTER 5

Relaxation Really Works

Ask someone to relax when they are sitting or standing, and you'll probably see them physically slump into an absolutely atrocious posture, with rounded shoulders, cramped chest and curved back. This, as you can tell them if you have learned the proper technique, is not beneficial relaxation. The real thing depends on re-educating your body, and it's something you certainly can learn to do either sitting or standing as well as lying down, though the action will be barely discernible since there'll be no slumping. On the contrary, you will automatically want to sit or stand upright with shoulders down and pulled back, and arms held loosely at your sides.

When you learn deep relaxation, the effect is not only to reduce muscular tension or calm the mind, though the technique certainly does those things. In addition, all the physical responses that come into play when you feel fear or panic or anxiety are calmed down. The heartbeat slows to normal, blood pressure is reduced, and the individual responses to tension – which may be headache in one person, bowel disturbance in another – will gradually subside.

Deep relaxation is quite safe and suitable for *almost* everyone. The exception occurs sometimes in people with specific phobias – the spider and snake haters, for instance. They might find that unpleasant images of their phobia come unbidden into their minds, and the momentary loss of control is obviously upsetting. When this is so, they may need professional help with their fears – see chapter 23 – before they can make good use of relaxation techniques.

By now, it will be clear that relaxation is not a matter of sitting in front of the television, or reading a book or going to sleep either, though with a little regular practice you'll get so good at it that you will be able to tell your body to calm down when you are driving or at a desk or at the kitchen sink. Just reminding yourself to relax will create an immediate effect. This means you can use relaxation when you need it, which is when you begin to feel worry or anxiety or fear or panic. It is a valuable tool, along with the even breathing or the 'floating' techniques which were described earlier.

In fact, all three are interrelated. Allowing feelings of panic or fear to float out of you is really another way of telling your system to relax. The ultimate aim is to make your body so accustomed to relaxation that when your muscles tighten up or you begin to feel tense you become sensitive to the physical and mental changes and will want to correct them.

Breathing plays a big part in relaxation. You can demonstrate the effect now. As you sit reading this, check whether your shoulders or neck feel tense and, if so, just try the slower, even breathing you have already learned without making a conscious effort to relax your shoulders. You will find that you automatically relax them as you breathe out. If you're not convinced, try tightening and tensing up your shoulders and then taking a slow deep breath in and a slower one out. It's almost impossible to keep those shoulders tensed as you breathe out slowly.

HOW TO ACHIEVE DEEP RELAXATION

The method used in yoga is a good, basic procedure. A yoga teacher in a classroom setting will talk people through the stages – and indeed learning yoga and practising it regularly is a good way to learn body control, remain supple and enjoy relaxation – but the steps are easy for anyone to follow on their own.

What you need:

1. Fifteen minutes of uninterrupted time. Unplug the phone if necessary.
2. Light, comfortable clothing.

3. A warm, draught-free room.
4. A carpeted floor or rug, though you can use a firm bed.
5. A thin blanket or towel which you can fold into a shallow, firm pillow.
6. A second light blanket to cover yourself with.

Getting ready:
Lie on your back on the floor or bed with the covering blanket up to your shoulders and with the thin folded blanket supporting your head and neck. Your shoulders should have contact with the floor, your chin should not be sticking up in the air. Try to make the back of your neck feel long. Have your arms set a little away from your body, upper arms moving outwards and palms facing upwards. Your legs should be slightly apart with feet falling outwards. Your eyes are closed.

First, take a couple of deep, slow breaths in and out, and then just let your body go, observing your breathing but doing nothing positive.

Now use the total-body relax check:

★ *Start by thinking about your feet.* Wriggle your toes and then let them relax. Check that your feet are rolled out and the ankles are relaxed. Feel your feet and legs 'spreading', be aware that the floor is holding you up and you don't have to do anything to help. You feel heavy, supported by the floor. Don't change your breathing at this stage, but be aware that as you breathe out you can 'spread' even more. Feel that air is spreading into your feet and legs. Carry the feeling up into your calves and thighs and through your entire body. If this is at all difficult, start again, concentrating on one foot and leg, then the other, and then both, then let your whole body soften and expand as you breathe out.

If you still feel there is tension, go over your body, deliberately tensing up and then releasing the muscles. Hold for a second and then let go. Repeat three times. You can start with your feet and ankles, then work up through the body ending with shoulders and facial muscles.

★ *Now transfer your attention to your abdomen*, again allowing yourself to spread and give way to the floor. Then think about your arms and fingers spreading and getting heavier, checking on one arm at a time at first, then both together.

★ *Shoulders are next*. Try to tuck your shoulder blades in against the floor under you. This opens up your chest and automatically makes breathing deeper. Feel the stretch as your shoulders move down and back. Then let go. Think about your neck feeling longer and smoother at the back. Consciously relax the back of your head.

★ *Lastly, think about your face*. Feel your forehead smooth out, allow your jaw to soften. Your lips can be lightly touching, teeth unclenched and a little apart. Make your eyelids feel heavy, your eyes turning down and sinking back into your head.

You may at this stage feel that the bits of your body you 'treated' first are now tensing again, so check yourself once more, letting your breathing soften any part that is not relaxed. Notice how different each part of your body feels now it is relaxed.

This part of the exercise should take about ten minutes.

Practise anti-panic breathing exercises:
Take a few normal breaths, then slowly take a deep breath filling the abdomen with air. Hold for a second and smoothly release the breath, taking time for the last little bit to go. Repeat once more then return to normal breathing for a minute.

Finish the session gently:
Open your eyes. Bend your knees up to your body and roll over to one side, turning your head as you go but keeping it on the 'pillow'. Allow yourself a few seconds before getting up slowly. Don't rush about immediately.

Repeat the relaxation procedure three times a week for a few weeks, and your brain will quickly respond to the *idea* of relaxation so that all you will have to do is let go, either lying down or sitting, and you will achieve relaxation without having to do any of the body-checks. You will be able to tell your body to relax in the face of any fears, and know that even if you slip, you can always instruct yourself again.

If you feel this is a lot to remember and have a tape recorder, then record all the steps, speaking deliberately slowly and quietly. Then you can play the tape back as you relax. Alternatively, cassettes are available which will take you through the stages of relaxation (see addresses and contacts at the end of the book). The methods may differ slightly from that given above but will achieve the same results.

CHAPTER 6

Do-It-Yourself Massage

One of the results of getting tense is tightened muscles. Those in the neck and shoulders are particularly vulnerable, often causing stiffness, pain and limited movement. Even deep relaxation won't stretch muscles that have contracted in these areas, and often the tightness exists for years alongside poor posture like rounded shoulders. To add to the discomfort, a cold draught or just sitting still too long in one position can produce acute muscle pain.

The best solution for muscle stiffness is massage, and it is something you can do yourself. Giving yourself a massage is not as good as getting someone else to do it for you, and there are parts you can't reach, but it's convenient, costs nothing and you can do it on a regular basis, working on specific muscles that you know have a tendency to tense up.

Here's a simple routine to try daily.

What you need:

1. A warm room and ten minutes uninterrupted time.
2. Some baby oil or sweet almond oil (available from chemists).

Getting ready:
If you massage through clothing, you lose half the effect, so work on bare skin, making sure that clothing on surrounding areas does not come into contact with the oil.

First make sure your hands are perfectly clean. You will use only one hand at a time for the massage so, assuming you will start with your right hand, put a few drops of oil into the right palm and on the pads of the fingertips before you begin. You can top up when you feel you are rubbing on your skin and creating friction.

The shoulder and neck squeeze

There is no single 'best' position for this. You have to find the one that gives you the best access. Here are some suggestions:

★ Sit upright on a chair *or*
★ Sit with your left elbow on a desk or table with your head supported on the left hand *or*
★ Lie on your back, either flat or on a pillow *or*
★ Lie down on your right side, legs slightly bent, right arm resting in front.

Then follow these simple steps:

1. Choose your starting position and then consciously relax your neck and shoulders – it should come easily after your relaxation practice.

2. Turn your head towards the right or, if you are supporting your head on your left hand, bring your head forward if you can. Now cross your right arm in front of you and take your right, oiled, hand to your left shoulder. You'll have your thumb by your left ear, palm facing down on top of the shoulder and fingers pressing into your back.

    If you are lying on your right side, cross the right hand in front of you to reach over and massage the left shoulder.

3. Keep your fingers still, as much as possible, and push with the heel of your hand so that the flesh gets pressed together. Raise the heel of your hand a little and squeeze again. Repeat four to six times, working the heel of your hand up till it virtually touches your fingers. (If you find access difficult with the heel of your hand, use the length of your thumb instead, keeping your fingers still.)

4. Now start at the top outer edge of your shoulder, and work inwards in small movements up to the side of the neck.

5. For your neck, sitting up is best, left hand doing left side. Switch to your first and second fingers at the back and your thumb in front, using the thumb in place of the heel of the hand and keeping your fingers still. Gradually work along the back of your neck to the centre.

6. Repeat steps 1 to 5, using more pressure if you can.

Then repeat this entire procedure changing hands to massage your other side.

Back of head pressure points
You won't need any oil on your hands for this one. Simply sit upright.

1. Bend your head forward and use the fingertips of both hands to locate the base of your skull. It's the slightly bumpy, bony area behind the ears and across above the back of your neck. At the centre there is a hollow. You will feel where the sensitive pressure points are on either side and above this.

2. Use the pads of the fingertips of both hands to make small circular movements. You'll start from the centre and work outwards toward both ears. Make three or four circles at the centre and then move your fingers along just a little and repeat till the fingers arrive each side behind the ears. Alternatively, work with your right hand from the centre out to the right ear and then do the same with the left hand.

3. Repeat the procedure two or three times. You may want to go higher and lower to cover all sensitive areas.

The upper-arm massage
You can sit resting one arm on your lap or on a table in front of you for this.

1. Rest your left arm and put a few drops of oil in the palm of your right hand.

2. Take your right arm across in front of your body and put your hand over the very top of your left arm in the same position as the first step in the shoulder squeeze.

3. Keep your fingers still and squeeze with the heel of the hand, gradually closing in towards the fingers as with the shoulder squeeze.

4. Bring your hand down gradually using the same movements till you get to the elbow. Take care not to leave out sections; it's better to overlap.

Repeat the procedure three or four times on both arms.

HOW AROMATHERAPY HELPS RELAXATION

Aromatherapy makes use of what are known as essential oils, extracts from the fragrant-releasing parts of plants, in order to calm the mind. The powers of these oils have been known from the most ancient times: references to balms and unguents occur in the Bible and the anointing with special oils is central to many religious ceremonies. Museums all over the world exhibit jars and pots that once held precious oils derived from plants and used for healing and soothing. Research in recent years has shown the scientific effect on the brain of such oils. Many have a sedative or stimulating effect, backing up the claims of aromatherapists that they can be a useful aid to relaxation or can act as an anti-depressant.

The benefits tend to be subtle rather than dramatic, and a combination of two or three essential oils is likely to be more effective than one, especially as individuals respond to different fragrances. Aromatherapy oils are most commonly used in the bath – a few drops are all that is needed. But a single oil can also be

Do-It-Yourself Massage

used for massage, combined with sweet almond oil. Here is a small selection of oils and their effects. All should be obtainable from health food shops or from mail order companies specialising in alternative health products.

★ *Camomile* is said to have a profoundly calming emotional effect, helpful for the hyperactive, for those who worry or are hypersensitive. It is appropriate for premenstrual tension too. In large doses it may have too much of a sedative effect. It blends well with jasmine, lavender, rose and geranium.

To use in the bath: up to ten drops
As a massage: six drops combined with one tablespoon of sweet almond oil
For general relaxation: a few drops on a pillow or on night clothes or on a handkerchief
As a nightcap: only in the form of dried flowers (a dessertspoonful to a pint of boiling water) or in the form of bought camomile tea

★ *Jasmine*, according to aromatherapy practitioners, works as an anti-depressant, is uplifting and warming. And it's said to be an aphrodisiac too.

To use in the bath: five to eight drops
As a massage: two drops each jasmine and sandalwood or camomile combined with one tablespoon sweet almond oil
For general relaxation: use in an oil burner or added to pot pourri or apply as a perfume, though if you have a sensitive skin try a little to start with as it can, rarely, cause an allergy reaction

★ *Lavender* is thought to be relaxing, calming, soothing. As it also has a sedative effect it's best used in the evening.

To use in the bath: five to ten drops
As a massage: two drops each geranium, rose and lavender combined with one tablespoon sweet almond oil
For general relaxation: add to pot pourri or put a few drops on the

pillow or put on to a handkerchief and inhale to relieve headaches or faintness

★ *Geranium* is thought to be an anti-depressant and to stimulate the lymphatic system, thus helping to fight infection, as well as reducing nervous tension.

To use in the bath: five to ten drops
As a massage: two drops combined with two drops rose or lavender and one tablespoon sweet almond oil
For general relaxation: add to pot pourri or put a few drops on the pillow or put on to a handkerchief

CHAPTER 7

Give Yourself Positive Thinking Power

We can carry around some horribly negative thoughts about ourselves without even knowing we're doing it. Think back to chapter 1 and that exercise exploring how you felt about your hidden fears. Remember words such as 'crazy' or 'inadequate' or 'ashamed'? Such words reflect our state of mind. They also reinforce it.

At this stage you know about the anti-panic measures and relaxation techniques covered in the previous chapters, and may already be using them. So how positive is your current state of mind regarding your fears? Check out on the following:

'It's all too difficult.'
'I'll never remember.'
'I don't have the time.'
'I know it won't work for me.'
'I've tried it before and it didn't work.'

Any of these, if it's an echo of your own thoughts, is more like self-sabotage than self help! Time then for a change to positive thinking or, more specifically, to positive self-talk.

The messages above are clear examples of negative self-talk, so it's easy to understand what positive self-talk means. Teach yourself with thoughts like these:

'The anti-panic measures and relaxation techniques are surprisingly easy.'
'With a bit of practice I will remember them.'

'This is worth making time for.'
'They will work for me.'

You get the message. Add this one too:

'I will not let discouraging thoughts get in the way.'

No, of course it isn't easy to stay positive. Anyone who lives with a sense of defeatism will understand the following conversation:

'All this stuff is just brain-washing. You're kidding yourself.' (Negative self-talk)
'Why should thinking about failure be more truthful than thinking about success?' (Positive self-talk)
'Because I've failed up till now. So failure in the future is surely more likely than success.' (Negative self-talk)
'But you've always used negative self-talk to reinforce failure and what that does is to create a self-fulfilling prophesy.' (Positive self-talk)

In other words, give positive self-talk a try. You've got nothing to lose that's worth holding on to.

Now think about something that brings out fear in you – perhaps picking up the telephone or going into restaurants alone or going into the supermarket or encountering a spider. Imagine you are going to face this fear.

Write down the negative self-talk statements that fit with what you feel

They may go something like this or you may identify other negative self-talk:

'I will get palpitations, my legs will turn to jelly, my hands will tremble.'
'I'll get tense thinking about my fears for days before I try doing anything about them.'
'The worry will make me feel exhausted.'

'I lack the confidence to believe that people want to hear from me.'
'People will notice me making a fool of myself.'
'I will reveal my vulnerabilities.'
'I will be terribly embarrassed.'

Now transform your own list of 'downers' into positive talk

'I know I won't collapse even if I do get uncomfortable physical sensations.'
'I'll just accept the sensations.'
'I'll be able to use the anti-panic measures if and when I need them.'
'If I find I am tense or worried, I'll use the relaxation techniques and the self-massage.'
'I'm equipped to deal with the situation and I can face the fear.'
'If I make a fool of myself it doesn't matter to anyone else, so I won't let it matter to me.'
'I don't despise people who reveal their vulnerabilities, so it's all right for me to reveal mine at times.'
'I don't have to care about what people might think of me.'
'I can make mistakes and forgive myself.'
'I believe in myself as an effective person.'
I have choices. I don't have to be driven by certain feelings.'

Even if you still harbour negative self-talk or rebellious resistance, just ignore it. Don't fall into the self-pity trap: 'I can't . . . I'll never . . . I'm hopeless . . . I'm an outsider . . .' Accentuate the positive with 'I can . . . I will . . . I feel purposeful . . . I feel strong . . .' If you do this every day, and also do it whenever you feel negative, you will gradually feel stronger and more purposeful for longer and longer.

Simply say 'STOP'
Take your mind off negative thoughts with this mental reminder. You feel worried, tense, discouraged and just can't get into a positive frame of mind? Then:

Pleased to meet you. You don't frighten me at all. In fact, I no longer care what you think of me. Did I say that out loud? Silly me, not the end of the world though...

1. Say the 'S' word to yourself, out loud or under your breath: 'STOP.'
2. Take a couple of slow, deeper breaths.
3. Tense up your shoulders and then relax them.
4. Breathe normally, observing your breathing.
5. Stay quiet for a few seconds before slowly resuming whatever you were doing. With practice just saying 'STOP' will be sufficient.

Practise positive thoughts, repeating them when doubts creep in. Notice how they feel – strange at first maybe, contrived, unbelievable. You will gradually get used to them. Practise self-talk regularly after you've done the relaxation. You've lived a long time with those negative thoughts. They've become a habit. Positive self-talk can become a habit too.

CHAPTER 8

Exposing Yourself to the Fear

When we get involved in a minor accident – in a car, perhaps, or falling off a bicycle, or when we suffer an injury using everyday equipment, our instinct is to use the offending object or revisit the place where the incident occurred as soon as the shock has worn off. The instinct is a good one. Confrontation will usually reduce fantasy and bring everything back to reality. The sooner and more regular the re-encounter, the less likely it is that fears will grow.

Many deep fears and phobias start through avoidance of a situation after it has proved frightening. The horse rider who falls off and thereafter avoids horses, the performer who gets stagefright and then refuses work are at greater risk of developing a persistent fear than they are of breaking their neck or forgetting their lines.

Nowadays, confrontation or exposure therapy is one of the major forms of treatment for persistent fears. A leading proponent is clinical psychiatrist Dr Isaac Marks of the Institute of Psychiatry in south London and author of a book on behavioural treatments *Living with Fear*. Dr Marks successfully treats patients with a wide range of fears, phobias and obsessions, using exposure therapy. He is convinced that if we confront our fears determinedly, they will diminish and in time disappear. His most encouraging finding is that the majority of his patients, even those with deeply embedded fears or obsessions, can successfully treat themselves after brief medical supervision. People with less intense fears can use his programme too, without any medical supervision.

Dr Marks does, however, qualify his claim. Anyone who suffers from serious depression, or is alcohol dependent, or taking high doses of sedatives is unlikely to respond to exposure treatment. Anyone who has a condition that could worsen through stress – such as heart disease, asthma, peptic ulcer, colitis – should not use exposure techniques without medical supervision. Anyone experiencing major difficulties at work or in their marriage is unlikely to succeed with exposure therapy without professional help.

The treatment works best for people who know they have *specific* fears, and not for those who are anxious most of the time or have a history of psychological problems.

Exposure therapy doesn't have to mean going in at the deep end. For most people, that is too much of a challenge, especially if they are doing it on a self-help basis. Instead, you can make up a programme for yourself so that you start off with a 'mini' exposure and gradually work up to the more serious business.

The best way to do this is to write down a list of fears or worrying situations in order of their severity. Decide to tackle the least-threatening situation first. Choose a suitable time and prepare yourself mentally by reminding yourself of the techniques you have learned – relaxation, even breathing, anti-panic measures, etc. In later chapters, you will find specific preparation advice adapted to suit various different phobias and fears. You will learn how to match the technique to your individual needs.

Exposure treatment works with careful pre-planning and weekly targets. This programme has helped a man who could not travel on the Underground:

★ Days one to three: Stand outside the station, lengthening the time each day.
★ Days four to seven: Go to the station and buy a ticket.
★ Days eight and nine: Go down into the station and get on the train, then immediately get off.
★ Day ten: Go one stop on the train.
★ Day eleven: Go two or three stops.

When this part of the programme is complete, it is important to carry on, gradually travelling longer distances.

After each day of exposure, the person has to write down and keep a record of reactions, comparing how they change.

For those who cannot bring themselves to quick confrontation, there are other methods.

Visualising and desensitisation

With this method, the fear is approached slowly, and only in the mind, before the person progresses to true confrontation as above. There are several steps to follow:

1. Write down a list of frightening situations in order of importance, with the worst first.
2. Use your relaxation techniques to reduce panic reactions.
3. Imagine the least threatening situation and mentally approach it, getting nearer and nearer, just for a few seconds.
4. Gradually try imagining increasingly difficult situations.

This technique works better for some people than others. And sometimes it works best after having a real-life exposure experience, going over the most stressful parts and thinking about a different way of coping next time, perhaps with more relaxation or appropriate self-talk.

It can be helpful for simple phobias. Someone frightened of spiders could start by imagining they are outside their front door, knowing there is a spider in the sitting room. Then in imagination they progress into the hall, then into the room and may even eventually imagine allowing the spider to crawl on their arm.

Once they are ready to move on to the real-life programme, they might make use of a plastic spider or photographs of spiders, then trap a spider in a plastic box, then let it free.

There's a risk with slow desensitisation of going nowhere. You are in danger of prevaricating and putting off the evil moment till you get disappointed and discouraged. Here's where a little self-talk will be useful, but remember not to be hard on yourself. Doing things slowly is better than not doing them at all, and with self-talk you will be able to replace disappointment and discouragement with motivation.

Neuro-Linguistic Programming (NLP)

This American technique was developed by a mathematician, Richard Bandler, and a linguist, John Grinder, who wanted to explore why some people excel at a skill while others are merely competent. They bypassed the obvious answer – that it all hinges on natural ability – and focused on how to change the current behaviour of any individual from the competent to the outstanding.

Courses for individuals are costly, but their ideas can be adapted and used on a self-help basis, particularly for people with social fears, though the aim may be for competence rather than excellence.

NLP is presented here as another tool in the fight against anxiety. The approach is to regard words as one way to describe experience, but by no means the only way. There is also body language to project certain messages.

For instance, when we want guests to go home at the end of a visit, we may sit on the edge of the chair, or stand up, or move towards the door, and the guests usually respond whether they are aware of the 'hints' or not. If we want to give these messages but refrain for fear of seeming impolite, the evening can drag on too long and may not, in retrospect, be considered a success. Similarly, we can assess when the guests want to go by sensing their body movements and can respond accordingly. Or of course if we want to keep them there longer we can employ new tactics: we may offer more drink or food or put on some music.

Then there is the ability to 'read' the underlying agenda. We do this all the time. When we hear a wife complaining of her husband we may interpose in our reception of her words our own ideas about that relationship, even if we give nothing away in the conversation. It can be useful to be aware when we are doing this.

NLP breaks down any skill or behaviour into three elements:

1. Our external behaviour: what we say and do.
2. Our internal process: what we think and the way that we think.
3. Our internal state: what and how we feel.

Exposing Yourself to the Fear

People who give out an aura of confidence have particular ways of expressing these elements. They do it in their body language, in the way they use their voices, in the way they project their thoughts and ideas. NLP suggests that the less competent (or the merely competent) can model themselves on these successful versions.

You can model yourself on someone else by observing their style and mode of presentation. This is no easy achievement, though once you are aware that 'style' is important, you may learn through observation. It can be easier, on a do-it-yourself basis, however, to learn from yourself. You learn by observing what you do in circumstances in which you feel comfortable, and then use them in more threatening circumstances.

For instance, a person who is happy and confident having a conversation with one other person, but dries up when more are present or dreads speaking in a wider group, could adapt the feelgood factor from the happy and confident situation and use it to reduce the discomfort in the more threatening situation.

Here are some statements that provide clues to positive social behaviour, either yours or that of someone you'd like to emulate:

★ It is the informality that makes chatting to one person feel OK.
★ It is the fact that I know and trust that person.
★ It is through nods and smiles and murmurs of agreement or dissent that I establish rapport.
★ It's the way I stand or sit during an easy conversation – diagonally or face to face, using arm movements, perhaps leaning forward when especially interested or relaxing in the chair.
★ When I am listening I can get deeply involved in the discussion and then I forget any self-consciousness.
★ When I am relaxed I am able to brush it off as inconsequential when I forget what I was going to say, or get confused or am interrupted.

These for most people are examples of competent behaviour. How can you adapt them to speaking in public or in a group?

★ You can recall the overall sense of confidence – 'If I can carry it off there I can do it here too. After all, the only difference really is that there are more people present.' The sense of informality can be created by copying what you did in the one-to-one situation, both physically and mentally.

★ Tell yourself that other people are unlikely to be critical if you show friendliness towards them.

★ Pretend to yourself that you are addressing one person when you are actually addressing a group.

★ Concentrate on one person in the group who you know is sympathetic or merely looks sympathetic (perhaps because she or he is nodding and smiling and showing interest).

★ Catch the eye of someone in the group or listen to the speaker while nodding and showing interest.

★ Smile when showing disagreement, to indicate that you want to stimulate discussion and are not inviting aggression.

★ Use body language by sitting in a relaxed manner or in an intensely interested manner when appropriate.

Changing to positive behaviour in this way can be used for specific phobias. Think of how you feel and act when you are in the presence of some non-threatening animal or insect or object, and then psych yourself into the same behaviour when in the presence of a threatening one. When in any specific anxiety-making situation, make yourself act in the way you do in non-anxious situations.

NLP will help some people and not others, and is an option to be used along with the other techniques in this book.

CHAPTER 9

The Alternative Way – Herbal and Homeopathic

They may sound like a witch's brews, but many people find relief through using homeopathic and herbal remedies now widely available in chemists as well as health food stores. Homeopathy is based on the principle of 'like curing like', though the dosage of the remedy is always a minute much-watered-down version, and the connection between the substance and the ailment is not always obvious. Remedies come from herbal, animal or mineral sources and are non-toxic because of the extremely low amounts involved.

Two compilations containing a mix of homeopathic ingredients are the Bach Rescue Remedy and Jan de Vries' Emergency Essence, both developed by respected homeopathic practitioners. They claim that the remedies will calm fears in emergencies and counteract stress. Both are available in chemists and health food stores.

Homeopathy is used to treat emotional and psychological problems on the same basis that it treats physical problems. The remedies aim to restore overall well-being. Buying over-the-counter will obviously be hit and miss compared to individual prescribing by a practitioner who will take a full case history and consider the 'whole person'.

The following list of individual homeopathic remedies for fears and phobias has been compiled by Lynne Crawford and Salah Ben Salim of London's Hale Clinic and is published with their permission. They suggest the remedies should be used for acute and emergency situations as well as for long-term problems. See the Remedy Profile for specific doses. If symptoms persist after the recommended course, they suggest seeking professional help from a homeopath if you wish to continue this type of treatment.

First, below, are the conditions with suggested remedies listed under them. To select appropriately, refer also to the Remedy Profile.

CONDITIONS AND REMEDIES

Panic attacks
Aconite, argentum nitricum, arsenicum album, gelsemium, kali-arsenicum, phosphorus, pulsatilla

Agoraphobia
Aconite, argentum nitricum, calcarea carbonica, gelsemium, lycopodium, natrum muriaticum

Claustrophobia
Aconite, argentum nitricum, natrum muriaticum, pulsatilla, stramonium

Fear that 'something will happen'
Causticum, nux vomica, phosphorus, tuberculinum

Fear of flying
Aconite, argentum nitricum, calcarea carbonica, natrum muriaticum

Fear of failure
Argentum nitricum, arnica, carcinocin, gelsemium, lycopodium, nux vomica, phosphorus

Fear of driving
Aconite, argentum nitricum, calcarea carbonica

Fear of animals
Calcarea carbonica, stramonium

Fear of spiders
Calcarea carbonica, gelsemium, natrum muriaticum

Fear of doctors and hospitals
Aconite, argentum nitricum, calcarea carbonica, gelsemium, natrum muriaticum, phosphorus

Fear of dentists
Aconite, argentum nitricum, calcarea carbonica, gelsemium

Fear of blood
Nux vomica

Social fears
1. Afraid of being humiliated: lycopodium, natrum muriaticum, staphysagria
2. Afraid of rejection: natrum muriaticum
3. Afraid of strangers: lycopodium

Sexual fears
Impotence: lycopodium

Fear of heights
Argentum nitricum, calcarea carbonica, gelsemium, natrum muriaticum, staphysagria

Fear of the telephone
Viscum album

Obsessive compulsive disorders
Arsenicum, carcinocin, medorrhinum, natrum muriaticum, nux vomica, pulsatilla, staphysagria, syphilinum, thuja

THE REMEDY PROFILE

See which type matches best your condition or personality

Aconite
Fear of crowds, great anxiety, agonising fear and restlessness.

Sudden panic, palpitations. Shock. Nervous and anxious state, dread of ordeals. Fear of death or injury. Fear of public places because there is a fear of death or injury. Dreadful foreboding.
Take one tablet in 30c potency up to three times a day for two or three days or before facing a difficult situation.

Anacardium
Loss of will, cannot control vocabulary. Thinking becomes difficult, memory weak. Lack of self-confidence.
Take one tablet in 30c potency twice a day for one day a week, over a period of four weeks only.

Argentum nitricum
Anticipation, anxiety and fear. May suffer diarrhoea at dreaded prospect. Nervous hysteria. Severe anxiety. Lack of self-confidence. Fear of crowds. Irrational fears and ideas. Timidity and anxiety. Migraine through anticipation. Better in cool fresh air and in motion. Fear of heights and looking down, also sight of high buildings. Feel buildings are closing in either side of street. Exam nerves, fear of death, stage-fright.
Take one tablet in 30c potency up to three times a day for two or three days or before facing a difficult situation.

Arnica
Trauma remedy, for loss, grief or shock. For people with great fears, often of crowds or public places. Night fears.
Take one tablet in 30c potency twice a day for one day a week, over a period of four weeks only.

Arsenicum album
Scared of thieves and death. Nervous, anxious and restless. Unable to be alone. Fear of doing themselves bodily harm if alone. Excessively neat and tidy.
Take one tablet in 30c potency twice a day for one day a week over a period of four weeks only.

Calcarea carbonica

Apprehensive, prefer to stay at home. Overwhelmed by worry. Anxiety with palpitations. Fear of disaster. Obstinate and irritable. Self-conscious, feel people are staring.
Take one tablet in 30c potency twice a day for one day a week over a period of four weeks only.

Carcinocin

Fear of the future. For 'nice' people who suppress their anger or those who want to fit in or lack self-esteem. When upset cannot communicate with others. Fear in pit of stomach. May be fastidious, suffer insomnia, fear failure, suffer Obsessive Compulsive disorders.
Take one tablet in 30c potency once a day for one day a week over a period of four weeks only.

Causticum

Anxiety, over-concern for others. Typical characteristic is to prefer cold drinks rather than hot ones.
Take one tablet in 30c potency twice a day for one day a week over a period of four weeks only.

Gelsemium

Confusion. Person wants to be held. Tremors or twitching of single muscle. Dazed, emotional and fearful state. Possible dizziness or weakness of knees, shaking with fright. Possible diarrhoea or incontinence or desire to pass quantities of urine. Panic through fear of insects or spiders.
Take one tablet in 30c potency twice a day for one day a week over a period of four weeks only.

Hyoscaymus

For nervous, excitable, irritable people. Those fearful of being alone in case they are pursued, or have fear of being poisoned, fear everyone, are prone to nervous muscle twitching, suspicious or jealous.
Take one tablet in 30c potency twice a day for one day a week over a period of four weeks only.

Kali-arsenicum

Sudden noise throws body into terror.
Take one tablet in 30c potency twice a day for one day a week over a period of four weeks only.

Lycopodium

Indecision, timidity, apprehension. Fear of being alone. Poor self-esteem, dependence on others. Fear of undertaking anything new yet goes through it with ease. Fear of meeting new people. Fear of public speaking. Weak memory, possible dyslexia. Improves on being mobile and with warm food and drink.
Take one tablet in 30c potency twice a day for one day a week over a period of four weeks only.

Medorrhinum

For great feelings of sadness. Tearful. Fear that they will never recover or are going insane. They feel that time passes slowly, they are distanced from reality, things seem strange. Loss of concentration, poor memory, tendency to repeat things. Better at night. Lean towards drugs, sex, late nights. Also for Obsessive Compulsive disorders.
Take one tablet in 30c potency twice a day for one day a week over a period of four weeks only.

Natrum muriaticum

Dislike of company or of being consoled. Desire to retreat behind emotional and physical wall, or to be alone to cry. Fear of narrow places. Possibly depressed and introverted, dwelling on past unpleasant memories. Irritable and fearful of rejection. Awkward speech patterns that make for difficulty socialising. Possible clumsiness.
Take one tablet in 30c potency twice a day for one day a week over a period of four weeks only.

Nux vomica

For irritable, ambitious, hard-working people. The nervous and excited, angry and impatient. They like stimulants, coffee, alcohol,

etc. Dislike being consoled. Have a fear that something will happen, suffer fear of failure, may have fear of blood. Also for Obsessive Compulsive disorders.
Take one tablet in 30c potency twice a day for one day a week over a period of four weeks only.

Phosphorus
Highly imaginative. Fear twilight, thunderstorms and lightning. Startle easily, fear future, need much reassurance and sympathy. Suffer mental fatigue, symptoms worse at twilight. Anger brings on anxiety.
Take one tablet in 30c potency twice a day for one day a week over a period of four weeks only.

Pulsatilla
For timid, mild, emotional, moody or tearful people. They feel better in open air and when in gentle motion. Prone to panic attacks, lack of self-esteem and claustrophobia. Never thirsty.
Take one tablet in 30c potency twice a day for one day a week over a period of four weeks only.

Staphysagria
For very sensitive, nervous people, easily hurt by people saying the slightest thing. Anger and insults make them feel ill, there may be a history of verbal, physical or sexual abuse. Anger is suppressed through fear and there is always a desire to make peace. Poor self-image, often shy and apologising, unassertive. Feelings of injustice suppressed. Fear of heights, fear of being humiliated. May suffer Obsessive Compulsive disorder.
Take one tablet in 30c potency twice a day for one day a week over a period of four weeks only.

Stramonium
For those who dread the dark and have a horror of shiny things. Prone to mood swings from joy to sadness. Feel better in company, especially at night. Fear of suffocation or claustrophobia and of animals. Feel isolated and separate. May have difficulty urinating.

Take one tablet in 30c potency twice a day for one day a week over a period of four weeks only.

Syphilinum
For people who suffer night fears or fears of insanity or feelings of hopelessness. Extremely restless people who wake up feeling wiped out. May be anti-social at times. Suffer Obsessive Compulsive disorder such as repeated hand washing.
Take one tablet in 30c potency once a day for one day a week over a period of four weeks only.

Thuja
For those with fixed ideas who are in a hurry and suffer bad temper. Worse at night when in bed – imagine seeing things with closed eyes. Fear of being followed. Feel they can predict time of own death. Sexual fears. May suffer Obsessive Compulsive disorders.
Take one tablet in 30c potency once a day for one day a week over a period of four weeks only.

Tuberculinum
For people with intense fatigue who constantly seek change. May be melancholy, depressed, have an intense inner yearning to seek spiritual truth. Burn candle at both ends. May have loathing for cats or dogs. Prone to colds, diarrhoea. Feel hopeless and anxious.
Take one tablet in 30c potency twice a day for one day a week over a period of four weeks only.

Viscum album
For the restless and nervous who are sad or dwell on past. May have obsessive dwelling on one thought or one unpleasant occurrence. Fear of telephones.
Take one tablet in 30c potency twice a day for one day a week over a period of four weeks only.

Homeopathic remedies may be bought at many health food stores or ordered from Helios Pharmacy, telephone 01892 53725 or Ainsworth Pharmacy, telephone 0171 935 5330.

SECTION 3

Finding Freedom: Best Ways to Tackle Specific Fears

CHAPTER 10

Getting Out of the House

The well-known name is agoraphobia: fear of open spaces – but in practice it covers going shopping, travelling, being in crowds, going anywhere unknown. It's the most common of all fears and phobias, with many more women affected than men.

Women are usually in their twenties or thirties when the problem starts. They are likely to be at home looking after young children, often with a husband who will do the shopping or take the children to school. They may not even be able to get out of the house to visit the doctor's surgery.

Husband and children may watch and worry, taking over all domestic tasks and treating the person like a frail invalid. Some men even need the dependence of a woman to boost their own ego, and almost collude with their partners to emphasise feminine 'weakness'. When a woman in this situation does find the courage to go out, get a job and make new friends, the balance of the partnership can change dramatically, with the husband sometimes resenting his wife's new-found independence.

Men too can suffer from agoraphobia and in different ways from women. They may find it very difficult to accept dependency or to admit to vulnerability. Instead, they might find excuses like headaches or tiredness are more acceptable when they have difficulty in leaving the house.

Agoraphobia often leads to depression. Travelling to work becomes an ordeal and continued absenteeism may mean that the best solution is to give up work altogether. For some, home then becomes a prison.

Milder forms of fear are more common. A person can travel to work, but not in the rush hour. Buses are acceptable but not trains. Local routes feel safe but not motorways. Corner shops can be entered but not supermarkets.

The fear is of going to places alone, of getting lost, perhaps of being attacked or of expecting some catastrophe to happen. In short, the fear is of the unknown. The physical reaction is always to do with feeling panic or anxiety, perhaps fainting or losing control.

HAZEL'S STORY: 'A VISIT TO THE SUPERMARKET TURNED INTO A NIGHTMARE'

Hazel is thirty-six, married with two young children. Her fear of going out was partly due to depression as well as agoraphobia.

'I got depressed when my daughter Beth was about six months old. I said it must be post-natal depression and expected it to go away. I don't really remember why I started feeling anxious when I was out of the house. Before I was married I'd worked in an architect's office and going out had never bothered me. I read somewhere that you might just be a bit self-conscious and think someone is looking at you, and then you get embarrassed for no real reason. And then you begin to get worried when you are going to the same place another time and eventually you dread going there.

'One day in the supermarket I thought I was going to faint. I felt my legs would collapse under me. I had to wait till the panic was over before I could get myself home. After that I would go to the corner shop though it was much more expensive. My husband was annoyed when he discovered I had stopped going to the supermarket. He thought I was lazy and I couldn't tell him the truth at the time. Finally, it was even a nightmare going to the local shop. I said I was tired, and my mum came round to help with the baby. She'd take her out and I'd say, "You may as well do the shopping while you're about it." My neighbour collected my little boy from school.

'Then my husband was made redundant. I said he would have to take Beth to nursery since he had nothing else to do. So it was easy to avoid going out. I didn't realise myself quite what was happening. I was so tired and getting headaches, and I had no energy to do anything. We had arguments about it.

'My husband got angry with me and said I needed to see a psychiatrist. I said there was nothing wrong with me, but I was beginning to realise that I was very depressed. When he got a job, I found I was dreading having him away from the house all day, and finally I told him and I agreed to see my doctor.

'It was a relief to talk. The doctor suggested some anti-depressants. I took them for a bit, though I hated the idea. They didn't seem to help very much. I tried going out and just felt terrified. Finally, my doctor sent me to the local hospital where I saw a psychiatrist. He asked me to use exposure techniques and explained what I should do.

'First I had to imagine going out, walking down the road and going to the supermarket. I was able to do this when I was talking to him, but when I was at home, it was really difficult. It was hard to concentrate, and really I didn't want to think about things that frightened me.

'He also gave me things to do, like going out a little way to the shops, then to go to meet Beth from school, and so on. I'd walk there trying to control my breathing the way I knew you should. I dreaded going, and sometimes I got into a panic, but I felt wonderful when I managed it.

'You're supposed to have someone to help you, but I felt better about doing it myself. The first time I tried going to the supermarket was a failure. I panicked before I even got there and almost ran home. But I knew by then that there would be some bad days and I'd have to live through them. The important thing is not to be discouraged, and honestly the thought of going back to my old hermit existence was too awful.

'My husband became more understanding eventually too. Instead of blaming me or making me feel as if I was insane, he began to encourage me to go out. He realised he'd not been helpful by letting me keep the whole thing a secret.

'Now, I look back and see how I was locked up in my shame as well as the fear itself. I didn't want to face the world and it was so easy to hide behind being a housewife. I've got a part-time job now, and I've learned to drive. I still lose confidence in myself at times, but I've learned to be much more independent. Is that a cure? I wouldn't want to be that sure about it. I do feel much much better.'

Helping to change the habit

Getting out into the world if you suffer from agoraphobia doesn't necessarily need professional help. You can adapt to your own needs the techniques already covered in this book.

★ *The desensitising/visualising technique* can help reduce the legs-turned-to-jelly syndrome. Like many people who suffer from agoraphobia, Hazel felt faint and thought her legs would collapse when she had her first major panic attack. This is a very unlikely thing to happen, and even if it did it wouldn't be the end of the world. Use visualisation to imagine going into a supermarket on trembling legs and think about what might happen if you fainted or whatever is your worst scenario. Don't evade the horror thoughts. Remind yourself that you can stop thinking at any moment, but choose instead to continue.

★ *Remember to breathe evenly* and use the anti-panic and relaxation measures that you have already learned should anxiety levels start to rise.

★ *The floating technique* will increase a sense of liberation when imagining or trying to go out in real life. With this, you accept the sensation and allow yourself to float into the shop, even floating right through the door and along the aisles if you want to make free with your imagination. Allow yourself to float past whatever thought or object is obstructing you.

★ *Don't forget self-talk*. Tell yourself that you can beat this fear and you will do so. You have the tools to get you through. You will take your goals step by step. You will think of the immediate task in front of you, and not the one that lurks ahead. So you will concentrate on getting the few yards to the garden gate and not think about the supermarket door till you arrive at it.

Getting Out of the House

★ *Give yourself some goals* and make them specific. Buy a notepad and write down your goals. Ask a helper to come with you on the first trips. Hazel's list might have gone something like this: 'I'll start with a walk to the corner.' The second goal, after a few days, might have been: 'Go to the nearest shop.' Her third goal: a trip to the nursery to collect her daughter. Later goals, each one attempted when she felt comfortable with the previous one, might have included going out alone and buying some groceries, going to a supermarket and spending half an hour, then an hour in there even if she completed her shopping in less time. It doesn't matter how small the progression is or how many times a goal is repeated so long as the next one is on the agenda and the exposure programme is continued with least interruption. Always have your anti-panic measures in mind ready to use.

★ *Start with something simple*. You may have several 'fear' points, so take the simplest one first and progress to the most difficult later. Quiet streets are easier than busy ones, walking is usually less challenging than using public transport. Going by car or getting on to a bus tends to be less difficult than taking a tube or train.

★ *Give yourself time*, both beforehand and when you are out. The last thing you want is to feel harassed and rushed before a planned outing. Use relaxation exercises before you go.

★ *Use a prop* to get yourself out into the street. A walking stick, a shopping trolley or a pram provide something to concentrate on and are also a real physical support. Dark glasses can be relaxing, chewing a sweet can be comforting. For most people, having something in their hands provides a sense of security, but for others, having hands free is more helpful, in which case use a rucksack instead of shopping bags.

★ *Face out the fear*. Plan to stay in your frightening situation for about an hour, even if it does mean hanging around outside the nursery or in the supermarket. If you do panic, stick with the experience, timing yourself to see just how long it lasts. The more prepared you are to face the fear the sooner it will go.

★ *Try not to care what others might be thinking*. Use self-talk for this. The ideal would be: 'What they might think is not really important . . . this is my goal and I have a purpose and there's no reason for other people to know it.' If this is too much, and you feel self-conscious when your goal is walking to the front gate and back or going halfway down the street, tell yourself you only went out to see if it was raining, or you have to go back because you have forgotten something. Choose goals like going to empty the dustbins, going to post a letter. If your goal involves hanging around in a shop, tell yourself that you have to wait for a friend so you may as well browse or sit and read a paper. At the end of the time, you can arrange for a friend to meet you or you can look at your watch and decide to go.

★ *Write down how you felt* when you get home, and keep a record of all your experiences, noting whether you felt panic, describing the physical symptoms and how you felt when you had used any self-help techniques. This is important because you will want to repeat your previous day's goal if things did not improve, and use the things that helped most for future goals. Remember the typical exposure programme described in chapter 8, planned for a man afraid of travelling on the Underground, which repeated each goal for several days. And be prepared to take a whole afternoon to complete one goal.

★ *Tell someone about your fears*. You will relieve yourself of the unnecessary burden of secrecy and also be in a position to ask a trusted friend or relative to help you achieve your goals by accompanying you on outings.

★ *Don't be fainthearted*, even if you do experience setbacks or find the first encounter very frightening. Use self-talk to restore your courage and optimism. You have no need to run away from your panic any more. You know you can look it in the face and live through it.

CHAPTER 11

Feeling Hemmed In

It's called claustrophobia, and it means a fear of confined spaces like lifts or the Underground or attics or cellars or telephone booths or aeroplanes. It's the confined space itself that triggers the fear, but claustrophobia can overlap with other fears. For instance, a fear of being confined in a plane may be just one aspect of a fear of flying, and a fear of being in a small room may be partly connected with social discomfort

Reasons, as with other phobias, may go back to some childhood experience, or may follow a bad experience in adulthood like panicking in a lift that has stuck and never wanting to repeat the feeling. As with other fears, psychologists have found that the exposure techniques and self-help programmes are quicker and more effective for most people than long-term psychotherapy.

If you suffer from claustrophobia, there can be a lot of things you don't like doing. Travelling can be a problem, or going to the theatre or cinema. Windows that don't open or heavy curtains that block out the light can pose a threat. Some people can't cope with bunk beds or even heavy bedcoverings because they feel smothered or over-enclosed.

JANET'S STORY: 'I WOULDN'T ENTER ROOMS WHERE THERE WAS NO NATURAL LIGHT'

Janet is thirty and works in a department store. A television programme led her to the realisation that she could be helped with her claustrophobia.

'When I was a child, I got locked in the lavatory. I know that sounds a joke, but it must be the reason for what happened later. I've gone over it many times. The lock had stuck. I was about six or seven. They couldn't get me out and had to call for the locksmith. My brother put a thin pad and pencil under the door, and I sat on the lavatory seat drawing. Funnily enough I don't think I felt anything at the time. I must have repressed it. When the locksmith came and let me out, they made a big fuss of me.

'Some time later I started to feel bad. I had a couple of nightmares, and I wanted my bedroom door open at night and the curtains too, so it was never pitch black. My mother was very good about it, but no one connected it with me being locked in, and I never thought to talk about it.

'I grew out of needing the door open, but I always kept the curtains open just a little to let in a chink of light. Then, somehow, when I was in my twenties, I started to get frightened again. It wasn't a very strong fear, but I wouldn't go into bathrooms or toilets where there was no natural light, no windows. And I wouldn't go into cupboards or cloakrooms where there were no windows. I could just about manage hallways as long as there was a light switched on. And I could go into places like cinemas or theatres. I could travel anywhere and wasn't bothered.

'None of this was a major problem. I could find ways around it. Toilets in public places like restaurants or cinemas may be in the basement or have no windows, so I learned to avoid them. I didn't like having the worry at the back of my mind and from time to time I'd tell myself that I should try to overcome my fears.

'I never thought of it as claustrophobia. I tried to understand what I felt. I knew it was only panic – that terrible trapped feeling – but it seemed to trivial and unimportant to do anything about it. I could never have gone to my doctor and talked about it because it wouldn't have been worth bothering him. Though come to think of it, if someone had said to me that it was claustrophobia, I might have done something earlier. But you don't always recognise the restrictions you place on yourself, and don't realise that people would take them seriously. And anyway, it still didn't occur to me to tell anyone.

'Then I saw a television programme on claustrophobia, and there was a sense of recognition. I saw how the psychologist got people to face up to what frightened them. I bought a book on relaxation, and then I did the most important thing of all. I told my flatmate about myself. Doing that made me realise two things. One was that the problem wasn't so unimportant. In fact, it was very important to me, and affected my life in small ways. The other was that it was a perfectly acceptable example of human weakness, and I didn't have to feel embarrassed about it.

'The first time I "exposed" myself was in the house of a friend of my flatmate's. She had this internal bathroom, and we went round especially so that I could try out facing my fear. The first time, I looked in the door. I didn't like the feeling so I came away immediately. I felt foolish and somehow also depressed. It discourages you from going on. But the second time we went round, I suddenly seemed to make this leap, as if my mind was preparing itself, I just opened the door and went in without hesitation.

'On my next visit I was able to half-close the door, and finally I was able to stay in there with the door shut for a few minutes. The first time I went in properly, I looked at myself in the mirror and I appeared just, well, ordinary. My fear didn't show at all. That was very reassuring.

'I have progressed to using a toilet in the basement of a restaurant. I've done that a couple of times now. I still have to expand my activities, but already I feel absurdly pleased with myself. Anybody would think I've climbed Mount Everest!'

Helping to change the habit

★ *Write down your fears*. If you can't go into a lift or other enclosed space, make a list of the reasons why. Maybe you fear feeling stuck, or think that the lift door may open when it is in the shaft. What do you think you would do? Lose control? Bang on the doors and shout? Try to jump out of the lift? Fall down in a faint? Write down the list of fears and your reactions in order of importance from one to ten and treat them in turn to the following, from easiest to most difficult.

Hidden Fears

★ *Desensitising/visualising*. Start by picturing in your mind the place or situation you fear. It may be an enclosed room or a lift or cupboard or bathroom. If there are several places, think first of the one that is least threatening, the one you could actually see yourself entering. If you get sensations of panic, start to breathe evenly and notice your physical sensations. See how long they take to subside. When one image is desensitised, work on another, continuing till you get to the most challenging.

★ *Use anti-panic measures* to reduce the fears. You know the physical reactions can be controlled and if you feel you want to do something dramatic like jump or bang on the doors you will be able to detach yourself from these wishes. Use the STOP trick on pages 49–50 to divert your thoughts.

★ *The floating technique* can help you to visualise an enclosed space. You can feel yourself floating over it, and experience the sense of calm and control this technique can create.

★ *Give yourself some goals*. Buy a notepad and write them down. Janet paced herself so that gradually she was able to enter the bathroom and stay there with the door closed. You can take the easiest goals first, practising them step-by-step till you feel confident to go to the next stage. Take a trusted friend with you when you first try out something in a public place, and don't be discouraged if you need several repeats.

★ *Give yourself time*, both beforehand and when you are out. Plan a relaxation session before you go, and remind yourself of the anti-panic measures.

★ *Face out the fear*. Take it moment by moment. If you panic, stick with the experience, timing yourself to see just how long it lasts. The more prepared you are to face the fear the sooner it will go.

★ *Invent a trick*. When Dr Robert Sharpe was accompanying a claustrophobic patient to the Underground, he noticed that the

Feeling Hemmed In

---

patient stamped his foot in response to his anxiety. The doctor immediately incorporated the action into his anxiety management programme. Later the patient merely had to think about stamping to control his fear. Find some similar means of reassurance and use it when approaching an anxiety-making location.

★ *Write down how you felt* when you get home, and keep a record of all your experiences, noting whether you felt panic, describing the physical symptoms. This is important because you will want to repeat your previous day's goal if things did not improve.

★ *Use self-talk* to boost your courage and optimism. You know that lifts don't get stuck very often, and the doors rarely open in the lift shaft. You know that panic subsides if you detach yourself from it. You know that bedclothes won't smother you and the dark is just the dark. Tell yourself these things. And don't forget to tell yourself that to be discouraged is temporary. You will progress.

★ *Write reminder cards*. Write your fears on one card; your reassuring self-talk on another, or on a series of cards. Take these with you to read as you approach a threatening environment, or when you are in one.

CHAPTER 12

When You Suffer from Social Fears

The basic problem for people with social fears is being noticed. Going into a restaurant, eating or drinking in front of other people, dining in other people's houses, going to parties, talking in groups of people, even writing a cheque in public or buttoning up a coat can cause self-consciousness that leads to panic. People with social fears often feel clumsy and awkward, dropping shopping bags, mislaying tickets. They may get anxious about losing passports or tickets, even though they have just located them in a pocket or handbag. They may have difficulty looking people in the eye or talking to people of the opposite sex.

Travelling can become an ordeal, too, not in the way that it hits those suffering from agoraphobia, but because it may entail sitting opposite other passengers or having to pass a queue or walk down a narrow aisle. The fear here is of being observed, though the end result can be staying at home to avoid potential panic.

People with social fears are not just shy, they are mega shy, and there are an awful lot of them about. Around 40 per cent of the population admit to being shy or having some kind of social fear, while 3 per cent, that's one million, come into the category of having a social phobia and probably need treatment so that they are no longer cut off from the world.

Typical social phobias come in two categories. The most common is the social set: being introduced to strangers, meeting people in authority, eating or drinking in public places, participating in small groups, entering a party group, being teased. The other category is performance: speaking in public, writing or signing a cheque in front of others, acting, etc, giving a report, expressing disagreement.

Hidden Fears

The most common symptoms experienced by people with intense fears of these situations are, in order of prevalence, palpitations, trembling, sweating, tense muscles, sinking stomach, dry mouth, feeling hot or cold, blushing.

The problem may begin in childhood or mid-teens. The small boy who sits at the back of the class and never puts his hand up, may develop social fears in adolescence, especially if the teacher homes in on him and he stutters out an inadequate response, not because he doesn't know the answer, but because his mind goes blank and he panics. The reclusive teenager who stays in his room and has few friends is further along the line. While the family think they have a moody and unfriendly adolescent on their hands, he or she may be anxious, depressed, possibly suicidal. School performance, work, family relationships, marriage, friendships may be severely affected in people with social phobias.

The shame and sense of inadequacy are often so great that the victims never reveal the true reason for not joining in, or refusing invitations or avoiding promotion. Often they are not fully aware of the handicap themselves. 'I'm just boring . . . nobody is interested in me', are the kinds of self-defeating things they tell themselves.

ROY'S STORY: 'TO ME TREMBLING AND BLUSHING IN PUBLIC WAS TERRIBLE'

Roy is thirty, unmarried and working in local government. He found help through a local group.

'I think I was always a bit shy and self-conscious as a child. I don't remember any single incident that worried me, but I used to watch other people to make sure I did the right thing, and I never liked the teacher drawing attention to me in school.

'I was about eighteen when it really began to be troublesome. I tried to chat up this girl, and I made a mess of it. The thing still embarrasses me when I think about it. After that I began to find it difficult to accept social invitations. I made excuses. I was very quiet in groups and when I did say anything I immediately felt I'd made a fool of myself. If anyone contradicted me or said something that gave an opposite view I would feel they were criticising me. I would go over in my mind what I had said and what they had said for days after, and I always felt I'd done the wrong thing and maybe other people were criticising me or saying I was stupid. I went into a shell.

'Then I started making myself go out again and I began to feel more confident, but again there was a scene with a girl. We were in a restaurant and I felt nervous. When it came to paying the bill I couldn't sign the cheque card receipt. My hand trembled, I felt I couldn't get it down to the piece of paper. I felt terrified. I said something about paying with cash instead, but I didn't have enough, and then the girl offered to pay. I sent her a cheque the next day, but I was really embarrassed. I avoided social outings after that. I felt very depressed and I began to drink, and that worried me because I had an uncle who was an alcoholic.

'I went to my doctor, and he prescribed tranquillisers. I couldn't bring myself to explain what was really wrong, but I felt I didn't want drugs. It was in the doctor's waiting room that I read about a local group for people with social fears. I felt very foolish about contacting them and I didn't tell anyone about it, but I finally plucked up courage and went to a meeting. It changed everything. I had this revelation that all the turmoil inside me was a part of lots of other people's experience too. It was an enormous relief to realise you're not alone, and you can somehow put your problem into perspective. At last I was able to tell my family and friends about it.

'The first thing I learned was that trembling and blushing in public are not so terrible. Other people hardly notice, and even if they do, the whole thing passes in a few minutes or even seconds. You learn to breathe more slowly – I found that concentrating on expanding the abdomen made me relax quickly, and I use that kind of breathing if I have a sleepless night too.

'Talking to other people in the group made me realise that many people are shy and find it difficult to speak out. I gave myself a set of aims, just basic things like deliberately starting up a conversation with someone at work. I asked if she had watched a television show the night before, and when she said no, instead of leaving it at that, I told her about it. I knew it could be difficult to end the conversation, and I did feel awkward doing it, but I wanted something positive to report back to the group so I just did what I could. When I saw her later in the day I made myself say "hi" quite casually, and that somehow made the thing better.

'In the group, I learned how to make better eye-to-eye contact. I'd avoided looking at people before, and when we tried avoiding and then looking in role play I could see the first way is very off-putting. It actually makes other people feel shy and awkward too.

'I found ways to make things easier for myself. After I told my family and one or two friends about the problem, I started going out with them. I carried enough cash till I gave myself the task of writing out a cheque in public. I started going to restaurants and I ate things like risotto which only needed one hand – my right hand always seemed less shaky than the left. I found drinking from a glass easier than using a handle on a cup, so I avoided asking for tea or coffee.

'I wouldn't say I'm a totally confident person yet. Maybe I never will be. But I actually quite enjoy the challenge of setting myself aims, and I feel wonderful when I've achieved them.'

Helping to change the habit
Use the self-help techniques and tips already covered, adapting them to your needs.

★ *Desensitising/visualising technique*: Imagine being in the social situation that upsets you. Try the least threatening ones first. Then let yourself imagine your way through a particularly 'humiliating' situation – like Roy's experience when paying the bill. Imagine the consequences if things go wrong and keep on thinking about it till you begin to feel comfortable with your feelings. Think about what happened and realise that it caused no damage to anyone else and need cause no further damage to you.

★ *Give yourself some goals*. Plan to start a short conversation with someone, allowing it to last for no more than two sentences before you deliberately bring the conversation to an end. Agree to meet someone in a public place, preferably a pub or café (you don't have to stay there on the first or second attempts). If that's too difficult, meet in a park or at a busy train station and work up to pubs and cafés later. Arrange to meet at a public place and deliberately get there first. At a later stage, get there first and order a drink.

★ *Ask open-ended questions* in conversation, not questions that require only a yes or no in reply. Asking 'Where do you live?' is better than asking 'Do you live in Oxford?' and makes it easier for you to follow up with 'What's it like living there?' If the response is non-committal you can still respond by giving your opinion of the place or by talking of your desire to go there or by sharing some other information about yourself that is vaguely relevant.

★ *If you panic*, use the techniques you have learned in this book. Live with the panic (float over it). Label the fear in terms of severity from one (worst) to ten (bearable). Once you've neared ten, take a deep breath and then get on with your immediate goal.

★ *Use a prop if you feel you are on show in public*. Take a book, some knitting, do a crossword puzzle to keep yourself occupied when you are waiting in a public place. Keep tickets and coins easily accessible if a sense of awkwardness makes you feel clumsy. A belt bag or small purse that hangs from the shoulder may be suitable. Use cash till you are confident you can write a cheque without trembling (that can be one of your goals). Wear unfussy clothes and don't bother to button up coats. Choose foods that are easy to eat – not spaghetti, for instance.

★ *Learn the rules of eye-to-eye contact*. Staring is not appropriate. Instead, the norm is to make brief initial eye-to-eye contact, then look anywhere you wish, returning to eye-to-eye contact when you make a point and when parting. Practise at home with a trusted friend or relative. Concentrate on the current conversation and you won't worry about eye contact.

When You Suffer from Social Fears

★ *Remember to change your breathing level* and to relax in a social situation. Do this before picking up a cup or glass if you fear you will tremble. Concentrate on listening or observing or asking a question of someone – see the distraction method on pages 88–90.

★ *Test the water*. This one takes guts but it can be an eye-opener: do the thing you fear most and observe responses. Deliberately tremble as you pick up a glass, deliberately 'dry up' for a moment or pause when you are talking to a group or in public. Psychologist Dr David Clarke of the University of Oxford even tells his patients with fear of perspiring to wet their underarm shirt sleeves with water and then wave their arms about and watch for responses. Patients then realise that most people don't notice, or appear indifferent. (It helps to boost confidence if you let a friend in on this one before you do it.)

★ *Intentionally disagree* during conversation, planning to do so in advance. Observe responses and discover that you can do it without devastating effect.

★ *Make self-talk work for you* by banishing thoughts like 'I am just a misfit,' or 'Nobody wants to know me.' Tell yourself that being criticised is not a disaster. It's OK for you to dislike or criticise other people, and it's OK for them to do it too. You and they will survive. Tell yourself that you are allowed to fail (you allow other people to fail don't you?). Unpleasant, and even humiliating events are Not That Bad, they only seem so in your own mind. Remind yourself that even if people are looking at you, it doesn't matter.

★ *Cultivate a sense of proportion, and use it when you start to think negatively*. When someone gets up to leave the room as you are talking, it is unlikely to be a reflection on you. They are probably going to the toilet or getting a glass of water. Not everything that other people say or do is a comment on your behaviour. If someone seems to be staring at you, they are likely to be deep in thought, though they might, of course, simply find you fascinating in the nicest possible way.

★ *Take things slowly*. Give yourself plenty of time when you are going out on a social occasion. Remind yourself of the relaxation and anti-panic measures. A glass of wine or spirits, just one, may help you relax before you go out.

★ *Write down how you felt* when you get home, and keep a record of all your experiences, noting whether you felt panic, etc. You will want to repeat your previous day's goal if things did not improve.

★ *Free yourself from what other people think of you*. You don't really know what they think anyway. If you make a fool of yourself, the chances are that it only really matters to you. Practise forgiving yourself.

★ *Take an assertiveness training course*. You will learn new social skills – see more on this training on pages 159–61.

WHAT'S SO TERRIBLE ABOUT BLUSHING?

Getting red in the face is something that happens when we become overheated, often through exercise, or we may become flushed when we are angry. It also happens when we are embarrassed, which is when we call it blushing.

The body reaction is the same in all three situations: skin temperature increases and small veins close to the skin's surface become congested with blood, a process that actually enhances heat loss through the skin and aids cooling. Though we all have this protective device, the effect in some people is more visible than in others. It's particularly noticeable in those with fair hair and fine skin – we can see them flush up to the roots, and see them cool down again often within seconds.

No one minds a bit about flushing through exercise or anger, but we mind quite a lot about blushing through embarrassment. People with social fears may be prone to blushing, especially when they do something that they think will bring attention to themselves. And for some people, blushing itself is the focus of their fear, the thing that stops them going to parties or talking to people or eating in public.

It was blushing that stopped Brenda from being a bridesmaid at her sister's wedding: 'I knew I couldn't go through with it – the thought of all those people looking at me. It makes me blush just to think about it. Suppose I tripped going up the aisle or I dropped a tissue, and then I blushed? I'd be so embarrassed, and then I'd blush some more.'

This pattern is very typical: lack of composure leads to a minor social embarrassment which leads to blushing which in turn creates more blushing. The end result is avoidance.

Ways to stop blushing

★ *Paradoxical Intention*. This is a method used by some psychotherapists which you can develop on a self-help basis. It sounds distinctly odd, but it works. The idea is to try to blush deliberately. This is quite the opposite to Brenda's problem of blushing at the mere thought of being looked at in public. With Paradoxical Intention you put yourself in control.

Dr Richard Stern, consultant psychiatrist at St George's Hospital in London, reports a successful case in his book *Mastering Phobias*. His patient wore high-necked clothes because she said she would otherwise feel exposed and would visibly flush on her face and neck. She also blushed when someone called out her name in the office.

During a session with Dr Stern, the patient's boyfriend suggested a strange-sounding exercise. She would look at herself in a mirror naked from the waist up while he called out her name. At first, she said the mere thought of it would make her either die of embarrassment or die laughing, but she tried the experiment for several days and found to her surprise that she was unable to blush. She made a huge effort to blush in front of the mirror but nothing happened. She tried deliberately blushing in the office when her name was called out and found the trick worked there too.

There are three simple steps (and you don't need a boyfriend or therapist for them):
1. Tell yourself to blush, starting off at home when you are on your own, and practising daily as often as you can.
2. Start to do the same when you are with people. Try it out when you are on a bus or train.
3. Try the technique in a situation you would normally find embarrassing.

★ *Distraction method*. This technique focuses on redirecting thoughts so you are distracted from the idea of blushing. You start by trying to understand your behaviour, checking yourself on the following:

Q What are my first thoughts on meeting people?
(One answer might well be: 'I hope I don't blush.')
Q What do I first pay attention to when meeting people?
(Their actions, words, your own reactions, especially blushing?)
Q How do I feel when I know I am about to blush?
(Hope no one notices, want to get away?)
Q What do you feel when you know you are blushing?
(It's embarrassing, what must they think of me?)

Give yourself a fortnight to monitor your reactions in real life, recording your reactions and noting whether there are any changes along the way. Ask yourself why blushing is so embarrassing and what is the worst thing that could happen if you do blush.

Then progress to the next stage of self-questioning in which you pay special attention to the behaviour of others when you are talking with them:

Q What is the other person doing as we talk?
(The answer might be laughing or gesturing or looking serious or scratching their head.)
Q What is their voice like?
(High-pitched or low, loud or soft, foreign accent, fast, slow?)
Q Is the conversation on an equal footing or is the other person

dominating or are you dominating?

Q Do they seem confident or unsure or flustered? Do they blush?

This method aims to help you recognise your thinking pattern and directs your attention away from yourself on to others. It also helps you towards some positive self-talk, so you develop more life-enhancing answers to the first set of questions.

Use the above method along with relaxation techniques for a calming effect. And the floating idea will act as an anti-blushing aid too.

ALL ALONE ON THE TELEPHONE

Having difficulty using the telephone may seem like the opposite to a social fear, but it is still one. No one would see you blushing, but you don't get the feedback that occurs in face-to-face conversation: no reassuring nods or smiles or the sense that someone is listening seriously to what you are saying. A disembodied voice, if you are not too sure of yourself and have an over-active imagination, can sound non-committal or disapproving or menacing.

According to psychologist Dr Guy Fielding of Queen Margaret College in Edinburgh, 2.5 million people in the UK suffer from 'telephone apprehension', and 2.5 per cent of them are fearful to the point of being phobic. A panic attack can be triggered even when the phone rings, never mind about when you're contemplating using it.

Fear of having to speak, getting an angry or unwelcoming reception, saying the wrong thing, ending a conversation are also triggers for panic. Some people can only make calls to friends or relatives, but never to anyone official. Others, like Beverly who was mentioned earlier in this book, can only make business calls and don't have the social confidence to expect to be welcomed on the phone by friends.

How to feel happier about the telephone
Use any of the advice for social fears above, adapting it to your needs by, for instance, visualising yourself making a telephone call

and using self-talk to boost your confidence. Positive exposure is the best and quickest way to overcome the fear. Some of the questions in the Distraction Method above can be used for telephone conversations.

★ *If you've given up using the phone* altogether, start again by dialling the speaking clock. Practise relaxation first, get into even-breathing mode and then dial. Don't go on to each of the next stages till you are ready for them.

★ *Telephone a trusted friend* or family member, planning the call with them in advance so they can help you through any panic attack while you are speaking or listening.

★ *Get them to telephone you* at an agreed time and again stay with it through any panic attack.

★ *Progress to ringing*, and being rung, at unpredictable times. Practise the Distraction Method.

CHAPTER 13

Fear of Flying

Many people don't like flying. They feel jittery, on edge and watchful, no matter how cheerful the pilot sounds or how impassive the air stewards appear. There are two big bad things about flying: one, it doesn't feel natural, and two, you've got no control over the operation. No wonder then that dislike can develop into a phobia.

Could I have a seat near enough the emergency exit to get out fast, but far enough from it not to be sucked out if the door comes off?

Hidden Fears

Novelist Erica Jong, in her book *Fear of Flying*, summed it up for many when she wrote that every flight was an attempt to prove that the laws of aerodynamics are not flimsy superstitions, when in her heart of hearts she was convinced they were. Only her concentration, she was sure, kept the plane aloft.

How would such a fear of flying start? There's the basic distrust to begin with, which can easily be topped up with various negative experiences: a single bumpy journey, perhaps in poor weather conditions; a delay in departure, providing opportunity for tension to build up; and even when you land safe and sound, a host of unpleasant memories so that you perhaps approach the return journey with a sense of dread. Who would want to repeat that just to go on holiday?

Since most of us don't lead a jet-setting life, there's not much opportunity for a repeat try-out soon after. The bad memory stays and grows. Avoidance is easy. It's the perfect climate to trigger a phobia.

As with other irrational fears, there may, however, be no identifiable incident. Fears about flying can be part and parcel of several other fears, often in the agoraphobia or social phobia group. Feeling exposed or self-conscious in a strange and public place is just as potent as being distrustful of the laws of aerodynamics.

DINA'S STORY: 'IT FELT AS IF IT WAS ONLY A MATTER OF LUCK THAT THE PLANE DIDN'T CRASH'

Dina is forty-five and is a social worker. She went on a course to help overcome her fear of flying.

'I've always been scared of heights. Don't like to go to the tops of buildings, don't like looking out of windows, don't like lifts or bridges. There's this dizziness sensation, and my feet feel sort of weak. Still, I do take lifts and cross bridges. I seem to be able to make myself do things I don't like, and at least the suffering time is short.

'But planes are different. You are in them for a long time. I'd make myself fly. I'd always tell myself I could do it. When we booked for holidays I would feel OK about it and then the worry would grow till, say a week before the flight, I'd want to pull out, especially if the weather forecast was bad. And then my partner would be furious. So I'd feel guilty and miserable and swear we'd never fly again.

'My main fear was that I would run screaming down the aisle. Of course, I never did. I just sat white-knuckled in my seat, looking for signs of concern in the air stewards when there was turbulence or whenever there was an announcement from the pilot. I always avoided looking out of the window and felt terrified when we seemed to go on a slant. I was never reassured just because we made a safe landing. To me it was always pure luck that the plane hadn't crashed.

'All the same, I didn't want to avoid flying – all that extra travelling by land, and anyway I hate being restricted. The crunch came when my partner was going on a business trip to New York and I had the opportunity to go with him on a free ticket. I didn't want to refuse, so I decided to get serious about kicking the flying phobic habit.

'I did it the expensive way, enrolling on a day's course which ends with a forty-five minute flight on a British Airways jet. It cost £169 and what you get is a presentation by two BA captains and a psychologist. They tell you how aircraft fly. You get slides and technical explanations – really reassuring stuff. Now I know that going up on a slant is normal.

'There was also a lot of talk about fear of heights and going in lifts. It seems I am not unique! Losing control and being frightened of falling were things that other people in the group felt too. There was a woman who flew on business every week and suddenly couldn't; also a man who'd boarded a plane and had to get off at the last minute. He'd relied on tranquillisers in the past, thought he could manage without them and then took fright. A nightmare!

'In the afternoon we went on the flight, along with the psychologist and BA personnel. They gave a running commentary from the flight deck, explaining what the different sounds and movements meant. Quite a few of us had assumed that any change of sound or movement was bad news but they explained that engine change noises are normal. Turbulence was likened to driving on a cobbled road or rough-riding on a choppy sea.

'I realised my most awful moment was at take-off. It was then that I felt trapped. The answer to that is to try to stay relaxed, and one of the things you can buy through the course organisers is a cassette relaxation tape. They also do a video and a book dealing with flying fears.

'The thing worked! I went on that business trip with my partner, and yes I did have to rely on the relaxation tape. The people who ran the course offer a "special assistance service" to passengers going on British Airways from the UK. You tell the air stewards and they really do everything to reassure you. Since then I've flown a few times. I have to psych myself up for it but I guess I'm pretty well desensitised. I'm totally easy about lifts and bridges and it's nice not to have to tell people that I prefer taking the ferry to Spain.'

Helping to change the habit

★ *Fear of Flying Courses*: They are run from Manchester and London Heathrow airports by Aviatours, and cost around £170. A back-up book and video are also available from Aviatours, plus an audio cassette relaxation tape. A similar course is run by Britannia Airways from East Midlands airport at £105. (See details and addresses on page 176.)

The problem with trying to conquer a deep fear of flying is that you can't easily create a step-by-step programme by yourself. You need a plane to do that, which is what the special courses provide. But the self-help techniques already described in this book will help, and if the fear is not so severe, they may be sufficient. Adapt them to your needs in the following ways.

★ *Desensitising/visualising*. Start by imagining you are going on a plane journey. Think of travelling to the airport, the queues when you get there. Progress to checking in, waiting for the flight to be called, entering the plane, and finding your seat. Note which stages produce most fear. Write down your worries in a list, in order of severity, label them one to ten and work on the least threatening first. If you feel fear, use relaxation and breathing techniques.

★ *Give yourself goals*. Practise going in lifts or travelling over bridges, extending the time in these places over days or weeks. Spend an afternoon at an airport. Arrange to meet people off planes if possible.

★ *When you book a flight*, prepare yourself well in advance, practising relaxation, anti-panic measures, etc, daily for at least a week. Recall or read over your worry list and if you panic use the techniques you have learned in this book. Live with the panic (float over it). Use the STOP technique on pages 49–50.

★ *Plan everything carefully*. Make lists for packing; do everything slowly and methodically; have tickets and passport in an accessible place; give yourself plenty of time.

★ *Use self-talk to keep yourself calm on a flight*. Tell yourself to slow down, take everything step by step. Remind yourself to breathe evenly. If you find a message from the pilot or air stewards is ominous, ask yourself the following questions: 'Is there really any evidence for my worry, or am I looking for bad signs? . . . Is it reasonable to expect absolute assurances on safety? I don't do it in a car or train.' If you hear an unfamiliar sound or see what seems to be a loose rivet on the wing, again seek reality with such thoughts as: 'There is probably a good reason for that and my worrying about it is quite pointless. I cannot be in control of this plane any more than I can be in control of any other form of transport as a passenger.'

★ *Take along some suitable distractions*: a compulsive thriller that you have already started, a crossword puzzle, a book of quizzes or mental teasers, a personal cassette with music or relaxation tapes. Start on one of these as soon as you are settled in your seat and concentrate quietly. Take along sweets or chewing gum as extra soothers.

★ *If you can't concentrate during a flight*, keep your head still, close your eyes and incline the seat back, then practise relaxation.

★ *Avoid gas-producing foods*. Flatulence can build up because of pressure changes in a plane, so avoid beans, curries, cabbage and carbonated drinks before and during a flight.

★ *Forget the free alcoholic drink*. Alcohol can make you feel lightheaded and though a little may relax you, it could have the opposite effect and reduce your sense of control. Alcohol also increases dehydration, loss of body fluid in flight. Have regular non-alcoholic drinks instead to prevent fluid loss.

★ *Don't get stuck in your seat*. Make a visit to the toilet one of your goals. Check first that there are no trolleys blocking the aisles, and that the toilet is not engaged. If it is, and you still decide to go, be prepared to stand in a queue. Moving about a little helps reduce feet swelling, which is due to fluid retention, an effect of pressure change. Wriggle your feet and ankles to pep up circulation.

★ *If you get ear discomfort*, it will again be due to pressure change. Relieve pain by pinching nostrils and blowing against the pressure. Swallow, yawn, move your jaw from side to side or suck a sweet. If none of these work, ask the steward for two polystyrene cups half-filled with wads of cottonwool squeezed out in hot water. The cups placed over each ear can ease severe pain by providing warmth and change of air pressure.

★ *If the plane banks or slants*, don't go rigid – doing so won't keep the plane in the air. The movements are normal procedure and the best you can do is to be extra vigilant about keeping relaxed. Resign yourself to whatever happens next, visualising the worst if you can't let go of the anxiety. After all, if there is an emergency, there may be only two alternatives: to resign yourself to the fact that you can do nothing, or to keep yourself as cool-headed as possible in order to respond well to rescue instructions.

Fear of Flying

★ *If your flying fear is one of several fears*, read chapters 10, 11 or 12 which cover agoraphobia, claustrophobia and social fears.

"We are now cruising at an altitude of approximately 35000 feet..."

CRUISING?

CHAPTER 14

Who's Afraid of the Big, Fast Motorway?

Driving on motorways or major routes is an obstacle for some people. This is yet another example of the stresses of modern life, and it's especially difficult for some women. Fast driving may seem simple when compared to the stop/start of driving in towns, but can also seem relentless and competitive and bring out a great deal of stress and nervous tension.

The problem may be part of a cluster of fears – agoraphobia, claustrophobia or social fears. Driving involves being out there in a possibly threatening world, and also in a confined space, and the social element is the fact that you are cheek by jowl with other drivers who may appear to be hostile or who actually are hostile and impatient.

In many ways, however, fast, continuous driving is in a category of its own, like fear of flying. This one needs special care because you do want to avoid panic when in the driving seat, but, as with other fears, it is practice and experience that breed confidence and take the panic away.

BARBARA'S STORY: 'I JUST GOT OUT OF THE HABIT OF MOTORWAY DRIVING, AND THEN I COULDN'T DO IT'

Barbara is fifty and has been driving for half her life, but it has been mainly in towns, taking her children to school when they were younger, using the car for shopping, but rarely driving for long distances.

'When I was first driving, I'd go anywhere. It never occurred to me not to. I remember borrowing a friend's cottage and thinking nothing of driving my three children there on my own in my little secondhand car. I never went fast because the car wasn't up to it, and I hated being just behind the juggernauts, but I managed just the same.

'I remember feeling what I now can describe as panic, though I called it stress at the time, when I was scared to overtake. It sort of shook me up and made me tremble. I told myself that driving is a stressful business, and it was an easy thing to avoid because my husband has always preferred to drive, especially long distances. He gets car sick as a passenger.

'My friends would laugh, especially the ones who live in the country and are terrified of London traffic. They couldn't understand how I can drive round hectic places like Hyde Park Corner without worrying too much about it. I do worry a little, but on the other hand, London driving is familiar to me. I like the fact that you have to slow down at traffic lights. I can manage narrow streets and giving way to let traffic through. There's this thing that I've heard about called Buddhist driving. It means you always give way to other people and watch their amazement. I try it at times, though I think it can add to the confusion when you get into a tricky situation.

'I don't like feeling dependent, so I've been meaning to take myself in hand for ages, even though I've been lazy about getting round to it. I am trying to do something now, after all these years, simply because my daughter is moving to the country and if I want to see her regularly it would be useful to drive there.

'I don't get a lot of opportunity for motorway driving, but now I make the effort when there is an occasion. I've had three tries so far, always with my husband as a passenger, and always on a route I know quite well.

'The first time I tried, I made a huge effort to relax and keep cool, though I did feel tense and exhausted by the end. I found that after driving for a while at a steady speed, I wanted to take my foot off the accelerator, and I had to concentrate hard on keeping it there. That's still the main problem. It's because I'm so used to slowing down when driving in town that it seems unnatural not to.

'On my second try I started to panic because the flow of traffic was slowing slightly and I was uncertain whether to use the brake or just take my foot off the accelerator. I realise it's the kind of judgement you get with experience. All you can do with this kind of thing is stick at it and learn by your mistakes.'

Helping to change the habit

★ *Prepare yourself before you start*. Relax, remind yourself about even breathing, and choose a route you know, with a partner or friend as a passenger.

★ *Travel between two motorway junctions only at first*, choosing a quiet time.

★ *Keep a steady speed on the inside lane* and don't worry about overtaking till you become more experienced and assured.

★ *Don't worry about holding people up* either. If you are driving safely and steadily, overtaking is their problem. Use self-talk to remind yourself of this: repeat the previous sentence to yourself.

★ *If you have to pull out or change lanes*, concentrate on the task in hand and don't think about other drivers' reactions.

★ *If hesitations generate horn-blowing, use self-talk*: 'My goal is more important than their impatience . . . If they are thinking I'm a silly old dodderer or a typical woman driver, too bad. I have my own agenda, and it's more important to me.'

★ *Keep up your pace*. The steady, constant pace of motorways and major roads is less acceptable to some drivers than the slower stops and starts of traffic lights. Resist an urge to slow down by observing that your foot is steady on the accelerator and should stay that way.

★ *If your mind jumps ahead* to a difficult interchange or roundabout you know is coming up, bring your concentration back to the present and the immediate demands.

★ *Joining a motorway* can be a frightening moment, but again keep a steady pace. If you find yourself nearing the end of the joining lane, then slow down or stop till a safe space emerges.

★ *If you miss an exit* (a common fear that deters drivers from using motorways), then go on till you get to the next one. It's not a major disaster. Repeat that sentence in your self-talk. As you panic less, you will be able to make better sense of the signs.

CHAPTER 15

Insects, Animals and Objectionable Objects

It's hard to imagine that someone is frightened of rhubarb or buttons, frightened, that is, to the degree of phobia, so that the panic they experience makes them do anything to avoid contact with such objects. On the other hand, few of us are greatly fond of insects. We call them creepy crawlies and brush them away if they come too close, so it's not too hard to imagine they might trigger stronger reactions in some people. And even animal lovers may appreciate that not everyone likes dogs or cats or mice or pigeons. Yet fears of insects, animals or objects are quite similar. The reaction does not usually spread beyond one species or one kind of object, so it's different from social fears or agoraphobia which may involve fear of several situations.

A specific fear will probably go back to childhood. There may be a remembered reason, such as a frightening incident, but not always. It is quite common for small children to go through a phase when they fear spiders or dogs, though in time the majority grow out of it. For some reason, larger feathered birds are feared more than small ones, while the spider seems to have acquired an image of being loathsome and evil.

Dr Isaac Marks looked into the background of spider phobics and found that the majority were women, some of whom had 'caught' their fear from their mothers, but the families, on the whole, were stable with no particular history of mental disorder or emotional upset. If there was a triggering incident, it was likely to be quite small.

Though insect and animal fears are specific, the result can still be highly inconvenient. Like Brian, the architect who designed his house to act as a spider-detector, people may go to extraordinary lengths to avoid a chance encounter with the focus of their phobia. Fear of dogs or cats may entail choosing detours to shops or public transport in order to avoid streets where such pets live. Parks, the countryside, the beach, a country cottage may hold hidden terrors.

ELLA'S STORY: 'I DREAMT ABOUT SPIDERS – THEY WERE THE ENEMY'

Ella is thirty-five, a company director. She reached the stage in her 'treatment' when she could touch spiders.

'It's something I always felt ridiculous about. I can't remember a time when I didn't fear spiders, even very tiny ones. There was I, running a company, dealing with powerful men, talking to financial advisers and bank managers, and I'd go to pieces if I saw a spider.

'One night, I'd just returned from a trip abroad, and I opened the door to my bedroom and saw this huge spider. I just shut the door and put a towel against the bottom, to keep the thing in, and I slept on the sofa. Except, of course, that I didn't sleep. I lay there worrying all night, the lights blazing, getting up every so often to check that no spider had invaded the living room. And in the morning I had to go to a neighbour and ask her to examine the bedroom. When she couldn't find the spider, I wanted to move out. I actually slept in the living room for two more nights, which was quite absurd.

'I'd had recurring nightmares about spiders for years. I would wake up sweating, thinking the window had blown open – I always slept with the window closed – and feeling that somehow I was being attacked by a spider. Not quite attacked, but threatened. The thing was evil, it was coming for me. It somehow knew me. It was my enemy. That's how I felt about the big spider in my bedroom.

'It wouldn't have been any good to throw it out of the window, or even to get someone else to do it, because I was sure it would return to taunt me. The only way I could get relief, I knew from previous experiences, was to be certain that it was dead. I hated killing it and always thought that I didn't do it properly and that it would return. On this occasion, I never found it, my sleep was

Insects, Animals and Objectionable Objects

getting more and more disturbed, and finally I could see that I had to take myself in hand.

'I'd read about Triumph over Phobia, a self-help group for people with spider phobias, and I decided it was time to go to their meetings. I hadn't been one of those who keep their phobia a secret because basically I am a pretty confident person, but all the same I did feel a bit unsure about meeting other sufferers. I'm not really the type to share things in that way. But I liked the practical approach. We had weekly meetings and were given tasks to do.

'The first thing I was asked to do was to draw a spider from memory. Then I started going to the library and looking at pictures of spiders in children's books. I was encouraged to touch the pictures. Eventually, I was able to hold a toy plastic spider, then a toy furry one – and at a meeting I allowed myself to sit near a real spider in a transparent box.

'Finally, I could touch a real spider, though I had it at home for several days in a box before I did so. I could hardly believe myself. But there it was. And I actually felt perfectly comfortable with it. Now, I never think about spiders or whether they are hiding in my bedroom. They are no longer my enemy. We coexist.'

Helping to change the habit
Use the self-help techniques and tips already covered in this book, adapting them to your situation.

★ *Desensitising/visualising technique*. Imagine being in a familiar street or building where you have seen, or expect to see, the insect or animal or object that you fear. Visualise the setting and yourself approaching it. When this seems comfortable, get nearer, and in your mind stroke or touch it. These exercises will familiarise you with real-life encounters.

★ *Keep a photograph* of your fear-inducing subject in some prominent place where you can see it. Cut out pictures from newspapers or magazines. Look at these pictures fully. You may have to start by looking at them out of the corner of your eye, but make your goals progress to full visibility. Keep on looking, giving time for the panic, if it arises, to fade, so you are still looking when you no longer feel fear. Think of the achievement as staring out the feared object to the point when your only reaction is boredom.

★ *Go to a museum if you can*, and seek out the natural history department for encounters with stuffed models and other exhibits. Go to libraries or bookshops and browse through relevant illustrated books. Take a friend with you for support.

★ *Draw or trace the hated object*. If it's a spider, you can start off with just a circle, adding legs as you feel more confident. Drawing a rose, a button or whatever worries you may be an easier first goal than the techniques described above.

★ *The floating technique* can be used to overcome panic. If you feel the insect could attack you or overwhelm you or could do something unexpected like drop down on you (something a spider could do), then float over your feelings. Tell yourself, 'This is OK. I'm rising above it.' Similarly, float over fears about any object.

★ *Use self-talk*. Remind yourself of the harmlessness of spiders or dogs or cats or moths or buttons or whatever. Tell yourself that you can and will beat this fear. Remind yourself that you are not abnormal and you are not perfect either. It is all right to be less than perfect. Everyone has some vulnerability hidden away somewhere.

★ *Give yourself goals*. Those used by Ella can be adapted. A goal relating to a dog would be to go down a street where you know there are dogs. Stop and look at one if you see it. Sit in a park and watch the wild life. Talk to a dog or cat owner. Stroke the animal. Approach the object of your fear and touch it.

★ *Don't keep your fear a secret*. Sharing it helps get it into perspective. Ask a friend or relative to support your goals, or join a self-help group – see the contacts list at the end of the book. Fear of harmless objects may be difficult to disclose because other people often find it hard to understand. Rehearse what you will say. Avoid excuses or explanations or apologies. Remember your 'affliction' is not greatly different from confessing to having headaches. It may be more unusual, but it's not your fault, nor is it a reflection on your sanity.

★ *Go to a place free of spiders or whatever*, then go with a friend to a place where you know you are likely to encounter them. Note how you feel in these different circumstances.

★ *If you panic*, use the techniques you have learned in this book. Live with the panic (float over it).

★ *Write down how you felt* after your exposure, and keep a record of all your experiences, noting whether you felt panic, etc. You will want to repeat your previous day's goal if things did not improve.

★ *There's no need to hurry*. You can plan your goals slowly, progressing as you feel more confident, but do keep to the plan. If you drop it, you may have to go back to square one.

★ *You don't have to learn to love spiders or dogs*, and you don't have to go on touching or stroking them once you have overcome

she's such a slow-coach

your fear. You can wash a spider down the plughole or put it on a piece of paper and tip it out of the window when you no longer feel it is your enemy and will return.

★ *Use new technology.* If you have a personal computer and a spider phobia, try SPIDER PC, a program offering graded exposure which you operate at your own pace. Details can be obtained from SPIDER PC, Gwent Psychology Services, St Cadoc's Hospital, Caerleon, Gwent NP6 1XQ (01633 421121).

★ *Fit an insect screen.* This is not as good as getting over a phobia, but is useful while you're trying, not only for spiders, but for birds and animals too. Screens to fit standard windows and doors are available from Bug Stoppers, 65 St Helier Avenue, Morden, Surrey SM4 6HY (0181 687 1233).

CHAPTER 16

Anything Medical

Dentists, doctors, injections, diseases, ambulances, hospitals, any reference to death or injury may cause various degrees of worry or fear in some people. Sometimes, if the fear is very bad, avoidance of anything to do with medical procedures may mean never leaving the house, so that the problem looks and even feels like agoraphobia when it is, in reality, ambulances or hospitals or the doctor's surgery. Fear of injections can mean avoiding travel to exotic places if vaccination is necessary. Having a sample of blood taken can trigger terror.

A fear of medical procedures or disease can range from squeamishness, which is something we all feel from time to time, to an all-out phobia where even the word 'injection' or whatever can send anxiety levels sky-high.

Illness fears usually focus on the life-threatening or untreatable variety like cancer or heart disease. This is not unreasonable. If we hear of a friend who contracts cancer, or read about the disease in relation to some celebrity, we are reminded of our own mortality even when the person survives. The reminder may be tied up with getting older and becoming more aware of the possible breakdown of health. Fear of the future may play a part in the fear of disease.

One of the most complicated illness phobias is fear of AIDS. Along with being incurable AIDS is contagious and is surrounded by taboo and stigma. Someone who deeply fears it and is ever-alert for symptoms may be haunted by a sexual encounter from the past and feel guilt or anger or disloyalty to the present partner. The complex mix of emotions may be sidestepped in favour of a phobia against AIDS itself, which in some ways is easier to address.

Hidden Fears

People who fear there is something wrong with them, or focus on certain diseases or medical procedures tend to say that they had anxious parents who reacted with concern to the slightest cough or cold. There may be a childhood memory of a family member contracting a serious illness, with whisperings and significant looks passing between the adults, suggesting unmentionable, terrifying secrets to an impressionable child; or the dentist, with his shiny and unfamiliar equipment may take on an aura of menace and power.

If these memories are carried over into adulthood, a sober or indifferent glance from a doctor – often nothing more than poor communication skills – may be translated as Bad News. A dental surgery may be seen as a torture chamber. The medical profession comes to be regarded as a threat to equilibrium, not a source of assurance.

Please open your mouth Mr Brown. If I say I'm only going to have a look at this stage, I MEAN I'm only going to look... Nobody's trying to TRICK you!...

These attitudes could seriously damage your health if you ignored significant symptoms or avoided seeking professional help, so it is important to nail them on the head.

Avoidance is not the only way that people deal with illness or medical fears. For some, minor symptoms that are probably a sign of some local and temporary physical problem cannot be ignored till a doctor has been consulted and reassurance given. So breathlessness must mean heart disease; a headache is translated as a brain tumour; a cough is lung cancer; forgetfulness is Alzheimer's disease. Every disease highlighted in the media or talked about among friends gives rise to similar symptoms. Though a visit to the doctor is an essential part of this scenario, his or her reassurance will last only until the onset of new symptoms, when the old worries start to haunt all over again. Seeking reassurance becomes a form of addiction.

If you worry about several symptoms you may be said to suffer from hypochondria, a fear of illness itself. This fear is not usually hidden. People can be airily dismissive of any individual who seems to be a hypochondriac, especially when he or she is heard never-endingly complaining of symptoms and even appears to relish the attention received. For the hypochondriac, however, the problem is deeply distressing. Living with uncertainty, which is what most people settle for in the face of unwelcome symptoms and unwelcome thoughts about them, will not do for the hypochondriac or anyone with illness fears. They *have* to be reassured.

Oddly enough, should such a person contract the dreaded illness or some serious condition, the irrational anxiety often goes. Or perhaps it is not so odd – contracting the real thing and being officially diagnosed is an extreme form of confrontation and exposure therapy.

TONY'S STORY: 'I'VE ALWAYS HATED GOING TO THE DENTIST'

Tony is thirty-five, married with two children under five.

'My parents were very fussy about my health. I was at the doctor at the first sign of a cough. I grew up thinking there must be something wrong with me just waiting to be discovered. I dreaded school health examinations, especially the dentist. If I knew she was coming I would try to be away or get in late but it never worked. I would sit trembling at my desk till I was called.

'I had difficult teeth. Some of my first teeth didn't get loose and my second ones were impacted, so I was always having treatment, and in those days it was foul. The drill and the noise were terrible. The injections terrified me. There was one trainee dentist who drilled on one tooth for an hour and then put in a filling. And the next day it came out. I still fear the horror and the anger I felt then.

'I also remember being given gas as a child, and fighting it. I was frightened of losing consciousness. I thought I might never wake up. I used to think that one of the best things about growing up was that I wouldn't have to go to the dentist.

'When I did grow up, I stopped having check-ups, and I think my fear actually increased. I couldn't bear to see anyone in a white coat. I wouldn't visit anyone in hospital because of that. If I had to have injections before going on holiday, I couldn't sleep for nights beforehand, I was so over-wrought.

'It never occurred to me to tell anyone. I still don't see the need for that, though I suppose it wouldn't be a bad idea to mention it to the dentist. After about five years of keeping away from the dentist I got a very painful toothache. By then I was married and my wife couldn't understand why I put up with the pain. When my face started to swell up she made an appointment for me with her dentist and in a way I was glad because I was past making any sensible decisions for myself. It was a bit like going back to childhood and having my parents doing all that fussing around me.

'I expected the dentist to tell me off for neglecting my teeth. I actually lied and said it was only three years since my last visit. He didn't say anything except that I had an abscess and needed treatment badly. I had to see him several times. I was given antibiotics and had some fillings. I felt rather foolish and guilty, but the dentist bypassed all that. He explained what he was doing all the time and he seemed quite calm and unrushed. This was different from my childhood memory. The equipment had improved too. I don't think my own children will be afraid of dentists.

'I go for regular check-ups now and I can't say I like them. I put off making the appointment, but only for a couple of weeks, and I have to make the appointment at least two weeks ahead so I can acclimatise myself to the idea. I'm surprised to find that I stay calm when I'm being treated, though I still can't sleep for a couple of nights beforehand and I get pretty uptight before I get to the

Anything Medical

surgery. But at least I go. And I can tolerate injections. I think I'll always be a little put off by people in white coats.'

Helping to change the habit
Use the self-help techniques and tips already covered in this book, adapting them to your situation.

★ *Desensitising/visualising technique*. Imagine that you are going to the dentist, doctor or hospital, visualising the trip from the moment you would be leaving your house until you get to the door. Note your reactions. Use relaxation and anti-panic measures to reduce anxiety. As you familiarise yourself with the scene, venture nearer, observing and coping as before. Visualise being in the reception, waiting room or surgery. Imagine that your doctor or dentist tells you that you need to have some tests. Stay with this and observe your reactions even though you want to escape. Observe what you are thinking – perhaps you are imagining a fatal disease or some complicated treatment. If your mind is racing along these lines, again don't stop. Stay with the thoughts till they no longer have an effect on you.

★ *Look at pictures in medical books*. If you don't have any at home, get books from the library or buy an illustrated home medical guide. Familiarise yourself with pictures of doctors, dentists, syringes, thermometers.

★ *Read sections on illnesses in the book*. Start off with diseases or conditions that don't worry you, reading through the symptoms. Progress gradually to ones that feel more threatening, changing each day to a more 'difficult' one or repeating the last one if it still conjures up fear. Observe how you feel and don't try to escape. Repeat any difficult descriptions the next day. Plan the reading so that you do it regularly and progress steadily.

★ *Cut out newspaper health features*, tape or video radio or television programmes, pick up leaflets from the surgery and chemists. Concentrate on the subject matter you fear – cancer, perhaps, or AIDS. Read, listen or view when you are ready (having primed yourself on the preceding exercise). It may help to have a relative or friend listening or viewing with you.

★ *When you have made an appointment in real life*, use the time-gap to strengthen your relaxation skills. On the actual visit, use the anti-panic measures. Take everything a step at a time, dealing emotionally with whatever is immediately in front of you.

★ *Resist asking for reassurances*. If you have had clear reassurances from your doctor and know that tests have been negative, don't seek further confirmation. We all have to live with uncertainty over our health and must learn to trust our bodies and to sense when it is really necessary to seek advice. Don't ask relatives or friends to confirm that you are looking well. Get them to promise that they will always say: 'I'm not answering.' It's the only way to break the addiction and to tolerate uncertainty.

★ *Use self-talk to eliminate guilt and embarrassment*. If you need a check-up and fear that your doctor or dentist will reprimand you for not seeking advice earlier, imagine what his disapproval means to you – embarrassment, perhaps, or guilt. Tell yourself that these are not conditions for which you are being treated, and it is important that you *do* get treated. It's not the end of the world if he or she reprimands you. You have the option to say: 'I agree, but at least I'm here now,' or to reflect that it is more useful for a medic to be insightful and therapeutic than to be disapproving.

★ *Use self-talk to demystify medical equipment*. It is shiny because it has to be spotless and germ-free and that's for your benefit. It is complex and strange looking, but so is a food mixer or a toaster if you have never seen one before. Injections are over in a couple of seconds and they are not usually painful, only perhaps uncomfortable. Pain itself is kept at acceptable levels with the use of effective analgesics. Remind yourself of these and other sensible thoughts.

★ *The floating technique* can be used to overcome panic. If you feel fear in the consulting room, tell yourself: 'This is OK. I'm rising above it.'

★ *Don't keep your fear a secret*. Sharing it helps get it into perspective. Tell your dentist or doctor you are following a self-help programme. Ask if you can look at and possibly touch instruments in the surgery. Ask a friend or relative to support your goals, or join a self-help group – see the contacts list at the end of the book.

★ *Give yourself time*. You can plan your goals slowly, progressing as you feel more confident – but do keep to a plan. If you need time to make an appointment with the doctor or dentist, then prepare yourself with the self-help techniques you have learned from this book.

★ *If you are not ready for injections at the dentist* you might like to know that around eighty dentists in the UK are using lasers in place of drills. They need no anaesthetic, therefore no injection, are as quiet as a hairdryer and don't stimulate the nerve endings. Inquire through the British Dental Association, 64 Wimpole Street, London W1M 8AL (0171 935 0875).

★ *Consider dentistry under hypnosis*. British Medical and Dental

Hypnosis will send a list of appropriate practitioners. Address: 73 Ware Road, Hertford, Herts SG13 7ED (01992 582945).

★ *Relaxation using Virtual Reality* is a new technology approach. Dentist Phillip Wander has been experimenting by giving his patients goggles and stereo headphones and offering them distracting images on a Virtual Reality screen while he treats their teeth. Patients may get a waterfall or a Grand Canyon flight to soothe and calm them. He is also trying out hypnotic images and pulsating music on another machine which can boost alpha waves in the brain, putting a patient into a deeply relaxed state. Phillip Wander can be contacted in Manchester on 0161 834 1643.

FAINTING

Fears generated by blood, injections or injury often result in the person fainting. Some psychologists believe that people with these phobias may actually have a slightly dodgy cardiovascular system that makes them go into a faint more easily than is normal. Fainting, in other words, may run in families, along with the related phobias.

The more usual physiological response to a fear is for the system to go into overdrive, but with blood fears it works the other way. There is the initial rise in heart rate and blood pressure, but then both plummet, and the heart may stop beating for several seconds. Veins dilate, blood collects in leg muscles and the brain is temporarily starved of oxygen. Result: fainting, even when the fear does not seem all that intense.

Standard treatment for this is the usual exposure to the feared object. People may be asked to draw a pool of blood, then to handle a syringe, and later to watch blood being taken or to put an injection into an orange. Clenching the muscles of the arms, legs and buttocks will help pump blood to the heart and brain and reduce the likelihood of fainting.

CHAPTER 17

Body Functions

When people say that they don't like using a public lavatory for hygienic reasons, they may possibly be sparing with the truth. Not all public lavatories are unhygienic, and you usually can get a good idea which are before you even enter one. The truth may be that they avoid public lavatories for more irrational reasons.

The mere thought of things to do with body function occurring in public – abdominal noises, farting, swallowing, using the lavatory – can set up feelings of panic. Fear of having a body smell or bad breath may have no basis in reality, but can still haunt some individuals, no matter how much they are assured that there is no smell. The dread may transfer or extend to other people in the form of an aversion to hearing anyone sniff or eat noisily or snore, or even cough or sneeze.

Some of the body fears are connected with taboos. We share certain body functions in intimate relationships only, or they are personal and kept to ourselves. Should they be made public, they are potential sources of embarrassment, rarely referred to in what we still call polite conversation. We don't even have the right words for some of the activities or places connected with them – 'lavatory' is barely acceptable to some people, though it derives from *lavo* 'to wash', while other words are also euphemisms: toilet, WC (for water closet), the john, the privy, etc. The four-letter words which once described body functions or genitals have long been appropriated as expletives by those who want to shock. Now they are also used to demonstrate streetwise credibility, to be smart. Both these uses only serve to distance them from their original meaning. Far from sounding relaxed and uninhibited, they reveal self-consciousness and uneasiness.

Taboo words and taboo activities are excellent breeding grounds for phobias. Just because you shouldn't do something, it becomes a temptation to do it. The temptation can take over, so that, for instance, a fear of farting can become a fairly full-time worry or preoccupation, as can belching, tummy rumbling, going to the lavatory.

When people run to the lavatory several times a day and refer vaguely to a weak bladder, they may be suffering from a physical condition, or they may have an underlying agenda, an anxiety about losing bladder or bowel control in public.

Because these activities are so normal and yet are also a taboo, seeking any kind of help about them often becomes part of the phobia itself. You can't tell friends or the doctor. You may not even be able to write to one of the self-help organisations. Perhaps the fear is so deep, so unexpressed and so familiar to you that in a funny way you are barely aware of it and have learned to co-exist with it as if it is second nature.

So the first step to any kind of cure must be recognition. The fear may be tied up with claustrophobia or agoraphobia, even though the focus is on using public lavatories or whatever. Or it could be part of social insecurity or embarrassment – swallowing, retching, tummy rumbling, farting, for instance come into this category. Revulsion at other people's noises may disguise something entirely different – an unexpressed irritation or anger, or possibly sexual distaste. If this is the case, the true problem may not be a personal fear or phobia, and counselling or psychotherapy may be the most appropriate and effective forms of help.

SYLVIE'S STORY: 'I CAN'T SWALLOW FOOD, MY THROAT SEEMS TO GO INTO A SPASM'

Sylvie is twenty-six, married and works in a library. Her problem began when she was a child.

'I think I know the reason behind the difficulty. As a child, I was made to eat everything on the plate. When we went out to tea, my mother would tell me it was rude not to eat everything. I would chew and chew the food – sometimes just a piece of cake – and then, when no one was looking, I would spit it out into my handkerchief and screw it all up and put it in my pocket or in my sleeve. Revolting, when you think of it now.

'One of the worst things was crust. I couldn't get it down me and I dreaded going out to tea when there were sandwiches. I'd chew the bread and then put it in my pocket, or, I hate to say, just crumble it up and let it fall under the table.

'Maybe I was nervous, or rebelling against my mother. I decided in my mind that I had an especially narrow throat. It was awful when the dentist or doctor put a spatula on my tongue. I'd start retching and gagging. I felt I'd let my mother down in some way. Yes, it is quite complicated when you think about it.

'I've never really grown out of the problem. I have adapted to it though. I found meat difficult, and that had a simple solution. I said I was a vegetarian, though I can eat meat at home. I had to give up lots of foods – I never eat rolls or French bread, or tomatoes because of the skin. I peel fresh fruit. At work, for lunch I'll have soup and things like yoghurt which are fairly easy to manage.

'I have to be watchful of what I eat all the time. I admit it can be very tiresome, and my friends think I am faddy about food. Sometimes it takes me unawares. My throat seems to go into a spasm, and then I splutter and my eyes water. I suppose that's panic. For a while, it got worse. My throat felt ultra-sensitive. I would gag using a toothbrush and I couldn't even bear wearing a high-necked sweater because my throat felt so sensitive and constricted.

'I confessed about this to my husband, but I was disappointed because it took quite a bit of courage and he didn't seem to see it. He said if it bothered me that much I should go and do something about it. I feel that as long as it doesn't get too bad, I can live with it. I just wanted his sympathy. In an odd way it reminded me of my mother when I was a child. She didn't understand what was going on. But does it make any difference? It seems pointless to blame anyone at this stage.'

Helping to change the habit

No matter how far back a fear goes, it is always possible to change it. If there is a suspected physical condition, however – say something obstructing the throat or bladder weakness – then check it out with your doctor first, just to be on the safe side. Medical treatment could be the fastest way to eliminate the problem or at least reduce it.

★ *Desensitising/visualising technique*. Imagine eating certain foods that trouble you, picturing yourself in social settings. Imagine what would happen if you started to splutter and choke. Stay with the image. If body noises or smells or needing to go frequently to the lavatory are the focus of a fear, use the same technique to desensitise yourself by imagining the worst scenario and keeping with it till the panic subsides.

★ *Relax and use the floating technique* to help you ride extreme emotional reactions and make you feel more comfortable with them.

★ *Use self-talk to eliminate embarrassment*. Tell yourself that it's not a problem for anyone else if you do choke or splutter. Remind yourself that others might notice momentarily, but they are unlikely to be particularly interested. The same goes for body noises. Tell yourself that we all have them, and they are entirely harmless. We all pass wind every day, and it's normal gas produced by the digestive system. Ask yourself how often you actually make any kind of body noises in public. Reflect on how you feel when others do so. If other people's noises truly disturb you, remember that you can use relaxation techniques.

★ *Give yourself goals*. Plan a programme according to your personal needs. Try eating certain 'difficult' foods – first at home, later in public – taking one at a time. Deliberately chew on the food for a long time. Deliberately use a fork or spoon to take it out of your mouth and put it on the plate. For body noises, plan visits to challenging places and use the following technique.

★ *Paradoxical Intention*. Deliberately try to choke or make body noises. See the section on 'Blushing' in chapter 12 for a detailed description of this technique and the way it works to put you in control. The distraction method, described in the same chapter, may also be helpful. With this, you explore how much you are preoccupied with your particular fear by monitoring reactions. For example, your immediate worry may be tummy rumbling, and you may find that this dominates your thoughts rather than the conversation you are engaged in. After monitoring your reactions, the distraction method asks you to focus on other people and situations by deliberately posing questions to yourself about them and the interaction that is going on between you.

★ *Bladder training* will reduce the need for frequent visits to the lavatory. The following exercises are designed for women, though men can adapt them for their use too. Imagine you want to pass urine and pull up the muscles as if to prevent it. You should feel the vagina pulling up at the same time. Hold this position for a few seconds, and then release. Repeat the exercise daily any time and anywhere. When passing urine, try to stop the flow for a few seconds. Repeat this once or twice. It may be difficult to do at first but performance quickly improves. Retrain your bladder by 'holding on' rather than rushing to a toilet at the slightest need. A longer hold each day helps strengthen the muscles. Don't let the bladder remain full for long periods, however, even if you are 'retraining'.

★ *Use taboo words*. You don't have to do it in public. Try them yourself on your own. Say the words quietly, then louder and confidently. Now try them on a partner or close friend and note if they feel less 'taboo-ish' than before.

★ *If you avoid public lavatories*, give yourself a set of gradual goals, starting with those in other people's homes and then in less familiar places. Take plenty of time, deliberately deciding beforehand on a set number of minutes, and staying through any panic or fear. Extend the time as you grow more confident. Take in a book or newspaper if that helps.

★ *Don't keep your fear a secret.* Sharing it helps get it into perspective. You are likely to find that other people are sympathetic – especially if they see you trying to do something about it. But don't expect the telling to be a cure in itself, and don't ask too much of your nearest and dearest. Their reassurance is not important. It's your own inner assurance that counts.

★ *Social fears, agoraphobia or claustrophobia?* If social embarrassment or fear of strange places or fear of feeling hemmed in resonate with any of the fears above, read the appropriate chapters, 10, 11 or 12.

CHAPTER 18

Obsessions and Compulsions

We've all experienced occasions when we go back to check that the doors are locked or the gas is turned off, and then may have doubts again a bit later and perhaps double-check. Children can be ritualistic about hearing certain bedtime stories every night as a form of relaxation and reassurance. And who hasn't felt a spark of recognition over the famous A.A. Milne verse about the lines and squares formed by paving stones – if you walk on the lines, the bears will get you, so make sure you stay in the squares. Rituals like these are common in small children, though most grow out of them. Those who don't and those who adopt compulsive rituals later – usually in adolescence or in their twenties – are recognised as suffering from an illness that can become chronic.

Obsessive Compulsive Disorder as it is called (often shortened to OCD) takes the form of intrusive and irrational thoughts and ideas that gradually take a hold on otherwise quite normal people and force them to adopt pointless habits and rituals. About 2 per cent of the population are thought to suffer from OCD at some time in their lives – that's about one million people in the UK. Charles Darwin, Martin Luther and John Bunyan had versions of OCD. So did American tycoon Howard Hughes, who was so obsessed about hygiene that he gradually became a hermit because in the outside world he could not fulfil the rituals he needed to allay his anxiety about possible contamination.

The condition may be inherited – it is seen repeated in families – and stress or unhappy life events may trigger it. Once the disorder has developed, a chemical imbalance occurs in the brain, identified as changes in serotonin levels. Though sufferers sometimes despair, they are not mad. They are usually aware of the absurdity of their behaviour, but controlling it can become extremely difficult, and they may be secretive, and disguise their compulsions even though the immediate family may have to be let in on the situation.

> *how come millions of people, every day, step on the lines and survive?*

The most common compulsions are: checking that a gas tap hasn't been left on, excessive cleaning and handwashing, repeated seeking of assurance that a feared event will not happen, counting or repeated touching of objects to prevent a feared disaster, arranging objects in a certain order, repeated questioning or confessing to others, hoarding, pulling out hair on the head or body.

All the problems associated with agoraphobia, social fears or claustrophobia can be tagged on to obsessions, since the fear may curtail going out or being with other people. A person obsessed with cleanliness may not want to visit restaurants for fear of food being touched and 'contaminated' by strangers, or will not use public lavatories. Fears about health or medical procedures may actually be due to an obsession about a certain illness. In all cases the problem is not so much a fear of the situation as of the consequences that could follow if certain procedures are not observed. So, it becomes necessary to avoid handling articles that could pass on dirt, or all the sharp knives in the kitchen have to be hidden because they provide a compulsive temptation which could end in causing self-harm or harm to others. A compulsive need to hoard food, possibly for fear of starving, could lead to keeping items even when they have gone rotten or fill every corner of the house.

Following regular rituals reinforces a sense of control and relieves anxiety, though the relief may be short-lived and the repetition time-consuming. Those who feel compelled to follow rituals may lose their jobs because they can't get themselves to work on time after a start that includes say forty repeats of teeth cleaning or washing, changing clothes because they might not pass the cleanliness inspection, wiping door handles before and after touching them, or starting all over again because some part of the ritual was deemed less than perfect.

Small obsessions can be tolerated. They are minor nuisances that can come and go, and may even serve a useful function – being over-cautious about the locks, or double-checking that the gas has been turned off for instance. Medium ones can be intrusive, and can grow bigger. OCD may follow depression, and bouts of depression may recur when the disorder is established. A mild bout of OCD may improve with time without treatment, but moderate to severe versions may become chronic.

Self-help works best on obsessions of minor and medium intensity. If they are experienced as part of other phobias, the basic fear is the one that has to be tackled, and then the other fears – agoraphobia or a fear of doctors for instance – may resolve themselves. Deeply established, severe OCD needs professional help – see chapter 23.

DAVE'S STORY: 'I COULDN'T STOP WASHING EVEN THOUGH MY HANDS BLED'

Dave is thirty-two and now a manager at a supermarket. His obsession with cleanliness meant he had to give up his job till treatment put him on the right path again.

'I've always been very meticulous and a bit fussy in a way. I'm tidy and I like things to be clean and neat. I was in my teens and living at home when things began to get slightly out of hand; I'd arrange my room so that it was just so, and I got really angry and upset when anyone disturbed it. My mum wasn't allowed in to clean. I started doing it myself.

'I was cleaning every day when I got in from work. I couldn't stop. I felt everything anyone touched was unclean and unhygienic, so I had to clean other parts of the house as well as my own room. I'd hoover after guests came in and even wash the door handles with disinfectant. I was a trainee manager at the time, and it got more and more difficult to get in to work on time because I had to clean the bath before and after I'd used it. I used to spend a long time in the men's toilets at work too, and I always had a terrible urge to clean the place though I managed to stop myself.

'In the end I couldn't go to work. The strain was too much and I had to give notice. Being at home all day, I got very depressed. I had very little social life and hardly went out. My parents were pretty good about it all, but I could see they were worried. I was washing so much that my hands bled. I couldn't stop because as soon as I did they seemed to me to be soiled and could contaminate things, and then I would have to wash anything I touched. It was a vicious circle.

'My mum started to hide the detergents, but I would get into such a state that she had to let me have them again. I did all the washing, but as soon as it was out of the machine I would put it back in for another wash, just in case it had touched the door of the machine and could spread infection. My mum got me to go to the doctor's with her and he gave me some anti-depressants. They did help me feel better and he took me off them after a couple of months, but the cleanliness obsession didn't go away.

'Eventually he sent me to the hospital to see a psychiatrist. I must have been ready for it because I was really pleased with the treatment. You have to do things like let clothes get dirty and touch things you wouldn't normally want to touch and let your hands get dirty deliberately but not be allowed to wash them afterwards. I had to put up notices in the bathroom reminding myself not to wash the bath or turn on the taps. My mum agreed to hide the detergent and I had to get used to that. Then I was able to leave it alone when she got it out again. It took about ten weeks going to the hospital, and then I carried on with my own treatment.

'Getting a job and finding I could keep it was a big boost to my morale. The treatment was six years ago, and I don't think of it much now. If I ever feel I'm getting worried and fussy again, I do something like letting my hands get dirty, and then I look at them and it's reassuring to find that nothing disastrous happens.'

Helping to change the habit

Self-treatment for OCD differs from techniques used for other fears and phobias in that the challenge is often to refrain from doing something, rather than aiming to extend activities. The principle is still the same in one way: you have to face up to the fear and work at doing whatever's needed to bring it under control, such as stopping yourself from washing or cleaning or checking for diseases or whether the front door is locked. Remember, however, that self help may work best after a push-start from professionals, possibly including drug treatment.

★ *Desensitising/visualising technique may help.* First think of all the things you have to do or avoid. Make a list of them in order of importance and start on the least challenging first, imagining yourself resisting the ritual or activity. If you feel panic, use the relaxation technique and other self-help measures described in this book.

★ *Limit the rituals.* Allow yourself to wash only twice a day. Leave dirty or ruffled clothing on a chair or on the floor and do not touch it for twenty-four hours. Limit any other ritual or compulsive activity, such as checking locks, hiding knives, hoarding food.

★ *Make a programme* of all the activities you promise to resist or limit: for instance, no washing after 9 am, no wiping door handles, lock up and then check locks only once before going out, etc. You need to think through all the activities that affect you in order to make a comprehensive programme.

★ *Expose yourself to the risk*. Deliberately dirty your hands, touch switches, wipe hands on a towel and leave it untended, touch someone else's clothing or anything you feel is contaminated. Deliberately mix clean and dirty clothing. Wear yesterday's unwashed clothing. Do not wash your hands or things you have touched. Confine checking on locks, etc, to say twice a day, reducing gradually to once. Throw out rubbish that you have not checked over first, or unwanted food, again graduating from say one old newspaper to greater numbers as you feel more confident.

★ *Use self-talk*. First and foremost tell yourself that you are not mad. You are, or have been, at the mercy of rituals that can be controlled. Tell yourself that you can survive without the rituals, and that you don't need them. You will live without them just as everyone else does. Contamination is all right, a fact of life we all have to tolerate, and you will survive it. You can live without old newspapers or other documents – after all, how often have you referred to them in the past? You have checked the doors and know they are locked. When you have performed a function, like checking doors or washing hands, tell yourself to hold on to the memory of that. You can say, 'I don't need further checks.'

★ *Don't involve the family* in your rituals. Don't ask them for reassurance, and make a pact with them so they remind you when you do ask. They can say they will not reassure, as that is what you agreed upon. Practise with them so you get used to them saying this. You have to learn to reassure yourself.

★ *Enlist new help from the family*. Ask for their support as you try to cut down the rituals. It can help if they do an action once, like

Obsessions and Compulsions

washing and drying hands, and then you copy, again just once. Or they can help you throw out rubbish.

★ *Have patience and hold on to the belief in yourself.* You may have to go through quite a bit of discomfort, but you know you will win in the end. That's the most important piece of self-talk of all.

CHAPTER 19

Sexual Troubles

Being 'bad' at sex is a fairly new taboo. Sexiness is promoted so much today that we are in danger of forgetting that we all start off inexperienced and uncertain in these matters. Sometimes uncertainty or anxiety from other parts of our lives overflows into sexual performance too.

There can be a snowball effect. A disappointing sexual experience, and then another, can lead to avoidance of sex just as a panic attack in the street can lead to avoidance of going out. There may be an underlying cause in some cases. Sexual abuse in childhood, rape or an early bad memory of sex may be a basic cause of sexual anxieties, but painful intercourse, an inability to reach orgasm, lack of confidence or social skills, particularly in men, are other possible causes in their own right.

This chapter addresses heterosexual relationships, which does not mean homosexual ones do not have their problems. The final section of the chapter can help both. Before deciding that 'phobia' or even 'anxiety' are true descriptions for you or your partner, there are a number of possibilities to consider. First, you must eliminate the following:

★ *Marital or relationship stress* can interfere with sexual performance as well as desire. If you are angry with your partner you may want to reject advances or refuse to respond even if you don't at first see an obvious connection.

★ *Depression* can damp down responses simply because the person is unrelaxed, preoccupied or has no sense of joy in life.

★ *Alcohol* can depress sexual desire and performance.

★ *Medication* – some drugs cause impotence, including antidepressants and those taken for high blood pressure. Check with your doctor.

★ *Physical disease, hormone imbalance* or other abnormality can affect sexual performance. Pain during sexual intercourse may be caused by an infection, vaginal dryness due to the hormonal changes of the menopause, or some other physical condition like fibroids. Erection failure in men may be due to hormonal changes too. Hormone treatment for women or men can make dramatic improvements. Again check with your doctor.

★ *Doubts about sexual orientation or inclination*. You might need medical or counselling help for this.

The most common cause of sexual difficulties in men is lack of confidence which creates fear and anxiety. From this, other problems can arise: failure to achieve an erection or to maintain one; maintaining an erection but not reaching orgasm; premature ejaculation, ie climaxing too early. Because virility is so tied up with male expectations, any of these conditions may be psychologically painful for a man. If the partner shows resentment, the problem increases. If the man then blames his partner, anger as well as anxiety increase.

In women, sexual anxiety can begin because of an anxious partner. This is still no reason for blame. The only road to recovery is goodwill and cooperation. Fear of sex may make a woman find intercourse uncomfortable or impossible through muscle spasm – the official name is vaginismus. Inability to achieve orgasm or dislike of sex are other problems connected with fear or anxiety.

SARAH AND CLIVE'S STORY: 'IT WAS LIKE STARTING FROM THE BEGINNING AGAIN'

Sarah and Clive are in their late thirties. They have been married for two years and before that lived together for eight years. Sarah tells what happened:

'Our sexual relationship was never that great, even at the beginning, but we both seemed satisfied. Neither of us had had a great deal of experience with other people because we got together when we were young, and we both came from backgrounds where sex wasn't mentioned. I don't like too much physical contact, it somehow disturbs me. I've always had to be very relaxed to have intercourse.

'The trouble really started when we got married and moved house. There were a lot of financial problems. We both got home very late in the evenings and there seemed no time for each other.

'We tried for a baby, but nothing happened. That was more of a blow to Clive than to me. The doctor said it was because we were stressed. We went for fertility treatment and I had to take my temperature every day and we had to make sure we had intercourse at certain times of the month. I didn't like it – it felt contrived to me, and then Clive started to have problems about keeping an erection and I wanted to throw in the whole thing. It all seemed too much.

'It got to the point for me when I became frigid. I couldn't respond. There was this critical comment going on all the time in my head. I knew it was hard for Clive, but I didn't like sex, didn't want him to touch me, didn't want to get pregnant. I tried to talk about it, but Clive didn't want to know. It never occurred to me that he had some real problems too, and they turned out to be bigger than mine.

'In the end I said we'd better get help. We went to Relate, where they do sex counselling. We talked quite a lot about how we felt about sex before we knew each other. We both began to see that we had different problems. I was scared, really scared of getting pregnant, and that must have been why I could hardly bear to be touched. Clive is quite a shy person and I hadn't really seen that he didn't have very much confidence. He had got really anxious about his sexual performance and couldn't cope with any of it.

'The counsellor gave us exercises to do, like not touching each other in certain places at first and saying out loud certain words so we would be able to tell each other what we enjoyed. I know it's the standard sex therapy treatment. You have to give it time, several weeks, and I think it helps if you have a counsellor or therapist, though I know there are lots of books on sex therapy around. With a counsellor, it's easier to keep going and you have more confidence about saying things. But we did read some of the books, and they were useful too.'

Helping to change the habit

The programme for sex therapy that Sarah describes can be followed without professional help. It does, however, need the conscious cooperation of both partners. Both must agree not to blame or criticise the other, and to focus on their own needs. If you want to try and your partner isn't sure, be prepared to wait for several days or weeks to allow your partner to get used to the idea. Bring it up again in a relaxed moment, describe the process, but continue to be patient. And never, ever be critical.

★ *Name your problems*. Each of you write down what your problem is. If there is more than one problem, put them in order of importance and decide which you can work on first. Concentrate on yourself. A woman might say: 'It hurts when we have intercourse because my vagina feels tight,' and 'I can't relax when you touch me.' A man might say: 'I can't maintain an erection and I find penetration difficult.' When the list is complete, show it to your partner. Some of the problems will match with each other. Some will appear to reflect on the other's performance. Don't apportion blame. Read through the next stages and agree to start your programme at a given time.

★ *Set aside time*. You need an hour in which to relax. Use the techniques described in chapter 5. Wear loose clothing, make sure the room is warm and the lighting subdued. Play background music if you like. Don't touch each other at this stage. Just relax together.

★ *Write down the difficult words*. Do this at the next session, after you have relaxed. Start with all the words you know for female genitalia, and for male – all the words, including the four-letter ones. Write them down along with their functions. You can write separate lists and then share them. Better still you can complete a list together, saying the words as one of you writes.

★ *Mood setters*. After relaxing, watch an erotic film together. Read a sex manual together. Still don't touch. Plan a time for your next session and either repeat this or go on to the next stage.

★ *Further stimulation*. Allow your partner to masturbate you and offer to masturbate your partner – not to the point of orgasm, just to try it out in the relaxed, undemanding setting that you have both created. Also, privately if you prefer, masturbate yourself. Don't worry about achieving orgasm. Tell your partner about it. Or agree to watch each other. This shows you what kind of touch your partner enjoys best.

★ *Use the sensate focus technique*. This well-proven approach involves creating the relaxed setting, with both partners naked. The rule is that each can stroke the other anywhere except breasts or genitals. Take turns, starting with hands or toes and working from there. Ask how it feels, tell your partner how it feels. Use body lotion to make the skin feel extra silky. Find out what each of you enjoys most.

★ *Repeat the above as often as you can, for a month*. Go over things that feel difficult. You should be getting used to sharing your reactions by now. If something scares or worries either of you, discuss it. If that's difficult, practise saying it in your imagination first.

★ *Progress to touching the 'forbidden' parts*. Stroke breasts and genitals. Say what feels good and what feels wrong. Explore each other's bodies with lips and tongue. Concentrate on the physical sensation, how it feels to you, and listen with an open mind to the parallel comments of your partner. You can masturbate to orgasm, but don't see it as a specific goal. Use a lubricant if you fear vaginal dryness. Keep to this stage for several sessions.

★ *If you find you are fighting letting go*, try the floating technique, imagining you are floating over the fear and can accept whatever is happening without feeling at risk. Practise even breathing and check that you are relaxed.

★ *Make self-talk work for you* by telling yourself that sex is for pleasure, that you are finding pleasure, that you don't have to be pushed into anything you don't want to do. You are not performing, but sharing and exploring.

★ *Progress to orgasm* when you both feel ready, using a lubricant if necessary. Lead up to it by repeating what you did in earlier sessions.

★ *Take things slowly*. If you feel you need more time then pace yourselves accordingly, making allowance for the partner who is slower in progressing.

CHAPTER 20

After the Event – Post-Traumatic Stress

After a disturbing, often abnormal event in our lives, perhaps a serious traffic accident or an assault, or even after witnessing an injury, it is normal to have a strong set of reactions. Psychologists describe the reactions as Post Traumatic Stress, which may manifest itself in flashbacks, nightmares, feelings of emotional numbness, sleep disturbance, depression, panic attacks and disturbed concentration.

The emotional shake-up gradually diminishes and so do the symptoms after the first month, though they can take two years or more to fade into the background.

Sometimes, however, the intensity of the reactions does not fade, and then it is recognised as a new category of psychological disturbance called Post Traumatic Stress Disorder (PTSD). Usually, though not always, this is because the event was too big for the person to cope with alone. Rape, torture, serious personal assault, bombing, surviving a fire or other major disaster, experiencing or witnessing serious injury or death, experiencing sexual abuse are categories that put people at risk of PTSD.

The difference between the two conditions – Post Traumatic *Stress* and Post Traumatic Stress *Disorder* – is important, because the first is something that will respond to self help, while the second needs specialist therapy which is described on pages 161–2.

How do you recognise whether you suffer from the stress or the more serious disorder? Deborah Lee, deputy director of the Traumatic Stress Clinic in London, a national centre for assessment and referral, says that four weeks is long enough for serious symptoms to persist. If intrusive thoughts continue for longer than that, and they occur two or three times a week or more, even daily, then a referral from a GP would be appropriate. Other persisting symptoms such as avoiding the place of the incident and experiencing panic attacks are signs that the stress is not diminishing in intensity and the person is not functioning normally.

Self help works best when the trauma is recognised for what it is at an early stage. The earlier it is dealt with, the fewer complications there will be. To some extent, the severity or seriousness of the event is less important as a predictor of after-effects than the individual who experiences it. Someone who has good support from a partner, relative or friend is more buffered than someone who has no one intimate to turn to. Someone who is by nature able to cope with unexpected stress will react better than someone who is not. A history of psychological disturbance or alcohol misuse has been linked to more severe reactions to trauma.

As for the best way to cope, that too seems to depend on the individual. For some people, finding distractions to take their minds off the memories can be effective. A holiday or a week's visit to a good friend can provide the best kind of comfort, but there is the danger with distractions that the incident is denied and the trauma is not given sufficient thinking time. Those painful moments of recall are, in the short term, therapeutic, and if they are suppressed, they can suddenly pop up many years later with devastating effect – the 'cringe moments' which return to haunt people, according to Deborah Lee. She suggests that those who have tried several different ways of coping – such as taking tranquillisers, blocking painful thoughts, avoiding the place of the incident – have shown more depression and suicidal tendencies than people who have stuck to one approach. The inference from this is that the different strategies failed or proved inadequate.

People who criticise themselves or blame themselves for the event, a not uncommon reaction in rape victims, experience greater distress. Other factors which exacerbate symptoms are keeping feelings a secret, hoping that a miracle will happen, and wishing oneself in a better place. A high degree of self-control, especially if there is unexpressed anger, is also a factor working against fast recovery.

After the Event – Post-Traumatic Stress

When the symptoms do persist, they can continue for years, ruining lives and causing deep unhappiness. It is important to get the right diagnosis. A magazine reports a story of a man suffering from agoraphobia for eighteen years following an incident in which he was the victim of a raid at a London mail sorting office. He witnessed one colleague being viciously assaulted and was locked inside a tiny, airless vault for fifteen minutes before being rescued. The incident left him paranoid, prone to panic attacks, unable to sleep and ultimately housebound. Today he might have been diagnosed as suffering from PTSD. At the time he probably received some tranquillisers or an anti-depressant from his GP.

A recent newspaper report told of another case, this time the story of a woman of twenty-eight who came face to face in her home with an intruder dressed all in black. She developed an obsessive fear that the raider was following her, and never slept alone in her flat again. She gave up a promising career, was committed to a psychiatric hospital, and was diagnosed as suffering from manic depression. Two years after the incident, she committed suicide. Unfortunately, she too was not recognised as suffering from PTSD, though the syndrome was recognised in the eighties.

Self help for post traumatic stress

★ *Remember that stress is normal* after an emotionally upsetting event. Disturbed sleep, a return of painful memories, intrusive thoughts, emotional numbness, disturbed concentration, a re-living of the incident are all part of the process.

★ *This is a time to keep life on an even keel*. Go to bed early, eat sensibly and regularly. You need to re-establish routine in your life.

★ *Talk to relatives and friends*, tell them about the incident and how you felt. Be specific.

★ *Write down your memories and thoughts* about the incident and refer back to them from time to time. You should find that the memories become less painful.

★ *Practise relaxation techniques* and use the anti-panic measures described in this book.

★ *Use the other self-help measures* described earlier in this book, according to your personal need.

★ *Return to the site of the incident* if possible. Remember that the sooner you get back in that driving seat or whatever, the more likely you will be able to nip any phobia in the bud.

★ *See your GP if reactions persist* in intensity after a month. You may find that your menstrual cycle is disturbed or you have stomach upsets. These are signs that you are not returning to normal functioning. A short-term course of sleeping pills may restore healthy sleep patterns.

★ *Don't allow yourself to be prescribed* anti-depressants if you feel you have Post Traumatic Stress Disorder. Drugs may have their place in your treatment, but they don't usually solve the problem in the long run.

SECTION 4
Getting Help from Others

CHAPTER 21

Making Connections: the Self-Help Group

The setting is a community centre, in a modern, soulless sixties building, but the room is large and bright and comfortable, and the atmosphere is relaxed. A group of people are sitting in a circle round some coffee tables. There are sixteen to twenty of them, men and women from twenty-something to sixty-something, talking quietly over their coffee and biscuits.

This is a self-help group funded by the charity Anxia (formerly called Phobic Action). At least four in the group are volunteers, as is the leader, all trained in counselling and other skills by the charity. The rest have some kind of anxiety problem, and they meet together weekly in this informal setting to talk about their lives and think about changes they can make.

'It was such a relief coming here,' says a small, dark woman in her forties. She had been widowed suddenly a year ago and had gone numb with grief and shock, unable to go out or carry on a normal life. Now she can travel by car but has difficulty with public transport. She has made some good friends in the group and sees them between meetings.

One of her new friends is sitting next to her: 'I get terrible panic attacks, suddenly out of the blue. Coming here made me see I wasn't insane. I go to relaxation classes, but I need this too. And when either of us feels bad we go and visit each other.' She smiles at her new friend.

The woman sitting opposite, in her fifties, is not talking, though the volunteer beside her has tried to draw her into the conversation. This is her first meeting and she is looking tense, but she answers willingly when questioned: 'I've had a lot of things go wrong in my life recently, and it has brought back all my old fears and insecurity. I've been to groups before and I got much better, but all the good work has gone out the door. Now I have such low self-esteem I freeze when I try to pick up the phone, so I can't even make an appointment with the hospital where my doctor said I could go for some counselling.'

A gentle-looking man in his sixties edges into the conversation. He suffers from Obsession Compulsive Disorder, and whenever he feels depressed the condition gets worse. He finds the group a great help, a lifeline. He is also on one of the new anti-depressants, Seroxat, and that has helped a lot, he says.

The volunteers meanwhile make themselves available, listening and offering help. Some are in training and observing, others are providing the opportunity for one-to-one quiet counselling, perhaps making a date to accompany someone who can't travel alone on a bus or following up on other self-exposure work.

The talk is not only of problems. Many in the group have been attending for a year or more, though some come for only a few months. They know each other and also know quite a bit about each other. There is a buzz of conversation about work and family, children and friends, holidays and outings. Some, like the new woman, don't join in, but they are here, of their own volition, and that's saying a lot.

The group leader calls for everyone's attention. We are switching to the more formal part of the meeting. This is report-back time, and people are expected to contribute, though newcomers are let off for the first few sessions.

'Is it all right if we start with you?' asks the leader, pointing to a grey-haired man who has been sitting making small-talk with a trainee volunteer. 'You didn't speak last week did you?'

The man nods. He is fairly new, and briefly sketches in his problem for the group to hear. He has worked all his life, has been in his present job for thirteen years, and yet is miserable on his days off, going over in his mind what he might have said or done at work that was wrong or wondering what he could be blamed for. 'It happens every time, and I still think I am going to lose my job, which I know is ridiculous after all these years.' He

Making Connections: the Self-Help Group

realises that his endless worrying is pointless.

He gives another example: 'My dentist put in a new filling and asked me to test it for the bite. He asked did he need to grind down a little more, and I said I thought so. And then he asked again if it felt all right and I wasn't sure. So he went on grinding. After I left the surgery I started to have doubts. Had I let him do too much? Had I ruined my teeth? I went on worrying about it for a couple of weeks, but I managed not to go back to the surgery, and eventually I forgot about it. But then the other worries returned.'

Another member of the group nods. He recognises the syndrome. Exactly the same thing has happened to him.

The leader offers encouragement. The new group member did well to resist returning to the dentist. Perhaps next week he will reveal more, or a volunteer will encourage him to take specific action, but for now we go on to the next speaker.

She says tiredness brings back her problems. She is angry with herself when she takes a step backwards. Someone in the group says a good night's sleep makes all the difference. They discuss camomile tea, lavender sprayed on the pillow, the antidepressants that may or may not help. She says she used to think that the drugs made her lethargic in the mornings but now is convinced it is her own tension. That makes her feel better. She can do something about the tension. It's a dilemma if the drugs that she takes solve part of her problem, but also cause other difficulties.

Another group member talks about drugs. He has been on a low dose of Prozac for five months and doesn't like it. 'I get high as a kite on it. I've become this assertive customer throwing my weight about, but it doesn't feel like me and I think I'll panic. Is it me being positive or is it the drug? I'm sleeping better and the obsessions and anxieties are better though I still replay everything in my mind. I don't think any of it is really any good for my confidence. I'm not really learning to do it myself. The drug doesn't solve my underlying fear.'

The leader seems to have known this person for a long time. 'Think what you were like before. Why don't you make a note of the good and bad sides of it before you think about stopping the drug?'

Someone else suggests he should ask his doctor for a lower dose. And then we move on to the small dark woman who decides that being without her car next week will not leave her housebound. She will use a mini-cab instead. The decision makes her feel proud and positive.

Another woman tells how she travelled with a volunteer in a car for the first time for years and promises to attempt a bus in the next week or so. She too is pleased with her progress, and both women are warmly congratulated.

There has been very little emotion in all this. Several people say they feel better today and were much worse yesterday. Is it because they had been dreading coming to the meeting? Or had the achievement of getting there boosted their morale?

On the way out, the new woman says that she felt welcomed and at ease. She found this group much less formal than group therapy. She resolves that she will walk up to the hospital and make an appointment with a counsellor instead of waiting for some moment when her hand on the telephone 'unfreezes'. It has been a useful evening, nothing dramatic, just another small building brick towards recovery.

The major work still has to go on during the rest of the week. There may be drug supervision under the GP or psychiatrist, a self-exposure programme to follow, some counselling or psychotherapy. A self-help group is a much watered-down version of group therapy (see page 159). It offers more in the way of tea and sympathy, is more informal and opens up opportunities for friendships and socialising. As with group therapy there's the chance to talk about your own experiences and hear other people's too. More than anything else, there is the reminder that you are not alone and not insane.

CHAPTER 22

What Friends and Relations Can Do

Throughout this book, the message is clear: it helps to confide in someone. This chapter is addressed to the someone, or some people, whom you choose to confide in. Read it for yourself first, then hand it over ...

One man's meat is another man's poison, as the saying goes. It fits the way we tend to respond when we first hear of someone else's irrational fear. 'I can understand having a phobia about spiders, but cats – surely not,' we may exclaim, with an almost wilful lack of understanding. Or we might go one step worse and introduce our furry friend saying: 'Go on, stroke her, she wouldn't hurt a fly.'

This is not sadism. It's a misguided way of trying to be helpful. We want to demonstrate that cats are loveable creatures, because that's what they seem to us. But the true way to help is quite different. We have to pause and then take a leap of the imagination. We have to understand that the fear is real. Deadly serious. We may never be able to enter into it totally, but we have to use imagination in order to empathise with the person who suffers it. 'Empathy: the ability fully to understand and share another's feeling,' says the dictionary. It's a tall order to do it fully, but we have to try because otherwise we can't be of help and could even do damage to the people who have trusted us with their particular vulnerability.

Empathy begins with listening. Let the other person talk. If you want to interject, hold it till you've heard all that the other person wants to tell you. Don't dismiss the problem as trivial or nonsense, and never tell anyone to pull themselves together or snap out of it. If only they could! Never appeal to logic either, because we're talking here of somebody else's emotional reality, not the world according to the official rules.

For a friend or relative, hearing of the problem for the first time may well be an enormous relief and a revelation. You hear what you have always partly suspected, or can now make more sense of what you had previously seen as bizarre or unreasonable or cold behaviour. For instance, it can be a relief to learn that a disease phobia is the reason why you have never received sympathy from a friend when ill yourself, or that your invitations have been refused not because the person wishes to avoid you but because he or she has social fears.

When someone confides, they don't always want help. They may just want to be heard and to get the feel of coming out in public. So any urging to seek further advice must be done gently. It's no help, of course, to show astonishment or indicate that you consider the behaviour freakish. The first response may be: 'Is there anything you would like me to do?' – and if the answer is no, accept it till they return to the subject themselves. It's important that a phobic person makes a conscious and purposeful decision to overcome the fears and does not feel pushed into it.

They may need to tell several people before they feel comfortable about talking and confessing. This is no reflection on you. It's part of their exploration after what may be years of keeping their fears a secret. They may enjoy a sense of relief at confessing and then progress no further for some time. You may have to live with this state of affairs for quite a while. When you become impatient or frustrated or exasperated, as well you might, recognise that the only useful thing to do is get back to base and just listen.

Now comes the hard bit. You might want to 'rescue' the person, in other words do things for them that help them avoid their problem. The husband of an agoraphobic wife may do all the shopping or always collect the children from school. His motives may be mixed, not just protection but also concealment: he doesn't want the world to know that his wife is what he might think of as 'mentally ill'. The stigma inferred in this response is contagious, and reinforces the wife's sense of shame. In the same way, it may seem like a loving, helpful gesture to clean the bathroom and

What Friends and Relations Can Do

check it out for spiders for a phobic partner, but the act is also reinforcing his sense of helplessness. And a person who lies to cover up a partner's fear of accepting invitations is again supporting the need for secrets.

Another form of collusion is to accept that the phobic person is extra sensitive and needs extra special care. They might want extra attention and pity, but if you give it, you will be hindering recovery. The 'poor you' syndrome only serves to confirm a fragile victim figure. Non-emotional sympathy is fine but allowing yourself to be manipulated is not.

Old habits, then, may have to change, but not without discussion and negotiation. A new bargain will have to be worked out – no more collecting the children from school unless accompanied by the agoraphobic person (or some kind of compromise on this if it feels too drastic at first); no more cleaning out spiders in advance; no more cover-up lies when refusing an invitation, though not the whole truth either, unless you have permission. No more victim reinforcing.

A large part of a recovery plan is the setting of goals, and here's where a partner, friend or relative can truly support. You can help set up a programme, planning outings or exposure to frightening situations. You can then accompany the person to the 'forbidden' setting. This could be going on a train, entering a restaurant, going to a public toilet, looking at pictures of spiders or whatever.

This may require much patience and possibly quite a big input of time. You could be hanging around outside a supermarket for an hour, as your partner stays inside, riding the fear and getting used to being there. You don't want to do anything to hurry the plan. That could create anxiety and a powerful negative effect. Never imply that the task ahead is easy. It may be for you, but a huge effort and possibly a huge struggle is going on inside the other person.

Support and encouragement, a reminder of past achievements, and no hint of criticism are the key responses when there are setbacks. Praise is always needed, for yesterday's triumph rather than today's failure, and of course always for today's successes. When there is failure, don't try to speed things or encourage repetition of a difficult exercise. Accept that sometimes there is a great advance that can't easily be repeated. Instead, suggest a small step forward from the previous success. Read the anti-panic measures earlier in this book and remind the person to use them if they show or say they are feeling panic. Remind about slower or deeper breathing.

Another toughie for the helper to overcome is the desire to reassure. People who have obsessive fears about dirt or are addictive about their health, may want constant reassurance. Once given, they come back for more – and more. So a pact has to be made, which might go something like this: 'We agree that I don't say: "Yes you are clean," or: "Yes, there is no possibility of contamination. Instead I will remind you of this pact when you ask me.'

A person who is trying to overcome a cleanliness obsession may have to learn to wash hands only once or twice a day, or leave soiled clothing around, or leave the room uncleaned. That means the helper lives with the change of habit too. If the bedroom remains dirty, it's something you both have to tolerate. Soiled clothes or an untidy room need to be left untended.

Professional treatment for Obsessional Compulsive Disorder often enlists the help of the family in recording progress and achieving goals. Ironically, though reassurance is not on the agenda, demonstration is. You can wash your hands once, and then wait as the other person does so too, and then remind that there'll be no more washing till the evening.

Children may be included in the helping team. Dr Isaac Marks records how children pinned the notice 'touch me' on a laundry basket their mother had hitherto avoided because of her cleanliness obsession. Children need to be told, in simple and sympathetic terms, of the problem their parent is trying to overcome. Even quite young children can understand, and can be given simple tasks, like the one described above, to make them feel useful and as a way to express their love.

Professional help can mean a change of role for a partner. Sex therapy usually involves the couple, not the individual alone, as both partners learn new habits. It is important to enter such therapy without a sense of blame. Use self-talk to get you out of this trap: you can say to yourself: 'This is not a matter of blame or superiority. Such ideas are useless and irrelevant. The purpose of seeking help is that we should both benefit. We are in this together as a partnership.'

To sum up – Do's and Don'ts for friends and relations

- ★ Try to empathise, don't bulldoze a person out of the fear.
- ★ Take the fear seriously.
- ★ Listen to the other person.
- ★ Don't appeal to logic.
- ★ Be patient.
- ★ Don't try to 'rescue' the person.
- ★ Talk together about new ways to do things.
- ★ Help plan goals and help pursue them.
- ★ Give your time generously.
- ★ Praise past and present successes.
- ★ Encourage small steps forward after a 'failure'.
- ★ Remind about anti-panic measures.
- ★ Agree not to reassure.
- ★ Don't exclude the children.
- ★ Regard sex therapy, or any other therapy in which you are asked to take part, as something to enhance the partnership.
- ★ Think of the role of helper as a job you have agreed to undertake. Do it consistently and reliably.

CHAPTER 23

Professional Help

It's not always possible to work your way out of a phobia or severe fear on your own, even if you do follow a self-help programme or enlist help from your friends. To get things started, you may want or need professional advice, and you'll probably know yourself if that feels right for you.

Your first port of call should be your GP. This provides the opportunity to check that there's no physical cause for your problem. When you have agreed on the kind of treatment you want and need, the GP might be able to recommend a local practitioner. Many of the treatments described below are available through the NHS. (If not, there is a list of contacts at the end of this book which will help you find a qualified practitioner who is a recognised member of a professional institution).

Whatever kind of treatment you choose, it is important to use the initial interview with the practitioner to discuss how long the treatment is likely to last, what is involved, what are the risks or side-effects, what are the overall costs if you are going privately. Write down a list of questions before your first visit. If you are dissatisfied with the answers, you are under no obligation to commit yourself to treatment. If, after a few sessions, especially with a psychotherapist, you feel the treatment, or the practitioner, is not right for you, then you can terminate the arrangement. It is common practice amongst psychotherapists to suggest someone else if a client expresses dissatisfaction, due to a personality clash for instance.

There are several different kinds of treatments, bunched together here into five categories:

1. The psychological treatments: psychotherapy and counselling, behaviour therapy, hypnotherapy, group therapy and social skills training
2. Drug treatments
3. Physical treatments
4. Alternative treatments such as acupuncture and homeopathy
5. Newest techniques

1. THE PSYCHOLOGICAL TREATMENTS

Psychotherapy and Counselling

These two are the 'talking treatments'. They give you the chance to discuss your difficulties with someone who will listen and accept what you have to say and who will offer support in your attempts to overcome your fears. Counselling tends to go into less depth than psychotherapy, and is less concerned with what happened in childhood than in the here and now, but both treatments try to find the underlying causes of the problems.

A phobia will probably be seen as a symbol for some other, deeply repressed fear by a psychotherapist. Spiders are often linked to sexuality in psychotherapeutic theory, so childhood experiences and attitudes towards sex will be explored if the client has a spider phobia. A fear of going to restaurants may be linked to experiences of eating in strange places as a child, or observing social insecurity in a parent. An aversion to something commonplace like buttons may produce an early memory of being threatened by something or someone quite removed from this. In such cases, the fear is thought to be transferred to the comparative safety of the inanimate object.

The hope is that in time, the understanding and insight you have gained through therapy will lead towards a cure or at least a sense of control. Psychotherapy may involve a weekly session over months or years. Counselling is of shorter duration.

The talking treatments boost self-esteem and increase confidence. It is highly therapeutic to feel understood and to be allowed to express any feelings, no matter how negative or unacceptable or trivial they might seem outside the consulting rooms. You can express anger about a parent or partner or any person or agent who seems to be the cause of your fear. You can explore old anxieties and resentments and gain new insights into your situation.

However, knowing the reason for a fear or bringing to light the complex history surrounding it does not necessarily mean that you will overcome it. Today many psychologists maintain that non-specific psychotherapy is not particularly effective for specific phobias or for people with obsessive disorder. However, if it sounds like something that could appeal to you, then it is worth a try. You can make a commitment for a certain amount of time, say three months, and then review the situation.

Cognitive Therapy

This is a behaviour-based therapy which helps you to change your mood by changing the way you think. It usually includes self-talk, the method outlined in chapter 7 and elsewhere in this book, and also looks into the background of the person to help provide insight as to why the fears might have started. A course of treatment is of fairly short duration – a few months at most. Cognitive therapy teaches you to challenge self-defeating beliefs and develop positive ones. The process of change with this, as with other therapies, is not easy. You will probably do 'homework' between sessions which may include keeping a diary to monitor your thought patterns and taking on difficult tasks like telephoning a friend who you imagine/suspect may not want to speak to you. This last is a typical exercise to help highlight the difference between 'I believe' and 'I know'. If you realise that you *believe* your call is not wanted, but have no concrete *evidence*, you can begin to distance yourself from that belief and recognise it as a distorting idea. You can eliminate fear of disapproval or criticism in social situations by recognising that it is ridiculous to be concerned about the judgement of complete strangers. You can realise that the panic you feel when you go into a shop will not make you stop breathing or kill you. Cognitive therapy is considered helpful for depression as well as for phobias. It works well for people with social phobias.

Behaviour Therapy

This treatment has been used successfully for phobias, panic attacks and Obsessive Compulsive Disorder. Behaviour therapy does not go to great lengths to explore the cause of the problem, though some practitioners may engage in this initially if they think their client would benefit. Cognitive therapy, described above, may be part of the treatment.

The focus, however, is on practical forms of treatment which aim to modify your behaviour and help you overcome your fears. Sex therapy techniques described in chapter 19 work in a similar way, and the self-help techniques offered in this book are based on the behavioural approach. The underlying theory of behaviour therapy is that a fear has been learned and has created a pattern or a habit that cannot be shaken off. By teaching new patterns and new habits you can eliminate the fear.

What you get from a professional is not so very different from the help you can get from this book, except that it will be tailor-made to your needs and you will have the supervision of an expert.

The major tool is exposure treatment, which means that you expose yourself to whatever frightens you till you get used to it. When you practise visualising techniques to desensitise yourself to the prospect of a real encounter with the object or situation of your fear, you are using a type of exposure treatment.

Exposure therapy is not so effective for anyone suffering from serious depression or general anxiety, unrelated emotional difficulties, alcohol dependency or who is on high doses of sedatives. And people who have a condition that could worsen through stress, such as heart disease, asthma, etc, should consult their GP first.

A therapist may decide that the preliminary, visualising stage is not necessary for you. For mild or single phobias the sooner you take on exposure to the real thing, the quicker will be the recovery time. For most people with specific single phobias, a fear will start to diminish within half an hour of a real encounter, though the technique has to be repeated several times over the following weeks. A total treatment may add up to between two and twenty sessions. In each session, the therapist may literally be doing the hand-holding, perhaps accompanying his patient to a railway station or supermarket. A plan will be set out, with goals that have to be followed. These goals are worked out carefully and agreed between the therapist and patient. Where appropriate, the whole family or a relative will be included in the recovery programme. After the course of sessions with the therapist is concluded, a self-help plan will be set up.

An alternative form of exposure is known as 'flooding'. With this, patients are asked to imagine themselves in their most frightening situation continuously for one to two hours. At the same time, the therapist focuses the attention by providing a commentary describing the patient's most dreaded encounters. It sounds fairly brutal, and is not to everyone's taste, but a kind of immunity seems to build up often within half an hour. Panic is not a long-held reaction. The imaginary encounter actually becomes boring.

Psychiatrists also use videotapes to film patients with social fears while doing role play (this means the patients put themselves in an imagined, feared situation and act it out with the help of other 'actors'). Before seeing their performance, they are asked to assess it. When comparing with the filmed (and therefore factual) version, they realise that their behaviour is often normal and very wide of the mark of their assessment.

Hypnotherapy
There's nothing magic about hypnotherapy. We go into light hypnotic states more often than we think. When we daydream, get absorbed in a book, listen to music, watch television, dance or are involved in some repetitive sport, we are mildly hypnotised. The relaxation exercises described earlier in this book also induce self-hypnosis.

Hypnotherapy as a treatment for phobias is not a miracle cure: you don't go into a trance, get instructions from the hypnotist and then go away with all your fears eliminated. A hypnotherapist, as the name implies, is a therapist as well as a hypnotist. He or she will employ similar techniques to ordinary therapists, and the approach might be behaviourist or explore early history or be a combination.

When you are in a trance, you are at the same time usually

mentally alert and can recall the session afterwards. However, under hypnosis, you are also deeply relaxed and open to ideas that in other circumstances could produce anxiety. Many hypnotherapists use this state to help their patients go back in time to re-experience painful incidents. If you prefer a behaviourist approach, or a combination, you should ask about it either before making an appointment or at your first interview.

The behaviourist approach works something like this. The hypnotherapist uses visualising techniques and encourages a person with a spider phobia to imagine a spider in the room, crawling on an arm, etc. An agoraphobic patient may be asked to visualise going to a supermarket or wherever. And during the hypnosis, as they familiarise themselves with difficult situations, patients will be encouraged to think in positive ways which they can carry over into real life.

Another behaviourist technique is to work out an 'anxiety hierarchy' with phobic patients before putting them into a trance. This is called SUDS (Subjective Unit of Disturbance Scale) which is simply a list of anxiety-making happenings in order of severity. A patient with fear of flying might get a SUDS which includes aircraft taking off (rating 100 points), boarding aircraft (rating 80 points) and seeing a plane in the sky (rating under 5 points). The sessions are based on the list, starting with the least threatening experience. The hypnotherapist may then take the patient through an entire imaginary flight experience. As part of the treatment, self-hypnosis – a form of relaxation – is taught, to be used in real-life situations, such as when flying. A simple gesture, like touching your nose or rubbing your ear might be used as a reminder to relax during a tense moment.

Hypnotherapy for phobias usually requires under six sessions. Some people are highly resistant to being hypnotised, and practitioners say that the best subjects are people who are creative, or can get easily engrossed in a book or film or other activity. Some therapists maintain that their role is primarily to assist relaxation, reduce tension and increase confidence. All would agree that their treatment requires effort, commitment and determination on the part of the client, just as any other kind of therapy does.

Group Therapy

The main difference between a self-help group and group therapy is that the latter is supervised by a counsellor or psychotherapist or psychiatrist who will be expert at handling groups. The members of a group are likely to share a single problem or set of problems, rather than represent a mixed bag of phobias. Someone suffering from social fears will meet with others similarly afflicted, or a group may focus on agoraphobia, or claustrophobia or flying. All of these groups of fears are thought to benefit from group therapy. Fear of flying is well treated by group therapy, usually incorporating a visit to an airport and an explanation of the mechanics of aeroplanes.

What advantage, if any, does group therapy offer over individual therapy? In the first place, there are other people to relate to and to identify with, since all will share similar fears. You hear their attitudes and, whether similar to or different from your own, they broaden your perspective. Others may express thoughts you would not have aired in public or spark off ideas you hadn't thought of. People who have difficulty in communicating or who feel inferior in a group get the chance to test out social skills in a safe setting.

Some research suggests that people who have group therapy alongside individual therapy overcome their phobias faster than do those having individual therapy alone.

Family therapy is another way of working in a group, this time with only close family members present, along with the patient. The advantage of this is that all can have their say under the safe supervision of an experienced family therapist who will guide the sessions away from blame or despair to more constructive approaches. The family will gain insight into their own behaviour as well as that of the patient, and may have to learn new ways to respond.

Social skills and assertiveness training

Part of the problem for people with social fears is that they lack social skills. This may be partly due to the fact that they never developed them during early adulthood because they avoided social occasions and the essential learning experiences.

Social skills training is one way of catching up on the learning experience. The aim is to increase confidence and bring out a sense of effectiveness in those taking part. Assertiveness training is not about being aggressive but about valuing yourself as a person and making this clear to others.

Here is a set of NON-assertive beliefs that a course aims to eliminate:

1. The belief that you need the approval of others, or that others' judgement of your behaviour is more valuable than your own.

2. The belief that we are as we are and cannot change. The 'I'm' syndrome, as in: 'That's how I am . . . I cannot help it . . . it's in my nature.'

3. The belief that guilt and worry are an indication that we care.

4. The belief that we should only do things if we are going to do them well and are governed by the fear of failure and the unknown, and the need to be perfect.

5. The belief that there is an absolute system of right and wrong – the ought/should syndrome.

6. The belief that if you wait long enough, things will change without you doing anything about it.

7. The belief that you must take responsibility for others.

8. The belief that you have no control over your emotions, especially anger.

9. The belief that you are not worthy.

Together, these make an overwhelmingly burdensome package which assertiveness training aims to undo. Skills are learned through discussion and sharing of experiences. Exercises and role play give participants the opportunity to explore how they normally react and how they can change their responses by using certain techniques.

The focus is on choice. Instead of blaming oneself for not participating or mixing with people at a party, for instance, the new attitude might be: 'I choose to take my time and get used to the place first.' Much of the thinking is aimed at boosting self-esteem, as with the self-talk technique, but there are other dimensions. Conversation skills include learning to give criticism constructively and to take it constructively too. Criticism becomes something you are prepared to consider seriously rather than something to contradict in a defensive manner. This means saying something like: 'Can you tell me more about the things you don't like?' and showing that you are ready to listen even if, in the end, you decide not to agree.

Courses in social skills or assertiveness training can sometimes be offered through the GP, local psychiatric clinic or adult education institutes. A course may last six to ten weeks, one session a week.

Therapy for Post-Traumatic Stress Disorder

This is a fairly new speciality in therapy, and there are few clinics out of London providing treatment. The Traumatic Stress Clinic in London treats adults and children, and is a national referral centre, accepting people from all parts of the UK. There are several different treatment programmes. The simplest, which may be sufficient when a person gets to the clinic soon after the upsetting incident, is carried out in small groups or on a one-to-one basis. This programme is described as 'debriefing'. Information about traumatic reactions is given, and clients are encouraged to describe their experiences, speaking in the first person and in the present tense.

For further programmes, the account may be tape recorded, and clients are then asked to listen to it at least three times a week for an hour each time. In subsequent sessions, the therapist may ask a person to 'rewind and hold' mentally on very distressing parts of the event and to repeat or expand on certain details. This of course is a version of the visualisation and desensitisation part of self-exposure therapy.

Where possible, the client is later exposed in carefully graded stages to the original situation or an adapted version of it.

Debriefing and reliving of the incident may take six to eight sessions, followed by a focus on changing the disturbed thinking patterns, using cognitive therapy. A trial based on these programmes showed that half of the clients taking part were no longer classified as suffering from Post Traumatic Stress Disorder by the time they had finished.

For children, family therapy and longer-term follow-up therapy may be offered.

2. DRUG TREATMENTS

If you go to your GP seeking help for irrational fears, you might well be given drugs to relieve anxiety or depression. These will not remove your fears, but they may help for a short time. One psychiatrist has described them as offering a 'window of opportunity' for patients with depression and severe symptoms, especially with social phobias, before they progress to psychological treatment. Certain drugs, however, are accepted as part of active treatment against Obsessive Compulsive Disorder. Always ask your GP what kind of drug you are taking – what are its side effects, is it affected by foods, alcohol or other drugs – and say what other drugs you are taking, including over-the-counter remedies.

★ *Tranquillisers* provide short-term relief from anxiety. If you take them for a fortnight to a month, never longer, they can carry you through a bad patch. Doctor Isaac Marks suggests they may be used in small doses before facing a frightening situation, especially when attempting new goals, but he points out that the drug should be taken three to four hours before exposure to allow time for it to wear off while still in the situation. In other words, a tranquilliser can give you the confidence to get out of the house, but you need to be fully in charge to gain positive feedback from the experience. Tranquillisers can make you feel drowsy and affect concentration. Alcohol works in a similar way to tranquillisers. Both can of course be addictive and need increasing amounts to be effective if taken regularly for a long time.

★ *Anti-depressants* not only work against depression, they can work against anxiety too. Psychological disturbance following bereavement, Post Traumatic Stress or injury may respond well to anti-depressants. If self-exposure to difficult situations produces panic that shows no sign of diminishing, a course of appropriate anti-depressants will often help make the exposure approach more effective. It will take up to a month before the beneficial effects are felt, so a course of treatment lasts longer than it does with tranquillisers, perhaps up to sixteen weeks. Side-effects such as drowsiness, dry mouth, blurred vision or nausea are not uncommon, depending on the kind of anti-depressant prescribed. On high doses of certain kinds, impotence and delayed ejaculation affect up to half of men and lack of orgasm affects half of women users.

The favoured kind for social phobias is moclobemide, one of a group called reversible inhibitors of mono-amine oxidase. These have shown good response rates of up to 80 per cent in patients with social phobias, and an improvement in up to 60 per cent. Side-effects are found to be tolerable. The help from an anti-depressant is temporary. It doesn't, on its own and in the long run, remove anxieties or phobias. Psychotherapy or self-help measures, or both, are needed for long-term control over fears. Again, dependency can develop, and coming off the drug should be planned with a doctor's help.

★ *Drugs for Obsessive Compulsive Disorder* have been proved helpful. There are several types available, all within the category of anti-depressants. They have a specific anti-phobic action on the brain, and some of the most successful are Selective Serotonin Re-Uptake Inhibitors (SSRIs), which include Prozac, Seroxat, Lustral and Faverin. They work by increasing levels of a chemical messenger, serotonin, in the brain. Low levels of serotonin are linked to compulsive behaviour. Some possible side-effects are nausea, diarrhoea, headache, sleeping difficulty, difficulty in reaching orgasm – this last effect occurs in at least a quarter of women using SSRIs – and they also interfere with ejaculation in men. The side-effects often decrease after a few weeks. Another anti-obsessive drug, Anafranil, has a different biochemical action and more intense side-effects including dry mouth, blurred vision and constipation. None of these drugs are considered to be addictive, though a slow reduction is recommended if the client decides to stop taking them.

SSRIs are sometimes used for children with Obsessive Compulsive Disorder as well as adults. A high dosage course is needed for at least ten weeks for results to show. Again, other kinds of treatment involving personal therapy and behaviour techniques may be needed too. Research has shown that at least 40 per cent of patients fail to respond to drugs alone.

★ *Beta Blockers* are mainly prescribed for high blood pressure, but they are also useful for people with mild performance anxiety, including public speaking or presenting information to a group. They have the effect of reducing palpitations and hand shaking, two aspects of fear or panic which can seriously impair performance, especially in the case of actors or musicians. Anyone with asthma or vascular disease shouldn't take beta blockers, and as with other drugs they are best for short-term or occasional use.

3. PHYSICAL TREATMENTS

These are for the most severe problems when other treatments have failed. They usually involve a stay in hospital.

★ *Electroconvulsive Therapy (ECT)* is rarely given nowadays, following horror stories of unwilling patients and poor results that included memory loss, but it is still considered for anyone who is highly anxious and depressed and possibly suicidal. An electric current passed briefly through the brain produces mild convulsions which seem to provide relief. One theory is that the electric current makes the brain cells more receptive to serotonin. The treatment takes place under anaesthetic, and only one or two sessions will often produce benefits. The memory loss is said to be temporary and the medical profession still regards ECT as a useful tool for people who do not respond to other treatment.

★ *Surgical Treatment*, known as leucotomy (or 'lobotomy' in the US), has an even worse reputation. It aims to destroy a small part of the brain in the location where anxiety is triggered. Modern versions treat a small brain area, usually with an irradiating implant. The treatment is used very rarely for severely disabled patients with long-term chronic anxiety.

4. ALTERNATIVE THERAPIES

Various alternative therapies and complementary remedies have been used successfully by people with fears and phobias. Their success is mainly based on the fact that the treatments aim to reduce tension, aid relaxation and induce a state of well-being. Practitioners also quite often provide a degree of psychotherapy, listening to personal problems and advising on lifestyle, diet and a change from negative to positive attitudes. Fortnightly or monthly sessions over a period of a few months seem to be sufficient for most people.

Alternative remedies are unlikely to be effective on their own in the treatment of anxieties and phobias, but they work well alongside self-help measures. The following list of treatments is by no means comprehensive. There are many other alternative remedies available. No single therapy stands out as especially helpful. The choice is up to you.

★ *Acupuncture* is part of traditional Chinese medicine. It is based on detailed observation of how people change when they become ill, from which a distinct theory has evolved. Fine needles are used to stimulate channels of energy, said to run through the body. The aim is to restore a proper balance in the body which will have an effect on emotional and physical symptoms. People suffering from panic attacks have reported improvement in their mental state after being treated by acupuncture, and have subsequently been more able to face their fears.

★ *Aromatherapy* uses essential oils or plant essences which may be massaged into the body or inhaled, providing deep relaxation. There are at least 400 essences with different therapeutic effects. Suggestions for self-help use are given in chapter 6. If you choose treatment from a professional you will gain the extra benefit from massage which will work on stiff muscles and create a sense of relaxation and well-being.

★ *Homeopathy* is described in chapter 9 on a self-help basis. Practitioners use the same remedies but tailor them to individual needs. Treatment usually consists of an initial consultation during which a detailed physical and mental history is taken. Consultations are usually monthly, over several months. Choose a qualified practitioner – see the contacts and address section at the end of this book.

★ *Herbalism* uses plants to treat specific ailments, but like homeopaths the herbalist will take into account a person's lifestyle, attitudes and general condition. Alleviation of anxiety, stress or panic will form part of any treatment. You can buy herbal remedies to treat yourself, but some are potentially toxic and you are safer going to a specialist for any complex treatments.

★ *Healing* is often referred to as 'faith healing', but practitioners say that no faith is necessary. The healer's aim is to restore health by channelling energy so that the body, or mind, heals itself. Again, you'll get the 'whole person' approach as well as some version of a 'laying on of hands': the techniques vary, and some healers don't even touch the body. In a *Which?* magazine survey of alternative therapies, 75 per cent of people visiting a healer reported feeling much better after the treatment, and half said their condition had improved. These results were far more positive than they were for any of the other therapies surveyed – including acupuncture, homeopathy, aromatherapy and herbalism, but the survey did not specify the conditions treated.

5. NEWEST TECHNIQUES

★ *Virtual Reality* is part of the fun of new technology. People can view scenes on a television screen while wearing a special headset that enables them to interact with the happenings on-screen. Already, a software computer programme showing graded exposure to spiders is available (see page 108) but that is not interactive, in the way that Virtual Reality is. Manchester dentist Phillip Wander is using VR as a means to relax and soothe nervous patients (see page 116).

The most inspired treatment comes from computer scientists and psychiatrists in the UK, who have made use of the VR 'experience' to confront people with their fears as part of a programme of exposure therapy. There have been good results with people exposed to fear of heights, and the treatment is expanding to include other phobias. People with spider fears could 'design' images of the insects and arrange for them to crawl into their field of vision. Those who fear flying could explore the experience in detail before ever setting foot in a plane. It may be some time before VR exposure programmes become widely available, but they make sense as part of behaviourist therapy.

★ *Eye Movement Desensitisation and Reprocessing* – a mouthful rendered down to EMDR – seems like a miracle cure for phobias and Post Traumatic Stress Syndrome. All it consists of is a psychologist holding two fingers in front of a patient's face and flicking them rhythmically from side to side. The technique comes from American psychologist Francine Shapiro, who found that when preoccupied with disturbing memories people's eyes will jerk involuntarily from side to side. She perfected a technique whereby patients are asked to think of the memory that disturbs them – bearing in mind that unpleasant memory flashes are typical of Post Traumatic Stress – and at the same time to follow the movement of the fingers. It takes just one or two sessions to get relief, and the positive effect is so quick that doctors have been suspecting that it must be too good to be true. However, theories are emerging. The eye movements seem to replicate those in the dreaming phase of sleep, so perhaps the finger movements provide new information to the brain which reshuffles the painful imagery and replaces it with something more tolerable; or attention-switching may be a side-effect of the finger movements; or there is a mild hypnotic effect. Whatever the reason, psychologist John Spector, who introduced the technique to the UK, thinks that it can help people with long-standing fears, including agoraphobia. Spector, of Shrodells Psychiatric Unit at Watford General Hospital, says that patients need to be screened carefully for suitability before being given the treatment. It could be a hazard for anyone with epilepsy, eye problems or certain mental health problems.

WHERE TO GET HELP

First approach your GP to see if you can get help under the NHS. Any of the psychotherapies and counselling treatments described above may be available, depending on funds and local resources. Some alternative treatments may also be obtained under the NHS.

If there's nothing doing in that direction, then enquire through one of the charities or the appropriate organisation listed in the contracts and addresses section on pages 173–6.

CHAPTER 24

Keeping up the Good Work

You know now that you can reduce or overcome anxiety, panic, obsessive behaviour, phobias, by putting in some dedicated and determined effort. Nobody can guarantee a complete cure. Doctors cautiously describe a patient as 'symptom-free' after successful professional treatment. The same applies to you. Unpredictable difficulties and challenges do occur, and sometimes they can knock you sideways. What you have are the tools to enable you to pick yourself up and carry on through the bad times. You also have the awareness that will help you recognise when things seem to be slipping.

Stress can make you more vulnerable – know the danger signals

★ Are you rushing? Check whether you are doing things more quickly than usual: eating, talking, drinking.
★ Are you feeling under pressure?
★ Do you feel driven?
★ Do you have no time for exercise or relaxation?
★ Is your sleep disturbed?
★ Are you feeling tired most of the time?
★ Are you getting more aches and pains than usual?
★ Or more indigestion, constipation, diarrhoea, headaches – whatever disturbance you associate with stress?
★ Are you arguing more with a partner, or having more conflicts at work?
★ Do you flare up more easily than normal?

Hidden Fears

Some of these symptoms may be temporary and due to a recognisable event, which may be exciting as well as stressful. If you have several symptoms and they seem to have been growing and getting worse of late, then you need to give yourself a boost, recharge your batteries, and make sure that events won't overwhelm you or make you extra vulnerable to anxiety or panic should some unexpected challenge arise.

Protect yourself from stress

★ *Get back to regular relaxation* sessions. Observe your breathing during the sessions and bring it down to an even keel.

★ *Be a clock-watcher*. Remind yourself to stop work and check your anxiety levels every hour. If you can't set an alarm, try putting a red spot on your watch or clock to remind you.

★ *Create a symbol*. It could be a photograph of someone you admire or someone you love, or a photograph of a beautiful landscape or a houseplant. Have it in your field of vision so when your eyes rest on it you are reminded to relax, to smile, to think of the person or object with pleasure.

★ *Learn to say no*. Don't be pushed into doing more than you can. Delegate tasks, both domestic and at work. Say no positively, not defensively, when asked to do more than you can comfortably manage.

★ *Make a timetable* and a list of things to be done. Be realistic about what you can achieve. Decide on the priorities.

★ *Give yourself time for yourself*. Go on, indulge, pamper yourself. Relax in a hot bath, read, watch television, cut yourself off from daily obligations.

★ *Take some exercise*. You can go for a walk and admire the flowers in the park, take up tennis, go for a swim, tend the garden. Even if you don't feel like it, do it (make a date to do it with a friend, then it's more difficult to pull out). Physical exercise actually gives you energy and also gives your mind a break.

★ *Try something new.* A sport perhaps, or some voluntary work, a day or evening class, a lecture.

★ *Smile please* – yes, even if you don't feel like it. There's evidence to suggest that a smile on the outside reaches parts on the inside too. Laughter is even better, as it relaxes muscles, slows the heart and uses up adrenaline.

★ *If you still feel on the edge of anxiety*, give yourself some worry time – but make it only one hour a day.

★ *Remind yourself* that a panic attack is not life-threatening. It is not an indication that you are crazy either. What you are experiencing is an exaggerated version of normal bodily reactions to stress.

★ *Don't fight the feelings* or try to brush them off. Face them for what they are, and you will tame them.

★ *Think of the good times*, and the way you freed yourself from worries in the past. You can do it again, even if you have slipped a little.

Hidden Fears

★ *Remind yourself, it's recovery, not cure.* Life is about change, and often challenges. You may have to be vigilant in order to keep up with change in a positive manner, but it is never too late to try.

★ *If you haven't joined one of the self-help charities*, now's the time to do so. You can get lifelong support, up-to-date news of treatments, and the knowledge that you are not alone.

Remember the self-talk. Tell yourself the following:

★ **I have done it before and I'll do it again**
★ **I know it can be difficult, but I can cope**
★ **I will have the courage**
★ **I will succeed**

AND YOU WILL

nowhere does it say everyone 'EXCEPT JUDY' will succeed...

are you sure?

Contacts and Addresses

Voluntary organisations

MIND (National Association for Mental Health). Look up local branch in telephone directory or write with sae to: 15/19 Broadway, Stratford, London E15 4BQ. Publishes helpful books and leaflets. Will put people in touch with local groups concerned with phobias.

The Phobics Society, 4 Cheltenham Road, Chorlton-cum-Hardy, Manchester M21 9QN (0161 881 1937). Publishes newsletter, puts people in touch with others locally.

Phobic Action, now called Anxia, Claybury Grounds, Manor Road, Woodford Green, Essex IG8 8PR (0181 559 2551, helpline 0181 559 2459). Publishes many leaflets and books on various phobias, also videos and relaxation cassette. Runs national telephone helpline and some self-help groups.

Triumph Over Phobia, PO Box 1831, Bath BA1 3YX (01225 330353). Self-help group for phobic and obsessive problems.

No Panic, 93 Brands Farm Way, Randlay, Telford TF3 2JQ (01952 590545).

Depression Alliance, PO Box 1022, London SE1 7GB. Send sae for details.

Hidden Fears

The Thanet Phobic Group, 47 Orchard Road, Westbrook, Margate, Kent CT9 5JS (01843 833720).

Scotland: Stresswatch, Barn Community Flats, 42 Barnwell Road, Riccarton, Kilmarnock ST16 3AD (01785 211144). Charity with many groups throughout Scotland.

Northern Ireland: The Agoraphobia and Anxiety Group, South Belfast Beacon Centre, 84 University Street, Belfast (01232 439945).

Psychotherapy and Counselling

MIND (see address, page 173) will provide information on psychotherapy and counselling, including local practitioners and group therapy.

British Association for Counselling, 1 Regent Place, Rugby, Warwickshire CV21 3BX (01788 578328). Membership organisation for counsellors and counselling organisations. Write with sae for local resources and guidelines on how to choose a counsellor or psychotherapist.

The Hypnotherapy Register, 24 Rickmansworth Road, Watford, Herts WD1 7HT (01923 227772). Offers a list of qualified practitioners.

The British Society of Experimental and Clinical Hypnosis, Dr M. Heap, Department of Psychotherapeutic Studies, University of Sheffield, 16 Claremont Crescent, Sheffield S10 2TA (01742 824975). Provides information on doctors and dentists using hypnotherapy.

Relate (Marriage Guidance), Herbert Gray College, Little Church Street, Rugby CV21 3AP, or look up local branch in telephone directory. Offers sex therapy and counselling for couples and individuals throughout country.

Contacts and Addresses

Post Traumatic Stress Clinic, 73 Charlotte Street, London W1P 1LB (0171 436 9000).

Relaxation, social skills, etc

Relaxation for Living, 168–170 Oatlands Drive, Weybridge, Surrey KT13 9ET. Provides cassettes, etc, on relaxation techniques, information on relaxation classes. Write with large sae.

Neuro Linguistic Programming, Pace Personal Development courses, 86 South Hill Park, London NW3 2SN (0171 794 0960).

LifeSkills, Bowman House, 6 Billetfield, Taunton, Somerset TA1 3NN (01823 451771). Anxiety and stress management cassettes for flying, agoraphobia and other fears devised by psychologist Dr Robert Sharpe.

Alternative Treatments

The Institute for Complementary Medicine, PO Box 194, London SE16 1QZ (0171 237 5165). Has created a register of approved practitioners in homeopathy, acupuncture, aromatherapy, etc. Send large sae for information.

The British Holistic Medical Association, 179 Gloucester Place, London NW1 6DX (0171 262 5299). List of medically qualified practitioners in holistic medicine.

The Acupuncture Association and Registrar, 34 Alderney Street, London SW1V 4EU (0171 834 1012). Has list of approved practitioners.

The United Kingdom Homeopathic Medical Association, 6 Livingstone Road, Gravesend, Kent DA12 5DZ (01474 560336). For approved practitioners.

Flying fears

Aviatours (Charter) Limited, Pinewoods, Eglinton Road, Tilford, Surrey GU10 2DH (01252 793250). Runs special courses including flights for people who fear flying. Book, video and audio cassette available.

Flying With Confidence, Britannia Airways, London Luton Airport, Luton, Bedfordshire LU2 9ND (01582 424155). Courses including flights for people who fear flying.

Index

aconite 59–60
acupuncture 165–6
adolescence 17, 80
adrenaline 24, 25
agoraphobia 67–72
   case history 68–70
   homeopathic remedies 58
   self help 70–2
   vulnerability to 15, 18, 67
AIDS, fear of 109
alcohol 33, 132, 163
   when flying 96
alternative therapies 57–64, 165–7
   acupuncture 165–6
   aromatherapy 44–6, 166
   contacts and addresses 175
   healing 166–7
   herbalism 57, 166
   homeopathy 57–64, 166
anacardium 60
Anafranil 164
animals, fear of 103–8
   homeopathic remedies 58
anti-depressants 163
Anxia (self-help group) 143–6
anxiety
   breaking the pattern 32–4
   hormonal trigger 32, 33
   positive and negative effects 31
   Woody Allen Character (WAC) 32
argentum nitricum 60
arnica 60
aromatherapy 44–6, 166
arsenicum album 60
assertiveness training 160–1
   non-assertive beliefs 160
   skill 160–1
avoidance 1–2, 19, 24, 51

Bach Rescue Remedy 57
behaviour therapy 156–7
beta blockers 164
birds, fear of 103
bladder training 121
blood, fear of 59
blushing 82, 86–8
   stopping 87–8
body functions 117–22
   case history 118–19
   self help 119–22
body language 54, 55
body noises 117, 118, 120
bowel control 118, 121
breathing patterns and techniques 25–7, 36, 38

bullying 15
Bunyan, John 123

caffeine 33
calcarea carbonica 61
camomile 45
carcinocin 61
causticum 61
childhood, fears originating in 13–15
Clarke, Dr David 85
claustrophobia 73–7
  case history 73–5
  homeopathic remedies 58
  self help 75–7
cleanliness, obsession with 124, 125–7, 150
cognitive therapy 155
compulsive behaviour 123, 124, 125
  see also Obsessive Compulsive Disorder (OCD)
confiding in other people 10–11, 34, 72, 147–8
confined spaces, fear of *see* claustrophobia
confrontation *see* exposure therapy
contacts and addresses 173–6
conversation skills 84, 161
counselling 154–5, 174–5
criticism, accepting 161

Darwin, Charles 123
defining your fears 16–19
dentists, fear of
  case history 111–13
  homeopathic remedies 59
  laser treatment 115
  relaxation using Virtual Reality 116, 167
  treatment under hypnosis 115–16
depression 131
describing your feelings 9–10
desensitisation/visualisation 53
  agoraphobia 70
  body functions 120
  claustrophobia 76
  flying, fear of 94–5
  insects, fear of 53, 106
  medical phobias 113
  Obsessive Compulsive Disorder (OCD) 127
  social fears 83
Distraction Method 88–9, 121
doctors and hospitals, fear of 59
dogs, fear of 7, 8–9
driving, fear of 99–102
  case histories 7, 99–101
  homeopathic remedies 58
  on motorways 99–102
  self help 101–2
drug treatments 162–4
  anti-depressants 163
  beta blockers 164
  for Obsessive Compulsive Disorder (OCD) 163–4
  tranquillisers 162–3

electroconvulsive therapy (ECT) 164–5
empathising with the sufferer 147–8
erection failure 132
essential oils 44–6
exercise 34, 170–1

Index

exposure therapy 51–3, 156
  designing a programme 52–3
  'flooding' 157
  listing the fears 52
  role play 157
  unsuitable candidates for 51–2, 156
  see also desensitisation/visualisation
exposure to fear 51–6
  desensitisation/visualisation 53
  exposure therapy 51–3, 156
  Neuro-Linguistic Programming (NLP) 54–6
Eye Movement Desensitisation and Reprocessing (EMDR) 167–8
eye-to-eye contact 82, 84

failure, fear of 58
fainting 116
family therapy 159
Faverin 163
fears
  clusters of 9
  effects on lifestyle 19–20
  exposure to 51–6
  identifying 8–9
  irrational 8, 103, 154
  justifiable 7–8
  origins of 13–16
  those affected 8, 13
  types of 16–19
feelings, releasing 34
Fielding, Dr Guy 89
'floating' technique
  agoraphobia 70
  claustrophobia 76
  insects, fear of 106
  medical phobias 114–15
  panic attacks 27–9
  sexual problems 136
'flooding' 157
flying, fear of 17–18, 73, 91–7
  case history 92–4
  contacts and addresses 176
  ear discomfort 96
  Fear of Flying courses 94, 176
  group therapy 159
  homeopathic remedies 58
  origins 92
  self help 94–7
food hoarding 125
friends and relations
  children, help from 150
  collusion 148–9
  confiding in 10–11, 34, 72, 147–8
  desire to reassure 150
  do's and don'ts 151
  empathy 147–8
  support and encouragement 149–50

gelsemium 61
genetic predisposition 13
geranium 46
goals
  agoraphobia 71
  body functions 120
  claustrophobia 76
  flying, fear of 95
  insects, fear of 107
  social fears 83–4
GPs 153
group therapy 159

healing 166–7

heights, fear of 59
herbalism 57, 166
homeopathy 57–64, 166
   remedy profile 59–64
hormone treatment 132
Hughes, Howard 123
hyoscaymus 61
hypnotherapy 157–8
   anxiety hierarchy 158
   behaviourist approach 158
   self-hypnosis 158
   Subjective Unit of Disturbance Scale (SUDS) 158
hypochondria 19, 111

identifying the fear 8–9
illness, fear of 7, 8, 9, 18–19, 109–11
inadequacy, feelings of 1, 80–1
inanimate objects, fear of 8, 103, 154
incidence of hidden fears in the population 8
injections, fear of 109
insect screens 108
insects, fear of 103–8
   self help 106–8

Jan de Vries' Emergency Essence 57
jasmine 45
Jong, Erica 92

kali-arsenicum 62

lavender 45–6
Lee, Deborah 137, 138
leucotomy (lobotomy) 165
lifts, fear of 75

loud noises, fear of 14, 23
Lustral 163
Luther, Martin 123
lycopodium 62

marital stress 131
Marks, Dr Isaac 51, 103, 150, 162
massage, do-it-yourself 41–4
medical phobias 7, 8, 9, 18–19, 109–16
   case history 111–13
   childhood origins 110
   reassurance, seeking 110–11, 114
   self help 113–16
medication *see* drug treatments
medorrhinum 62
moclobemide 163
modelling yourself on someone else 55

natrum muriaticum 62
negative self-talk 47, 48–9
Neuro-Linguistic Programming (NLP) 54–6
NHS treatments 153
nux vomica 62–3

obsessions 1, 124, 125
Obsessive Compulsive Disorder (OCD) 123–9
   case history 125–7
   common compulsions 124
   drug treatments 163–4
   family history 13, 123
   homeopathic remedies 59
   professional treatment 150
   self help 127–9

Index

origins of fears 13–16
over-dependence 15, 18, 67

panic attacks 23–9, 171
  acupuncture treatment 166
  anti-panic measures 25–9
  breathing technique 25–7, 38
  homeopathic remedies 58
  symptoms 1, 23–4
  triggers 24
  vulnerability to 24–5
Paradoxical Intention
  blushing 87
  body functions 120–1
perfectionism 11–12
phobias: defined 19
phosphorus 63
physical fears 16, 18–19
physical treatments 164–5
positive behaviour, changing to 56
positive thinking power 47–50
  positive self-talk 47–8, 49
  STOP trick 49–50
Post Traumatic Stress 137–40
  debriefing 161
  distractions 138
  self help 138, 139–40
  symptoms 137
Post-Traumatic Stress Disorder (PTSD)
  causes 16, 137
  diagnosis 137–8, 139
  therapy 161–2
professional help 153–68
  alternative therapies 57–64, 165–7
  drug treatments 162–4
  newest techniques 167–8
  physical treatments 164–5
  psychological treatments 154–62
props 71, 84
Prozac 145, 163
psychological treatments 154–62
  behaviour therapy 156–7
  cognitive therapy 155
  counselling 154–5, 174–5
  group therapy 159
  hypnotherapy 157–8
  psychotherapy 154–5, 165, 174–5
  social skills and assertiveness training 159–61
psychotherapy 154–5, 165, 174–5
public lavatories, fear of using 117, 121
public speaking 55–6
pulsatilla 63

relationship stress 131
relaxation 35–9
  aromatherapy and 44–6
  breathing and 36, 38
  cassettes 39, 175
  deep relaxation 35, 36–8
  using virtual reality 116
restaurants, fear of going to 23, 154
ridicule 10
rituals 123, 125, 127

school phobia 15
Selective Serotonin Re-Uptake Inhibitors (SSRIs) 163–4
self-consciousness 79
self-criticism 11

self-forgiveness 34
self-help groups 143–6
self-hypnosis 158
self-talk 47–50, 172
  agoraphobia 70, 72
  body functions 120
  claustrophobia 77
  flying, fear of 95
  insects, fear of 106–7
  medical phobias 114
  Obsessive Compulsive Disorder (OCD) 128
  sexual problems 136
  social fears 85
self-tolerance 12
sensate focus technique 135
sense of proportion 85
serotonin 164, 165
Seroxat 144, 163
sex therapy 134, 150–1, 156
sexual abuse 131
sexual intercourse, pain during 132
sexual orientation 132
sexual problems 131–6
  case history 133–4
  homeopathic remedies 59
  possible causes 131–2
  self help 134–6
shame and embarrassment 1, 23, 80–1
Shapiro, Francine 167–8
shyness 17, 79
social behaviour, positive 55
social fears 16–17, 79–90
  case history 81–3
  drug treatments 163
  homeopathic remedies 59
  Neuro-Linguistic Programming (NLP) 54–6
  origins 80
  performance set 79
  self help 83–6
  social set 79
  symptoms 80
social skills training 159–60
'something will happen', fear of 58
'space' fears 16, 17–18
specific single phobias 16, 19–20
  therapy 156–7
Spector, John 168
spiders, fear of 103
  case histories 7, 23, 104–5
  desensitisation 53
  homeopathic remedies 58
  sexuality, link with 154
  SPIDER PC (exposure program) 108
stagefright 31
staphysagria 63
Stern, Dr Richard 87
stigmas 11
stimulants 33
STOP trick 49–50
stramonium 63–4
stress
  protecting yourself from 170–2
  stress signals 169–70
surgical treatment 165
swallowing, fear of 118–19
syphilinum 64

taboo words 118, 121
taboos 117–18
telephone, fear of using 89–90
  case history 7, 17
  homeopathic remedies 59

Index

self help 89–90
thuja 64
'top' (childhood) fears 14–15
tranquillisers 162–3
transmitting fears 14
Traumatic Stress Clinic 137, 161
travelling, fear of 79
tuberculinum 64

vaginismus 132

Virtual Reality 116, 167
viscum album 64
visualisation *see* desensitisation/visualisation

Wander, Phillip 116, 167
Weekes, Dr Claire 27–8
Whitenburgh, Michael 8

Yoga 36

Another Great Book from Headline

BODYPURE

YOUR COMPLETE DETOX PROGRAMME FOR HEALTH AND BEAUTY

Marie Helvin

What is the secret of Marie Helvin's lasting beauty and perfect figure? For more than twenty years Marie Helvin's exotic looks have graced the covers of innumerable magazines all over the world. Now she shares the secret of her own personal detox programme.

In our over-stressed, over-indulged and highly polluted lives, detox is the process of cleaning out the body and mind, giving everything a chance to repair and revitalise, and bringing it back to a pure and healthy base level again.

If your car or home deserves an occasional service, pamper and spring-clean, don't you?

Try Marie's detox to:

- spring-clean physically and mentally a few times a year
- kick-start a new diet or exercise regime
- deep cleanse and recondition after a period of stress, loss or illness
- help rid the body of the cravings for alcohol, nicotine, caffeine and chocolate
- relax deeply and clear the mind
- just give yourself a wonderful treat

In a series of different detox programmes designed to fit comfortably with people's lives, Marie Helvin includes delicious dietary tips, relaxation techniques, natural beauty treatments, and an innovative detox exercise plan.

Her personal experiences and enthusiasm for detox infuse every page. This book will inspire you to change your lifestyle for the better so that you look and feel wonderfully... *Bodypure*.

NON-FICTION / HEALTH / BEAUTY 0 7472 5075 7

More Great Books from Headline

HOW TO DEVELOP A PERFECT MEMORY

DOMINIC O'BRIEN
WORLD MEMORY CHAMPION

YOU TOO CAN HAVE A PERFECT MEMORY

Dominic O'Brien is the current World Memory Champion, having won the title two years in a row. He holds two *Guinness Book of Records* entries for memorising the sequence of thirty-five packs of shuffled cards in the staggering time of 55.62 seconds. How does he do it?

What is his system and how can it help you remember names, faces, telephone numbers, pass exams, learn languages and clean up at the Blackjack table?

HOW TO DEVELOP A PERFECT MEMORY will show you in simple language and easy stages.

NON-FICTION / REFERENCE 0 7472 4517 7

Headline Health Kicks

MIND OVER MIGRAINE Self help for migraine sufferers	Belinda Hollyer	£5.99 ☐
NOT TO BE SCOFFED AT Self help for eating disorders	Anne-Marie Sapsted	£5.99 ☐
BELOW THE BELT Self help for cystitis and thrush	Maggie Jones	£5.99 ☐
COMING UP FOR AIR Self help for asthma sufferers	Brigid McConville	£5.99 ☐

You can kick that problem!

All Headline books are available at your local bookshop or newsagent, or can be ordered direct from the publisher. Just tick the titles you want and fill in the form below. Prices and availability subject to change without notice.

Headline Book Publishing, Cash Sales Department, Bookpoint, 39 Milton Park, Abingdon, OXON, OX14 4TD, UK. If you have a credit card you may order by telephone – 01235 400400.

Please enclose a cheque or postal order made payable to Bookpoint Ltd to the value of the cover price and allow the following for postage and packing:

UK & BFPO: £1.00 for the first book, 50p for the second book and 30p for each additional book ordered up to a maximum charge of £3.00.

OVERSEAS & EIRE: £2.00 for the first book, £1.00 for the second book and 50p for each additional book.

Name ....

Address ....

....

....

If you would prefer to pay by credit card, please complete:
Please debit my Visa/Access/Diner's Card/American Express (delete as applicable) card no:

Signature .... Expiry Date ....

CW01113087

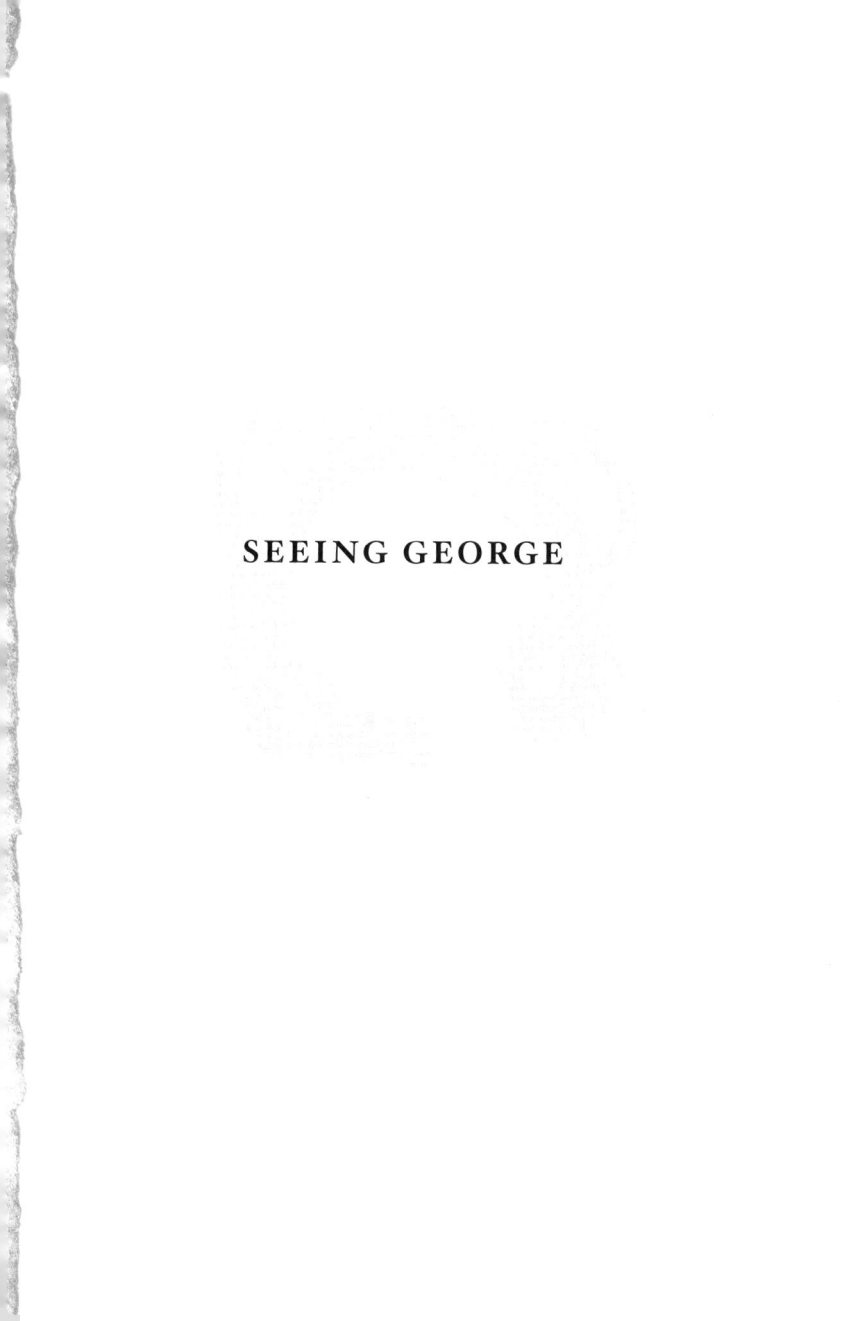

SEEING GEORGE

*For Adam,
who believes*

SEEING GEORGE

Cassandra Austin

KNOPF

A Knopf book

Published by Random House Australia Pty Ltd
20 Alfred Street, Milsons Point, NSW 2061
http://www.randomhouse.com.au
Sydney   New York   Toronto
London   Auckland   Johannesburg

First published in 2004
Copyright © Cassandra Austin 2004

All rights reserved. No part of this publication may be reproduced,
stored in a retrieval system, or transmitted in any form or by any
means, electronic, mechanical, photocopying, recording or
otherwise, without the prior written permission of the publisher.

National Library of Australia
Cataloguing-in-Publication Entry

> Austin, Cassandra, 1969- .
> Seeing George
>
> ISBN 1 74051 293 6
>
> 1. Man-woman relationships – Fiction. I. Title.

A823.4

Cover design by Greendot Design
Internal design by Greendot Design
Typeset in Filosofia 11/14pt by Midland Typesetters
Printed and bound by Tien Wah Press, Singapore
10 9 8 7 6 5 4 3 2 1

* 1 *

'I'm tired, Vi. Don't want to do this anymore.'

'Don't want to do what?' Violet looked up from her crossword puzzle. Frank was grating lemon peel into a small blue bowl. Unlike his limbs, his fingers were still dexterous. But the yellow fruit was tight with juice; he'd barely rubbed it twice before the pouting metal caught his knuckles.

'Shit.'

'You don't want to do what, love?'

He swung to face her, balding lemon in hand. 'Pretend.'

'Frank Rolden, I've never asked you to pretend anything in your life.'

He turned his back. Usually, he'd have been rattling on about how the chicken's rich fragrance – with its marjoram, garlic and lemon zest stuffing – would lure her appetite. But George was due in an hour, so Frank was being difficult.

Violet tugged at the left side of her wig. It kept listing and her swollen fingers weren't up to delicate ministration; the great brown mop slipped again as soon as she let it alone. She'd wanted a finer piece of European hair. All hand-tied. But they couldn't afford it and hers — machine-made, synthetic with a loose cap — itched and made her scalp sweat.

'Is he eating with us?'

'Well, what do we usually do, Frank?'

'You're got up differently this time.' His knife slid through the butter, making a soft click as it hit the plate.

Violet rubbed at the black velvet of her skirt, surprised he'd noticed. It was autumn, that's all. She needed thicker materials over her knees and a blanket was too dowdy for George.

She ran her tongue over her teeth to wipe off any inadvertent lipstick, thought better of it and spat out the top set of pearl and pink. No crimson marks. She pushed them back in. But her husband had made her nervous about her appearance.

Grabbing the top of a chair, she stood, then carefully clacked across the floorboards. Stupid to have bare boards in the kitchen; crumbs gathered in the grooves. Violet quickened her pace, aware that Frank's knife had paused as he watched her teetering high heels. By the time she reached the bathroom she was out of breath.

She was sorry she couldn't help out with things more. But Frank didn't mind. That was his saving grace after fifty-three years of marriage – that he really didn't mind her.

She sighed to see the plastic chair left in the shower stall and dropped the lid on the toilet to perch there instead. The vanity mirror showed her wig lunging forward on the left side. Underneath, there was a large patch on her head where her skull was pinking through. No traction. Though it would have been worse had she accepted the chemotherapy.

'Frank. FRANK.'

She could hear him whistling.

'Love, don't forget to put on a tie!'

'It's not Christmas.'

In the silvered glass her eyes looked large and frightening. She'd rimmed them with kohl as best she could, but they should have been pronounced, not bruised. Clutching the towel rail, she stood and walked toward her reflection. Closer up, the heavy kohl set off her brown irises, and the deep red frills on her blouse animated her face. She poked a small underarm bone from the corsetry into a less irritating position and worked another metallic bracelet over her hand. Tonight's costuming had a gypsy feel. To complete it she sprayed one of the numbered Chanel perfumes into the air, then flapped her skirt into it.

When she looked this beautiful she no longer saw bowed shoulders or a neck as crumpled as the greaseproof paper

Seeing George

Frank wrapped around her leftover lunch. She could almost believe she was young again. And even if the wig wasn't right, it would do.

She walked gingerly back down the hallway to Frank's room, intent on fossicking around in his wardrobe. A coat-hanger limbed with several wide-headed ties swung from the dowelling, alongside a faded cardboard diagram of How To Tie A Windsor Knot. She couldn't remember what colour shirt he had on, so chose a boring matt brown. Back in the kitchen she laid the tie discretely over a chair and picked up the candlesticks.

Frank had done a lovely job with the dining room table; best blue-printed crockery, silverware and fluted crystal. It was only after Violet had arranged the candlesticks and stepped back to admire, that she realised he'd set it for two.

In the kitchen she drew a chair out from its moorings and sat.

'Which two?'

'Guess.'

The chicken was in the oven and her husband was peeling kiflers, his shoulder blades tensely moving up and down.

'It's only once in a while, Frank.'

'Then once in a while I'll sit outside with Gretel.' He smacked on the tap and rinsed the potatoes under cold water. She waited until he shook his hands and wiped them on the tea-towel tucked into the top of his trousers.

'You're behaving like a six-year-old, love.'

Facing her, he nodded. 'I am.'

'Why?'

He opened his mouth at the very moment the doorbell rang and promptly turned back to the sink.

George's large shape was split into horizontal bars by the crenulated glass in the front door. Violet accepted a kiss on the cheek, then, shivering in the autumn air, ushered him in so quickly she almost caught his tail in the door.

'You look radiant,' he said, holding out a bedraggled bush of daisies and a bottle of cellared claret. He wore an Irishman's cap – hats being one of the few pieces of clothing he actually enjoyed – and a tuxedo.

'George, you've got no style.'

'Nonsense, I'm just too tall for top hats.'

'Go on down. Frank's in the kitchen.'

Violet clutched the flowers to her chest and took her time, not wanting him to see her hobbled steps. She was hoping the bottle of wine would soften Frank's mood, but George was grinning tightly through his rows of teeth when she entered the room and the brown tie was protruding from the bin flap.

'Cold, isn't it?' George pulled at his collar when neither of them answered.

Violet fetched a vase from the back of the pantry and held out the secateurs so Frank could snip the roots off the daisies. She sat for a bit to let her breath catch up, fussing with the vase.

Seeing George

'What'd you do — just take them from someone's garden?' Frank asked. The sink was covered with dirt by the time he'd chopped off the vein-like tendrils.

'I got them from the park.' George winked at Violet. 'That Grange is a good drop —.'

But Frank interrupted, shooing them through to the dining room. Violet set her mouth at her husband's manner, then forgave him upon spying the extra plate he'd set. It all looked lovely by candlelight. She put down the vase of daisies and waited while George play-acted being a gentlemen: tucking in her chair, shaking out her napkin.

'Frank all right?' He pulled off his cap and sat.

'His football team lost.' Whatever happened between she and Frank should stay between them. Problems shared multiplied.

'I still don't understand why team sports upset you all so much.'

'Loyalty, George.'

'Over-rated.' He grinned at her. 'I've got some news.'

'Oh, good. Pour me a wine, please.'

He picked up the bottle Frank had left to air. 'I've begun —.'

'No, no, save your news for when Frank comes. Just the wine.'

George's nostrils flared slightly, but he nodded and they sat in companionable silence for the couple of minutes it took for Frank to ladle up the curried pumpkin and apple soup. Then the three of them broke crusty rolls, breadcrumbs flaking over the white tablecloth, and Violet ripped hers into smaller bits to dunk in the soup. She smiled at Frank, delighting in the picture the three of them made around the small formal table. Almost like a family.

'You cook better than anyone else I know, Frank,' said George, after his first mouthful.

'Who else do you know?'

'Frank.' Violet's voice was a warning. Her misshapen hand wound around the stem of her wine glass, raising it.

'I'm just asking George about the other people he visits.'

'Violet was talking about your football team. Why don't we all go and see a game? It's about time I learnt the rules.'

'That's a marvellous idea,' said Violet.

Frank spooned up successive mouthfuls without pausing.

'I've been hoping we could catch up on our walks too, Violet. I've discovered a pretty little park in Caulfield I think you'd like.'

'She doesn't get out much these days, George. Or hadn't you noticed?' Frank wiped a linen napkin across his nose then stuffed it into his trouser pocket.

George laughed, dropping his spoon in his bowl. 'You two only *think* you feel the cold. It took me centuries to get out of the habit of hibernation.'

Frank stood abruptly and collected the partially emptied bowls inside each other. Violet waited until he left the room, then she patted George's hand. 'We're a dreadful bore when we fight.'

'Yes, you are. What the hell are we going to do for the rest of the evening?'

'Pour me another glass.'

Frank came to stand in the doorframe, arms crossed. 'The bird's not ready.'

'George has some news.'

'Yes!' Their guest slapped the table. 'I'd forgotten. I've begun my writing, or journal-keeping, to be more precise.' George lifted his glass, looking from one face to the other. 'Violet, I'm finally writing you up.'

'Hurrah!' she shouted.

Frank walked back into the kitchen.

2

It was late in the working day and Violet stood at Spatler & Smith's filing shelves with her face buried in the crook of her arm. She let the tears drip a moment before mopping them with the sleeve of her blouse.

Frank would be back from Adelaide tomorrow night with a month's worth of beard. Back from deserting her. And sitting in the house by herself this past month, Violet had realised that they should have been fighting about their secret, not tiptoeing around each other.

She sniffed and twisted her thin gold wedding band. It dug into her flesh, painfully ignoring her weight gain. Apparently neither of them had the courage to fight. Two years of marriage and everything was still too new. And too old. She didn't feel nineteen years old, she felt one hundred: the prospect of an entire life of just she and

Seeing George

Frank threatened to take away the horizon.

She couldn't imagine years of watching him take the newspaper into the toilet because he refused to eat enough preserved fruit, and thinking about getting out of bed to make sure her face was on before his 5 am starts — just thinking about doing that for the rest of her life — set her teeth on edge. All those mornings of just each other.

Violet's eyes watered again. She blotted them with the receipt she was supposed to be filing, and started when a male voice beside her asked, 'Are you all right?'

'Bit of dust.'

She made a show at dabbing her eyes, then turned towards the voice — and screamed.

It was leaning an elbow against the metal shelving, propping up at least six foot five inches of pinstripe-suited girth. Facial scales, purple and emerald, shimmered slightly under the fluorescent lights and its eyes were terribly large and bulbous. It looked like a dragon.

She clutched the receipt to her chest and slowly backed away.

'What's happened?' Betsy was striding toward them from the other end of the aisle. 'We could hear you in reception.'

'Betsy —.' Violet's voice was urgent.

'There was a mouse,' the dragon loudly interrupted.

'A mouse?' Betsy couldn't keep the amusement from her voice, although her tired brown eyes peered at the floor. 'George's going to think we're an office of silly girls. You've got them all panicking.'

Sure enough, Edward and Lila were also squashing into the narrow aisle.

Violet watched, bewildered that none of them seemed perturbed. This must be a hoax: an elaborate rubber suit. Any minute now they would start laughing, letting her in on the joke. Or maybe it was a promotional? But Betsy had the others more interested in finding the invisible rodent and Violet could feel the dragon staring at her.

'Can't you see it?' she whispered to Betsy.

'Well, it's probably run away, dear,' the elderly woman replied. 'But you look so pale. Was it a rat?'

Lila, who was now behind Betsy, looked down at her high-heeled feet, all skittish.

'I mean that. Him.' Violet inclined her head towards the dragon, using her free hand to continue pressing herself against the furthest part of the shelving.

'George? Of course we can see him. Did you bump yourself?' Betsy put a cool hand to Violet's forehead.

The dragon offered a small smile.

'No.'

'Well, what's the matter? Haven't you been introduced?' Betsy angled her shoulder to negotiate the cramped space a bit better. 'This is George — he only arrived yesterday. Transferred from Spatler & Smith's Shepparton office. George, this is Violet. Our secretary. And very lucky to have such a position of responsibility at her age.'

Seeing George

'Oh, come on.' Violet lurched forward to pull at the green facial scales.

'Violet!' Betsy was angry now, and when the scales didn't yield like cloth, when the dragon winced, Violet snatched her hand back to cover her mouth. It just wasn't possible. But the dragon grinned. Rows and rows of pointed white teeth.

'Let's get Mr Spatler.' Lila shifted her chewing gum from one cheek to another.

'No, it's my fault,' the dragon said. 'I gave her a fright.'

'Now look, Violet, none of us knew about the transfer,' said Edward from the back of the small grouping. 'But he seems nice enough. You'll excuse me George, talking in front of you like this. Clearly it's a bit of a surprise to someone.'

There was a rush of exchanged glances that Violet couldn't decipher and the dragon said, 'Why don't I help her with the rest of the filing? Give her a chance to get to know me.'

'No.' None of this made sense and Violet couldn't get a handle on which part of it was wrong: the way the others *weren't* reacting, or her own fear. Didn't know whether to laugh or cry.

'Violet, don't be silly, dear.' Betsy touched the dragon's scaly hand. 'Are you sure, George? You know it's nothing personal. Just goes about things backwards sometimes.'

He nodded, so Betsy backed away, heralding the return to the main office. Lila and Edward were reluctant to pass up this exciting diversion, but a telephone could be heard ringing, so they turned and walked off, Lila still looking for a mouse.

George plucked the crushed receipt from Violet's grasp and began straightening it against a shelf. 'Well,' he said, 'this is unexpected.'

Looking down at the floorboards, Violet didn't answer. She inched her way around him, then turned to run down the aisle.

'It's too late for that,' he called after her.

3

'Besides their endearing belief that foreigners are to be duped, the one thing I'll never get used to in China is all the spitting.' The flickering candlelight enlarged George's features. 'The trains are the worst. Right at your feet.'

'Of course they can't see *your* giant feet properly,' added Violet.

'Precisely. So half the time I end up feeling like a spittoon.'

'Sounds a bit racist, George.'

'Oh, Frank.' Violet downed some more claret. When it came to his travels, George only ever bothered with the stories. No postcards or souvenirs or red-eyed photographs; only his voice. Usually, even Frank appreciated his talent. Violet's grin froze as her hair slipped. 'Excuse me.'

The dining room fell silent as she made her way into the

passage. Frank wasn't making any effort tonight. He'd let his chicken wing sit cold and barely puddled in the roasted vegetables. Usually he drank a little. Jollied the talk along for her sake. Apparently even that was too tiresome this evening.

She squinted at herself in the bathroom mirror. Her cheeks were a dark flush of rose and the foundation hadn't caked, but her dark wig keeled – exposing lengths of her own thinning, grey and brown tresses. She tried to raise her arms to fix it, but they wouldn't go, no strength in them at this time of night. Tears of frustration pearled in the corners of her eyes, until she spied the plastic chair in the shower.

Dragging it over to the mirror she sat on it, then slowly tipped her head forward until it rested on the edge of the vanity. With her head almost parallel to her shoulders it was easier for her weak arms to manoeuvre the wig. She had to keep lifting her forehead a couple of centimetres off the vanity to shift the hair around, but in between times she rested and the job was soon done. She pushed bobby pins into the capping, and smiled at her reflection.

Frank was putting down bowls of dessert as she returned to the table.

'Did you know rhubarb means "barbarian food"?' George lowered his snout to the fruit and sniffed.

'I hope Frank wasn't in the kitchen the whole time I was gone?'

Seeing George

'We were talking about the purgatory of Mexican taxicabs, actually.' George had fiesta-ed in Mexico after China. 'Every time I got into one of those cabs I'm sure I crossed a time zone. I never seemed to get out except to feel exhausted or manic.'

'Where to next?' Violet asked, using her fingertips to nudge the hot custard onto her spoon.

'And when?' asked Frank.

'I was thinking of visiting some ancestors in Ireland, but I'm not sure what they've been told and I'd hate to go all that way only to find out they won't speak to me.'

They all ate silently for a moment.

Rapid scratching accompanied a whine outside the back door. Violet smiled. 'The dog'll be happy you didn't finish your dinner, love.'

Looking at his wife's colour, Frank stood to turn up the gas heating.

'You'll be cooking us soon,' said George, fanning himself. 'Honestly, you two live in a hothouse.'

'Getting old,' said Frank.

'Well, you've gone grey, but Violet's a spring chicken. Look at her.'

She raised her glass a little way into the air. 'Salute.'

'Prost; Skol; Chan ley,' said George.

Frank just drank.

'Seriously, old man. You act as though tomorrow were Armageddon. You've got to relax.'

'Take up yoga,' offered Violet.

'Yoga. There's an idea,' said George. 'Something to help you see things a different way. Never done it myself, but they say it's marvellous.'

'Oh, for pity's sake,' said Frank and left the table.

George's brow shot toward the ceiling and Violet put down her spoon.

'Should I go?'

'No.' Violet raised her face and smiled. 'We'll just ignore it.' She pushed her glass toward George, urging him to give her the last of the wine. They could hear Frank in the kitchen: turning on the radio and beginning to stack the dishes. Violet slowly drank her full glass, then George, who had apparently been waiting for her to finish, stood and plucked his hat from his pocket.

'Sorry,' he said.

Violet set her mouth into a hairpin of displeasure and gave a stiff nod. 'You can find your own way out.'

'Don't make this more difficult.'

But she just waved her hand, dismissing him.

George walked through to the kitchen.

'I'm off then.'

Frank remained facing the sink. 'Another soirée, I take it?'

'No. No.'

Frank half-turned. 'You wore the tuxedo for here?'

George nodded, pulling on his cap.

'Bit overdressed, aren't you?'

Seeing George

'See you next time, Frank.' George headed down the corridor.

'Go and see him out,' called Violet.

Frank started whistling. He ran water full bore and pulled on some bright blue gloves to wash the dishes. But as soon as he heard the front door shut, he peeled off the gloves and shut off the taps. He walked back into the dining room and flicked on the light.

The candles were almost melted down to their silver holders and Violet was resting her head on the table. An empty wine glass sat in front of her. She tried to lift herself up as she heard Frank's steps, but managed only to prop her chin on her hands. She smiled and shut her eyes against the brightness.

'You're a disgrace, Vi.'

Her smile flattened. 'He won't come around anymore.'

'That's too much to bloody hope for.' Frank tucked his hands under her arms and pulled her upright. It made him pant a bit: not as young as he used to be. He fetched the knitted throw from near the fireplace to wrap around her knees. She sighed deeply, reaching to pat his hand as he bustled about her.

'I'm all right, love.'

'You want to wake up to yourself.'

'Shhh.'

'Prancing around as though there's nothing wrong. And he's got his head in the sands of the Sahara bloody desert. When are you going to tell him?'

She lifted her arms. 'Take me to bed, darling.'

Frank's expression was pained. 'I can't carry you anymore.'

'That's not what I meant.'

While she stood – letting the blanket drop to the floor – he picked up her shoes. Then as she began swaying he put an arm about her waist and walked her forward.

'Be nice to me,' she whispered.

He flicked off the light, leaving the small candle-flame to splutter in the darkness.

In the morning, Violet had a frown stitched to her face and her mouth pulled as though she'd been drinking vinegar. She looked blearily at her strewn skirt and blouse, and at the dark wig hunched in the corner like an unwashed terrier pup. Frank wouldn't pick up after her when he was cross.

Now that last night's rush of excitement had faded, everything shifted back to its normal state. She regretted forcing her ankles up so high. They ached beneath the bedclothes, and she was sick and tired of aching.

She poked around on the bedside table until she felt the silver handle of the heavy hand mirror. She lifted it onto her chest and peered. Her eyes were dulled with the weight of sagging skin.

She nearly dropped the mirror as Frank barged tray first into the room. She was lying too low to see more than a glass vase with some lemon-scented wattle from the

Seeing George

garden. But the smells made her mouth water.

After edging the tray onto the dresser top, he slipped two big hands underneath her armpits and lifted. It bruised, but did the job. Upright, she reached for her knitted skullcap, not minding that Frank made a face. He insisted that he didn't care that she was balding, yet with each insistence she reached for a cap. If he truly didn't mind, he needn't say anything.

She waited patiently as he snapped the tray legs down and sat it over her lap. Smiling like a loon.

A muffin. Jam. A pot of peppermint tea. And an egg in an eggcup. She used the teaspoon to crack the egg and liberally sprinkled its yellow centre with salt and pepper. She never ate the egg. Never. Unless it was on toast. And it was never on toast because she liked the sourdough bread that came from an organic foodstore her husband refused to enter. According to him they sold only 'bird-seed'.

'Twenty-eight today.' Frank splayed open the paper he ostensibly brought in for her, but read himself.

She pushed the muffin around in her mouth, not caring to comment on the temperature. Her bedroom was consistently tepid and except for visits to the bathroom, she didn't much venture beyond anymore.

'I need to wash my hair today.'

'Before or after the niece comes?'

The paper cracked under her husband's fingers as he folded it down to the section he wanted. That's the way he read. Saw an article, folded the entire newspaper around it, then opened it out once more to search for the next article.

'I said, "Before or after Charlotte comes"?' Frank sucked at some food in his false teeth. He had a loose section he refused to have fixed. Nothing was rotting, so why waste the money? Violet watched his unblinking scrutiny of the financial section, deciding not to answer until he looked at her.

He finally lowered the paper. 'You hear what I asked?'

She nodded.

'Well, I vote we get it over and done with beforehand.'

'I'm not a thing you get over and done with. What time is Charlotte coming?'

'Thelma said midday.'

Thelma was Violet's sister. Younger by sixteen years. They tolerated each other like a pair of Siamese cats, both wanting to be the only pet.

Frank stood, the newspaper tucked under his arm. 'Don't you want the egg?'

Violet smiled.

He walked over to pick up the tray. 'I'll give it to Gretel then, shall I.'

It wasn't a question. Frank had long prepared a morning egg in the hope that Violet would find her appetite, but it invariably went to Gretel, their low-bellied bassett hound. It had become such a routine that Violet half-suspected the egg was now only brought in for her to refuse.

Seeing George

She waited to hear her husband's footsteps retreat all the way to the kitchen, then swung off the bedclothes. Her legs, as spindly as those on a card table, were a mapwork of blue and red veins. Edging sideways, she used the momentum to stand, then pushed her feet into the front portion of her slippers. Their backs were mashed flat — defeated without the assistance of a finger to curve them over her heels. She padded down the hall.

In the morning light the bathroom fittings were blatant pink. Not a light and gentle pink, but that ugly blue-pink that had seemed a revolution in the sixties. Frank had agreed to chisel off the wall tiles, but refused to pay for another sink or toilet bowl.

She dropped her dressing gown on the floor and waited for him to arrive. It wasn't humiliating anymore. Illness pared away emotions that weren't essential.

At first she had been angry with her ailing body. She wasn't able to wash her hair alone because it was too tiring to lift her arms above her head. And she could no longer bend her head far enough over the sink without blacking out. In a pique she had simply stopped washing her hair with soaps — just stood in the shower for half an hour trying to see whether more water would do the job. But she had such sebaceous skin. In the end, Frank insisted that she let him help because he couldn't bear her silent tantrums.

'Thought you were lost,' Violet said when Frank finally rounded the bathroom door. Suds had attached to the belly of his shirt; he liked to get the breakfast dishes done in the time it took her to get to the bathroom.

As he threaded her hands back through the sleeves of her nightgown, she stared at the white nakedness reflected in the mirror. Her arms and shoulders bent like a branch laden with fruit and her breasts and stomach had an over-ripeness that completed the image. However, the scar across her abdomen would never see the sun enough to fade.

She took her breasts in hand, weighing their doughy heaviness. Wishing she could prune them. This was always the way the morning after. No longer corseted into youthfulness, a seventy-year-old woman appeared.

'Hop in,' said Frank.

The hot water was on and steam billowed out past the plastic curtain. She gingerly grasped at the sides of the stall. Frank had secured a steel handle on the far wall but she hated to use it. She resented the unchanging element of the inanimate: wanted everything to age and be sickly. She had to seize the rail though, because her heels slipped on the pink porcelain.

Hanging her head under the beating water, she adjusted the taps, then lowered herself onto the chair. Frank pointlessly rolled up his sleeves as the water sprayed onto his shirt front. He lathered her hair, taking his time and not making any jokes about its thinness. She stood to rinse off. Once more for conditioner, and then she dismissed him.

'Yell out if you get into trouble.'

Seeing George

Violet didn't reply. She shut her eyes, enjoying the cascade of water down her face. Her long hair fell into a deep V down her middle back and for a brief while time stood still.

4

Reasons I didn't see a dragon:

Dragons don't exist
I've never seen one anywhere except picture books

She'd written these lines in her diary last night and they made sense. But they didn't explain the dragon at work.

Violet marked the diary page with her finger and looked outside the train window. Her breath was coming fast again and she needed the regular sights – cars, trees and blue sky – to help keep calm.

She'd made two lists in her diary last night, and either there was a dragon working at Spatler & Smith, or she was mad.

If she wasn't mad, then everyone else in the office was. Which was patently ridiculous, so couldn't be true. Which

Seeing George

meant George wasn't real. Was he? Violet closed her eyes and put a hand to her forehead to stop the same circles of thought she'd travelled all last night.

At home, alone, she had actually cried with the shock of it. And if she wasn't careful, if she didn't stop her 'silly self' as Frank called it, she'd cry now on the train. She'd wanted to call in ill this morning, but since no one else seemed to feel ill at the sight of a dragon, her colleagues would gossip and they hardly needed encouragement.

She wasn't insensible to the fact that she was considered odd. Edward, Lila, Betsy and even the mail-boy Sam, were always nodding politely then squinching their eyes whenever she offered her view on things. They took lunch without her. Yesterday would not have helped; it was almost as though they had *known* how she would react to the dragon. Didn't Betsy scoot down the aisle awfully quickly?

Violet opened her eyes, blinking at the glare of morning sun. Last night she'd wanted to dip into her and Frank's savings and make a trunk call to Adelaide. Hear her husband's voice. He would have been cross, but they were fighting anyway – if not talking counted as fighting – so it wouldn't have made much difference. What stopped her was that he would be home tonight. That, and the fact that she couldn't bear to hear the words, 'There's a dragon at work' come out of her mouth.

So she'd lain in bed, staring at the dim light leaking in around the sides of the window blind, and wondered why on earth a dragon was working at Spatler & Smith headquarters. Not that she had an alternate occupation in mind.

Violet pushed the diary down between her knees and concentrated on the rushing green of leaves out the train window. After her father died, her mother had suggested that she write down her feelings. Violet found her emotions too bald for the white page, so she wrote lists of thoughts instead. Many lists. But last night's 3 am scribbling really hadn't helped and this morning it just made her stomach heave.

Maybe I imagined the dragon?
Maybe the dragon is a big trick?
Maybe yesterday didn't really happen at all!

Frank joked about her diary. Said it was a way to avoid reality and that she had to stop believing in 'bigger, brighter, better' and just get on with things. But he had run to Adelaide at their first trouble, so could hardly talk.

Her husband didn't like the unexpected. He was too used to planning ahead, to building in contingencies. Of course, this was what initially drew her to him: Frank was always certain about what he was doing, what he wanted, while she wasn't even sure which meat to pick up for dinner.

But now he seemed naive, because some things just happened no matter how much care you took. Lately she felt older than Frank. Felt that even though he was

Seeing George

twenty-one and called her 'his baby', she had to look out for him and not the other way around.

The train eased into the station and the thicket of arms and legs began surging out the train doors. Violet joined the crush, liking the daily tide of coats and hats. She imagined she was part of a lovely sea spilling into the world where problems would just be swept along. She lifted her chin and swung her arms a bit, laughing at herself.

She could sort this out. She would sort this out before Frank got back tonight and show him what a splendid woman he had as a wife.

She didn't have to wait long for her chance; George was leaning against the front of Spatler & Smith when she approached. As she drew closer to the building he righted his hat and straightened.

Violet's arms faltered in their swing. Even at this distance his brilliant green and purple scales were gleaming. Taking a deep breath she marched towards the entrance.

George joined her, extending his neck downwards. 'Hello, it's me again.'

'Hello.'

'Beautiful day.'

'Isn't it.'

He kept asking her silly questions in the elevator. About her shoes and the office systems. She answered in monosyllables at first and then just ignored him altogether.

By the time she reached her desk, her heart was thudding and she had to wipe her palms on her skirt so as not to stain the morning's mail. But she couldn't concentrate so stole a look at him.

He was typing. Sitting awkwardly, his knees scraped along the roof of a desk that hadn't been used in over six months. And he was still wearing his hat. Perhaps sensing her watching, he gave a nod, so she quickly pointed to her head. He grinned and took off his hat, brushed it down and flipped it over his shoulder so it landed with precision on the hat-rack. Then he loosened his collar and resumed typing.

Typing like a maniac: whizzing the typewriter carriage across every time the small ping sounded, which it seemed to do entirely too frequently for someone with his oversized hands. Hands? Paws? Feet?

But in the middle of this inspection she became aware of the pungent smell of mothballs and quickly turned back to her typewriter. Mr Spatler was approaching.

She threaded a piece of paper into her machine and pepped up her shoulders, hoping Lila hadn't said anything about her screaming yesterday.

Mr Spatler stopped in front of her desk and plucked a newly sharpened pencil from its holder, placing the blunt end in his ear and twirling it. Violet looked down at her fingers locked into place over the space bar.

'All the banking went through on time yesterday, Violet?'

Seeing George

'Yes, Mr Spatler.'

'And the order for the hose attachments is complete? We don't want our stores left bereft —.'

'Yes, it's done, Mr Spatler.'

It was better not to interrupt him. Interrupting him could lead to a downward spiral where he felt obliged to keep listing tasks until he began inventing new ones.

'Very well then, I'm sure you've had a chance to meet our new staff member?' Mr Spatler now pointed the pencil towards George, who stood and bowed slightly. Violet didn't actually look at him, but gave a nod of acknowledgement, a blush lacing up her neck.

'He's going to be overseeing this section so why don't you see to it that he gets everything he needs?'

'Wouldn't Betsy be better —?'

Mr Spatler's eyebrows pinched and Violet's words died. Her employer popped the pencil into his jacket pocket before walking away.

George stood up from his desk and came towards her, while Violet fussed about with the postage stamps and envelopes. Usually in her top drawer, the items had spread over the desktop. But they weren't enough to keep her fingers busy and soon she had to look up. The sheer size of him caused her to draw breath.

But as she braced herself for whatever he might say, a flurry of colour near reception caught her eye and she said, 'Excuse me,' and slipped out from behind her desk.

Last night Violet had decided that she needed to ask

someone else about George and she couldn't prod information from Betsy or Lila. Betsy was a war widow and Spatler & Smith had her undivided loyalty. Lila, on the other hand, probably didn't know a thing, but whatever she did know soon everyone knew.

Joan was perfect. A tall woman with tight red curls that would take a trove of curling pins to set each night, she only called up to the office every Friday with the week's takings from the other city stores; but she organised the Friday night drinks, which kept her in the gossip loop.

Violet knew her to smile and nod at, but today, catching sight of the red poodle skirt, followed her past reception to join her in the lift.

'Looking forward to the weekend, Joan?'

'Always, kid. You?'

'Yes. You don't know anything about George, do you, Joan?'

'Who?'

'The new dragon up there.'

'No, I don't know anything. I'd hardly talk about him that way in the office though, Violet. Get yourself in a load of trouble.'

Violet hugged her arms around herself.

'Besides,' said Joan, noticing her colleague's discomfort, 'broad shoulders, gorgeous complexion; he's quite a dish, wouldn't you say?'

'I'm just wondering where he's from or why he's here.'

The willowy woman raised an eyebrow, but said nothing.

Seeing George

'Or anything about anything,' said Violet tripping over her words. 'I mean does anyone know about his previous workplace, home life, his —?' but she broke off when, to her horror, Joan winked.

'I'm sure you'll hear all about it given time,' she said.

'Oh look, Joan, no. Forget I mentioned it.'

'Nonsense. Don't be shy.' Joan pecked at the elevator button with a long nail. 'Why don't I ask around a bit? Someone's bound to know something. It's a tight ship.'

The doors opened and Joan said goodbye.

Violet plucked at the skin on her upper arms the whole ride back up. What had she done? Joan had the wrong idea completely; she was married for goodness sake.

She kept a low profile for the rest of the day, avoiding George whenever he loomed nearby and hiding in the toilets during lunch. It might be ridiculous to behave in such a manner but she didn't care. Unlike the others, she wasn't going to pretend.

But right on five o'clock, when she was making a cup of tea, Edward poked his head around the door and asked whether she was coming down to Clancy's Hotel for a drink. Even though she was excited to receive the rare invitation, she delayed, trying to determine whether George had been invited as well.

'Oh, come on. You need to get out more,' Edward said.

Violet sipped her tea.

'See you there, then.' He drum-rolled the doorframe and left.

Back at her desk, Violet picked up her hat and pulled on her new burgundy gloves. George, she could see from the empty chair, had already gone for the day. Perhaps she would go for a drink. Frank wasn't due back from Adelaide until seven o'clock and it was nice to think that her colleagues wanted her to have a drink with them. Perhaps she could even enquire about George. She tilted her hat at a jaunty angle and went out to the elevator.

5

After her shower, after Frank had gently dried her with a towel, Violet slowly dressed. Buttons were a damned nuisance. Elastic was a godsend. She never knew which part of herself was going to balloon up with the medications and it was better just to wear loose-fitting clothes. She compensated with the monthly dress-ups.

Violet went to sit in the lounge room, pleased that Frank didn't ask what she was up to as she slowly made her way past the kitchen door. He usually liked to know everything.

As with the bathroom, the lounge room decor was horribly old-fashioned; no one had a drinks bar anymore. Theirs had a lime green top with orange, vinyl barstools. It pulsated. She liked the room though, because it had wide, west-facing windows which invited the front yard in. Nearly as good as being outside.

Avoiding the old leather lounge suite – she'd never get out if she lowered herself that far down – she settled into the Jason-recliner. Her stomach pinched hard today and she looked about the room for something to take her mind off it. The drone of the lawnmower cut out and the sweet smell of grass drifted in through the open windows. Her skin warmed just looking at the way the sun stretched itself like a cat across the windowsill, and the hot light meant it was past midday. Charlotte was running late.

Violet fidgeted. Resentful of not being able to just hop in the car and fetch her niece. Or visit George. They had no idea how important they were to her day.

And Thelma was probably purposefully keeping her daughter busy somewhere. Plying her with knick-knacks so she would forget about her aunt. Violet and Thelma had been closer years ago. In adulthood, they had become more like sisters should be, gabbing about fashion and moustaches (Thelma liked, Violet didn't), and tolerating each other's weaknesses because weaknesses left a place for the other to shine.

Frank insisted that their new-found closeness had ruptured with Charlotte's arrival, but this made Violet scoff – she'd been at odds with her younger sister from the word go and it wasn't about to change because of a couple of convivial years. But it was true that Charlotte hadn't helped matters. Why Thelma had allowed herself to calve at the ludicrously late age of forty-six was beyond Violet. Only the fact that her niece adored her – presenting her with

Seeing George

daisy chains, feathers and hand-painted Easter eggs — provided consolation.

Violet sighed. Charlotte reminded her of herself. Painfully so. Apparently she had few friends, which was the only reason, Violet believed, that Thelma indulged the child's affection for her. Blessed with her great-grandmother's heavy blond hair, which shadowed her large eyes, Charlotte was unnaturally silent — completely without the childish tendency to regurgitate the moral judgements of her parents. She didn't belong in the category of 'little adult' either, though she might have done as an only child. In short, Charlotte spent a lot of time alone. Or on her own. Like Violet had done.

Besides all this, the girl seemed to know things about Violet that she shouldn't. Not at her young age. Her eyes sometimes looked right through the elderly woman, disconcerting her.

Violet pulled her dressing gown tighter and dabbed a flower of rumpled tissue at her nose. She was ready for her niece today. She'd asked Frank to rummage through a box of books she'd loved as a child; everything from May Gibbs to Enid Blyton. And she'd tucked an envelope into the side of the box. A plain one with Charlotte's name on the front. It contained one of her mother's brooches; a delicate filigree of gold with ruby settings meant to be pinned to a choker. Violet wasn't good at giving. She knew instantly when a gift wasn't liked and she had no idea how to handle gratitude when it was. Best to let Charlotte find it herself.

Violet's reverie was interrupted by Frank butting into the lounge room door with the lunch tray.

'There's something "Do not go gently" about you, Frank.' She pushed at the chair's wooden lever so she could sit up.

'Leftovers.' He arranged the tray over her lap.

'Have you heard from Thelma?'

'No.'

She tucked a napkin into the neckline of her nightgown. Cold chicken and salad including beetroot – her favourite – a glass of flat lemonade and a chocolate biscuit. She bit into the biscuit first.

'Are you eating with me?'

Frank shook his head. 'Too early for me, but I thought we might have a little chat later.'

Violet ignored the specific tone in his voice and tried to cut into the fleshy white breast with her knife and fork. The knife kept slipping sideways, so she laid down the cutlery and tore the meat into small pieces with her fingers. It reminded her of the picnics she and Frank used to take beside the park lake. They always ate with their hands, and once, only ten years or so ago when they'd forgotten to bring along a knife, he had used a credit card to slice the orange cake.

Frank carried a barstool over to the window and when he finally sat down, the sun threw a golden blanket over one trouser leg. 'It's hot outside.'

She held up her glass of lemonade, meaning to offer it

Seeing George

to him. But it started slipping from her grasp. Her knuckles were the size of grapes and when the fluid retention announced itself — owing to the medication — even the simplest of gestures was almost impossible. Today she had only a touch of it, but she wouldn't give him the drink now.

Frank didn't notice. He was fanning himself with his hat. Grey wisps of hair rose and fell with the small breeze.

'Get on with your chat then. Tell me I shouldn't bother with the fancy get up. No wigs. No frippery.'

'It's more than that, Violet. I want —.'

'I don't want to know what you want.' Violet didn't look at him as she interrupted. 'Let me eat in peace. And would you please give Thelma a ring and find out what time Charlotte is expected, if she's still coming, because I think I'll need a nap this afternoon?'

He stood and left the room.

Violet wiped her hands on the napkin and tucked long strands of hair behind her ears. She should wear a cap whenever she ate. Damned things. She suddenly hated them. Maybe she could borrow one of Charlotte's hair bands. She let her hair alone and dragged a piece of beetroot around her plate to drain off some of its purple moisture. She felt as though she was about to cry.

She knew what Frank wanted.

Why should she reveal her illness to George? Why spell out the ugliness of the fist-sized tumour they'd removed? It was *her* stomach, *her* scar — not Frank's. She'd do with it as she liked.

A quiet knock at the door broke her anger. Into the room slipped a seven-year-old whippet of a girl with an old scarf of Violet's draped around her slim hips. Violet supposed it was a substitute skirt: a copycat of Thelma's poor sense of fashion. It should have been vulgar, but the floral patterning frothed and billowed pleasingly around the little legs. Charlotte walked closer to the recliner and shucked off a backpack, before giving her aunt a gentle kiss.

Violet patted the skinny little arm. 'I've been waiting all day for you, cherub.'

'Your cheek's soft.'

'It's all the biscuits.' Violet waved her niece towards the lounge suite. 'What have you been up to?'

'I have to ask someone what people did before television for my English project.' The young girl swung her feet against the lounge suite's legs, her sandal buckle biting the wood.

Violet frowned. 'I don't remember.' Life before the blessed object – computer, CD player and so on – was always assumed to be bleak.

Charlotte leaned down to her backpack and fished around for a metal object Violet couldn't make out.

'What've you got there?'

'A digital camera. Mum said you and her –.'

'You and she.'

Violet smiled as Charlotte slumped back into the worn leather, her spine making a lovely but unhealthy curve. Couldn't stand being corrected.

Seeing George

'Never mind me, pet, tell me what you brought.'

'Pictures of my room.'

'Well, let's see.'

Charlotte slipped off the lounge suite and held the digital images in front of her.

'Too small for my old peepers. Go and fetch my reading glasses from beside the bed. And mind you don't knock anything else off the table.'

As the young legs ran from the room, Violet tried to get more comfortable. She wanted to lower the back of the recliner despite the tray across her lap, but she wasn't strong enough so had to be satisfied with twisting herself around a little.

When Charlotte came back with the glasses, Violet held the little camera at arm's length and peered expectantly. She still couldn't make out much. A bed covered in splodges of colour. Toys, presumably. Stupid idea to have pictures in the camera.

'It's a big room, isn't it, Charlotte?'

'Mum said you can come and see it if you want.'

'Oh, I've seen the pictures now.'

The child averted her face, clutching the camera to her chest, and Violet's heart seized at the thought she'd hurt her.

'Why don't you tell me a bit about school? I might get and see your classroom if Uncle Frank can arrange it.'

The child warbled on about the computers, a new girl who knew the answers to all the maths questions, and an excursion to the aquarium. Violet hung onto the last image, trying to picture a jellyfish gently ballooning its way through water to take her mind off the pain. But Charlotte halted too quickly and she was forced to rise to the surface again.

'We could look at your photographs of the old days, the ones before television,' the young girl said.

'Perhaps you want to go and ask Uncle Frank.'

A lower lip jutted. 'He won't be bothered with me.'

Just then there was a shuffling in the hallway and Frank put his head around the doorframe.

'You right, Vi?' he said, in his best gruff voice. 'Lottie not tiring you out?'

Violet didn't answer and Charlotte looked down at a scab on her knee, poking at it and hiding from Frank behind her thick blond hair.

'You finished eating?'

Violet's mouth was tight and she shook her head. Frank came fully into the room then. He walked over to the windows, shut them and ran his knotted fingers along the cracks, checking for draught. Watching him brought tears to Violet's eyes. It was all a fussy pretence, when what he really wanted to do was put his hand on her forehead and ask about her tablets.

He picked up her tray, looking down at the ragged bits of food still covering the plate. 'You've barely eaten anything.' He pushed at the wooden lever and using his elbow, nudged the chair into a more horizontal position.

Seeing George

Violet breathed heavily into the relief on her limbs.

Frank backed away to the door but didn't take his eyes off his wife, and Violet held her face steady for his benefit, concentrating on the colour of his eyes. Not the brilliant blue they once were. Cataracts settling in, probably. She'd have to hound him about making an appointment.

'Come on, Charlotte,' he said. 'Your aunt's tired.'

'I'll be quiet.'

Violet looked at her niece. 'You get on with your uncle. He needs you to help him mend a rift.'

The young girl slid out of her seat and walked to the door, where Frank put a large hand on her head and directed her out into the corridor. 'What's a "rift"?' she asked.

'It's a hole that will get much bigger if your aunt insists on poking it,' he said. 'Hop down to the kitchen.' He turned back to Violet. 'You get a kip.'

Violet smiled at him and shut her eyes.

· 6 ·

The late summer sun baked the streets and Clancy's Hotel was overflowing by the time Violet arrived; the Ladies' Lounge a hum of voices and bodies.

She perched on a stool to catch the publican's eye, intending to buy a non-alcoholic drink before wending her way through to her colleagues. Frank didn't like her drinking without him. But because she had to wait to be served she had a chance to look over the chalkboard and it seemed a shame not to try something fancy, so she ordered a pink champagne.

As she was getting out her money she was nearly knocked from her stool by an over-eager busboy, her coins tumbling across the counter. Once she'd managed to right herself and pay, she had to accept her fallen hat from George.

Seeing George

Putting the glass to her mouth, she swivelled away from him.

'I'm still here,' he said to her back.

She looked across hats and heads for the women from the office, still sipping at the champagne. But George flicked at the underside of her hat brim until it fell neatly over her eyes. She angrily tucked it under her arm and turned to face him.

'What'll we drink to, Violet?'

'Mice,' she retorted.

George threw back his head and laughed loudly, and Violet, overcoming her alarm at his teeth, smiled too. Pleased at her own wit.

He sipped from his martini glass and looked down at his olive without making any further conversation. Violet drank too. And each time she lowered her glass to see George staring silently at her, she immediately raised it again. It was only a matter of minutes before the pink champagne was gone, leaving her head all fluttery. Around them glasses clinked and people laughed and the overhead fans whirred, making the silence between them unbearable.

'Say something.' Violet slapped her gloves against the bar top. 'Tell me where you come from. Tell me when you're leaving. Anything.'

'I'm a farm boy,' he said. 'My father kept sheep, which was interesting because we're actually more comfortable –.'

She snorted. 'To eat?'

'I beg your pardon?'

'To eat. You know, did you keep sheep to eat?'

He hesitated a moment. 'Violet, have I offended you?'

She tipped her head right back to see him properly. 'No. It's just that –.'

As she stumbled over her words, Violet looked around the room and saw Joan and Edward standing together near a booth, looking at her. Joan raised her glass in cheer and Violet suddenly felt sick. She realised why she had been invited to drinks: Joan was helping her find out about George. How humiliating.

'I think I'll go now, George.'

She hopped down from the stool and started to weave her way through the crowded lounge, but when George didn't offer a 'goodbye' she realised he had put down his martini and followed her. She stopped suddenly and about-faced, forcing him to make a quick sidestep rather than bump into her. One of the aproned lads collecting glasses stepped on his tail and George grimaced, winding it up to rest on top of his shoe.

'Sorry, buddy,' the kid shrugged, indicating that he couldn't see where he was walking.

George gritted his teeth in a smile and turned his attention towards Violet. 'We really –,' he began.

'Monday.'

He held up his hands as though in resignation, but bent toward her ear. 'Violet, I'm not going to disappear.'

She made an effort to sober. 'Pardon?'

Seeing George

'Stop pretending you don't mind me.'

In her relief, Violet laughed. 'You've got it all backwards. It's no one else who cares and Joan thinks you're quite good-looking.' She flinched at this indiscretion. 'I screamed, remember?'

George looked solemnly at her. 'Mr Spatler, Joan and the others don't see me the way you do. I think you know that.'

She glanced over to where her colleagues were gathered. 'What do you mean?' He didn't answer and she put a hand on his suit arm. 'What do they see?'

'Just a man.'

'A man? Not a —?' Violet's voice rose. 'I see a dragon and there isn't one. Of course there isn't one. There are no dragons. I wrote that in my diary.'

'Calm down, Violet.' George fished about in his coat pocket for some toffee to offer her. But the wrapper had peeled away and small pieces of thread grew from it, so he hid it in his palm.

'I told Joan you were a dragon. I thought she —.'

'Let's go outside.' George held his hand near the small of her back to usher her towards the door, but she scooted forward avoiding his touch — very aware that their colleagues' eyes were upon them.

Standing beneath the green awning of Clancy's Hotel, Violet pulled on her gloves in an attempt to hide her shaking hands.

'I don't want to hear any more, George.'

'That's very intelligent.'

'Be quiet.' She paced a little. 'How did you know I saw you this way?'

'You screamed.'

'Why can't I see you the way the others do?'

He leaned against the red bricks. 'The question is, Violet, why do you see me as a dragon?'

His tone of voice made her stop fidgeting. He was serious, even though his expression seemed playful.

'Are you a dragon?' But before he could reply, she continued, 'That doesn't matter, actually. Because I see you as a dragon whether you are or aren't. Which means I'm mad.' Her voice trembled.

'You're not mad.' George dropped the toffee back inside his coat pocket.

'How am I going to tell my husband?'

George's facial scales darkened. 'Don't.'

'I have to. He'll be waiting for me, wondering why I'm not there waiting there for him, and he'll ask me how my day was, and –.' She sniffed, her nose running with the emotion.

George fetched his handkerchief and offered it to her as he moved closer, shielding her from the curious glances of people entering and exiting the pub. But she pushed his handkerchief away, opening her purse to fish about for her own.

'Why did you tell me this now?'

'What?'

Seeing George

'You must have already known that I was the only one, why didn't you tell me straight away — at the filing shelves?'

He looked over her head, didn't speak.

'Right.' She snapped the clasp of her purse shut. 'Stay away from me, or better yet, go away.'

He raised his brows.

'I mean it. Go away. I don't need this and I don't want to see you.' She began backing away from him.

'How am I supposed to arrange that?'

'I don't care.' And with that she turned and began to run.

Violet had been standing on her front verandah for the past ten minutes, trying to stop gulping air. Every time she thought she was fine another wave of panic rose in her chest. She couldn't let Frank see her like this. He'd wonder what was wrong and there wasn't any way to explain it and it was the last thing they needed on top of their fighting and —. Violet briefly squeezed her eyes shut. Took a few more deep breaths. She wasn't going to be able to calm herself, so may as well just get on with it.

She peeled off her gloves and rang the bell. And rang it again and again until her husband finally opened the door.

He smiled and wound an arm around her waist, pulling her close. 'Lost your key, sweetheart?'

'No.'

At her response, he held her slightly away. 'You're not still upset with me?'

She looked down, a tumult of feelings rising in her chest.

'I said I wouldn't take another interstate job, Vi.'

'That's not the point.'

He sighed.

'You just left me alone after we found out. I –.'

He tilted up her chin and her heart pounded at the familiar sweaty scent of him. At the endless blue of his eyes. And when he kissed her, even the straggly moustache and beard that he grew when he was away from her felt soft against her skin. But she wouldn't allow herself to be consoled that easily and she pulled away.

'Violet, what do you want me to do? I said I was an idiot.'

She didn't respond.

'What about if we erase the last month?'

'How?'

He stepped out onto the front porch, lifted her easily and carried her over the threshold. She couldn't help but smile into his neck, careful to kick off her shoes only once they were inside. He took her straight to the bedroom intending to drop her onto the double-bed. But her limbs clung to him, wouldn't let him go. So he fell gently on top of her body, nuzzling into her face until she laughed.

'Forgive me?'

She playfully pretended to bite him, but there were tears in her eyes. So he lay beside her and kissed her forehead,

Seeing George

her chin, her lips. Saying sorry all the while. Then he started unbuttoning her blouse, slowing his movements, deliberately looking into her eyes. And she finally reached for him, her hands up under his shirt. And they laughed at how awkward it was to take off their clothes while lying down, and finally they were naked together. Pressing against each other, into each other. Again.

Afterwards they lay looking at the ceiling.

'Tell me you love me, Vi.'

'I love you.'

'Tell me again.'

'I love you. But —,' she jumped off the bed, 'I don't love your horrid beard.'

'Come back here and say that.'

She ran from the room, barefooted and laughing, and by the time she retied the sash on her dressing gown, the sky was already dark. Not clear, but brooding. She stood at the stove and fried up a 'bubble and squeak' of vegetable leftovers for a late dinner. Kept returning to sit on his lap, metal spatula in hand, until she perched there with the two plates of hot food in front of them.

Frank was talking about starting up his own business in an outer suburb. It would mean more money, but also more travel time for Violet to and from work.

'It'd be really hard, Frank.' She spread her bread with the hot porridge of cauliflower and pea.

'Perhaps I could come and see Mr Spatler with you. Figure something out about different hours?'

Violet shuddered involuntarily. The last thing she wanted was for her husband to have contact with anyone at work. She looked down at her plate to hide her anxiety.

'Well, what then?'

'I don't know. But I have to work, Frank. We need the money.'

He forked some browned potatoes into his mouth at that, and Violet shifted from his knee to a chair. 'Sorry, love – but we do.'

She didn't mind a whit that Frank worked in a trade and didn't make as much money as his brother who brokered stock. She'd seen him on site, standing over blueprints with his arms folded as he mentally built the house, correcting easement and angle. Building was real and it was, strangely, a far gentler masculinity than stockbroking, which seemed to entail yelling and non-stop waving of bits of paper – all for speculation.

'Moving would give me a head start with these new concrete modules,' Frank was saying. 'And it'd be cheaper.'

'I don't want to shift further out. We've got enough to deal with as is.'

'It might do us good. A real change.'

'It'll just be us there instead of here.'

Frank used his thumbs to push away his plate. 'We'll at least consider it, Vi.'

'No.'

'Does everything we talk about lately have to end in a damned argument?'

Seeing George

'I'm not going, Frank. There's nothing in the suburbs. Only families.'

Unbidden, the image of children on bicycles came to mind. Tears welled beneath her eyelids. She dipped her head and blinked furiously, so her husband wouldn't see. But he laid down his fork and took her hand in his, and when that only made the tears fall faster, he pulled her back to his lap and held her there, rocking her as he stroked her long dark hair.

After that neither of them could finish their mash.

Violet ran herself a bath. As she lay in the hot water, skin pinking, she could hear Frank sharpening the old fibre needle, then pulling one of the 78s from his collection of worn brown paper covers. He wound up the gramophone his mother had given them as part of their wedding trunk. It was terribly old-fashioned but it used to be his grandfather's and he treated it with reverance. Music was magic to Frank.

Dame Melba's voice, singing some piece Violet could never remember the name of, floated in to greet her.

She closed her eyes, enjoying the singing and the rowdy intrusions as Frank set about tidying up the living area; putting away his workboots and tossing the magazines onto the side table.

If she had opened her eyes she would have seen him crouch down at the bookshelf where she kept her diary. He carefully placed a letter — its folds so thin they'd almost worn through — on top of the photo albums. Not hidden, but not quite in plain view.

Then he came to stand in the bathroom doorway, smiling at the sight of his tired wife, and he asked her to put aside a weekend a month or so from now, so they could talk about 'things'.

When he left, Violet looked up at the ceiling, tears forming in the corners of her eyes, so grateful he didn't come out and name it.

7

When Violet opened her eyes again she could hear Frank whistling *If You're Irish Come Into The Parlour*, and alongside this, her niece's tinny voice coaxing Gretel. Charlotte would be sitting cross-legged on the kitchen floor with the dog's head in her lap. She had heard Frank and Violet speak of Gretel as a 'sad-sack' and was determined to learn what was wrong. Violet wouldn't have been at all surprised if one day Gretel did open her mouth and spill out all the privations a well-fed, well-loved dog could suffer.

Violet stretched her fingers against her legs, amused at their curl even when she was doing her damndest to make them poker straight. The pain had eased with the velvet of sleep, giving her back some of the morning's mobility and she smiled to hear Charlotte's soft footsteps making their way up the hallway into the lounge room.

'Come in, poppet.'

Her niece's eyes were fixed on the tray she was carrying. Saliva flooded into Violet's mouth. Although her entire day consisted of one tray after another, she only ever managed to pick at food and was always hungry.

Charlotte tried not to drop the heavy tray onto the coffee table. There were two glasses of cranberry juice and a plate of biscuits. The weight was in the crockery. Crystal glasses meant for cellared wine that Violet had decided should be part of the everyday routine now that time had stopped feeling endless, and an elaborate dinner plate from her mother's collection. Charlotte liked the intricate gold flowers weaving round its centre.

'Where's your uncle?'

The girl carefully took a glass and walked over to the lone bar stool near the window. Only once she was safely seated did she speak.

'He just took Gretel walking.'

'And you didn't want to?'

'They go too fast.'

Frank did walk in great loping strides. It was a wonder Gretel could keep up anymore.

'Come and get a biscuit.'

Charlotte opened her palm to reveal a chocolate-coated Wheaton.

Violet laughed. 'Good for you. But you've still got to hop down because I can't reach anything from here.'

The child's face coloured as she slid down from the

stool. Using both hands she shifted the wooden lever, then put a glass of juice in her aunt's hand. Violet promptly rested it on her thigh.

'I was thinking about showing you our family photographs, petal. Mind you, I barely have any, just one album and I'll have to find it. When are you next visiting?'

'I don't know,' Charlotte said, with a mouthful of biscuit.

'Well, it's usually Wednesday. Do you think your mother will let you come straight after school on Wednesday afternoon?'

Charlotte shrugged her little shoulders and Violet sipped her ruby liquid. She knew better than to ask Charlotte about Thelma so directly. The child was very sensitive to the pointy elbows that characterised the relationship between her mother and aunt. It was only Frank who meddled.

Violet watched her niece stare dreamily out the window. That sweet face. When she'd seen Charlotte just after her birth, Violet had been overwhelmed. Held her tightly and wept. Knowing she was old enough to be the child's grandmother, knowing she was only an aunt.

Thelma had started crying too and Violet had managed the baby in one hand and clutched her sister's with the other. It was generally supposed that this would firm up their relationship, and Frank continued concocting reasons for them to be in the same room for years afterwards. But Violet's heart was attaching to Charlotte, not Thelma. And Charlotte had reciprocated.

In her most generous moments, Violet wondered

whether it hurt Thelma that Charlotte wanted to dress in her aunt's old clothes and insisted on imitating the way Violet spoke. The little urchin was far more like her than Thelma.

'I miss you when you're not here, Lottie.'

Her niece licked at the chocolate in the corner of her mouth, her eyes shining.

'You thank your mother for letting you come around today, all right?'

Charlotte nodded.

'Now why don't you go and pick out a couple of books from the box I asked Frank to leave in the passageway?'

The young girl nodded again, this time unconvincingly.

'Go on. You'll get square eyes if you watch too much television.'

'Okay.'

'There's something else in there for you too.'

Charlotte dragged her backpack after her, and Violet smiled to hear her rummaging through the various books. But before she could holler out a suggestion, a knock sounded at the front door.

Violet turned her face away as the young girl ran up the corridor, and she squeezed her eyes shut as Thelma's bright voice rang along the walls. Charlotte sang out her goodbyes, didn't invite her mother in, so then Violet got annoyed that her sister hadn't even *tried* to see her. It was better to refuse her than have Thelma not bother.

The house fell silent and after a couple of minutes Violet

Seeing George

wondered where Frank was. It wasn't like him to miss exchanging pleasantries with his sister-in-law.

The lounge room was bronzing with the setting sun and as much as she loved a sunset, Violet began shivering. The earlier sleep hadn't stopped her stomach feeling poorly. She tugged at the knitted throw, finally able to untuck it, and stood. Taking her time, keeping her head as low as she was able, she began the trek back to her bedroom – glass still in hand because she couldn't reach down to leave it on the coffee table.

She heard the side gate rattle and Gretel's nails clipping the concrete. Frank was speaking to the little dog, promising her some tucker.

Violet kept on to the bedroom, not feeling well at all. She sat to place the empty glass on her bedside table, then lay down on her bed. Frank had changed the cotton sheets during her morning shower and they smelt of a lavender laundry liquid. It was a smell she usually liked, but just now it was making her feel nauseous. She scrambled to sit up and groped for the little plastic ice-cream container kept beneath the bed.

As she held it beneath her chin, she retched. Fast footsteps travelling down the hallway meant Frank had heard. While she hunched over the green container, retching expectantly, he came to sit beside her and rubbed her back. But nothing came of it, and after a while she stopped leaning over so tensely and Frank took himself to the chair in the corner of the room.

She plucked a tissue from the box and dabbed at her mouth and nose. Then sat back and eased the bucket beneath the bed. When she looked across at her husband she saw he was agitated, fidgeting about in the chair as unsubtle as railway crossing bells.

'You missed saying goodbye to Lottie.' She was sorry she'd mentioned it, because when he looked at her his eyes were all watery. 'It doesn't matter, love,' she offered. 'She's coming back Wednesday –.'

'I want to talk about George.'

Violet folded her arms, preparing for another version of the conversation they'd been having for a week now. 'He knows, Frank. My stomach's like a bowling ball.'

'He's still planning walks in the park, for god's sake.'

Violet closed her eyes and sighed.

'I mean it. Your ridiculous frocks and wigs. I don't only want you to tell him about your stomach. It's more than that, Vi.'

She opened her eyes. 'Spit it out.'

'I want you to stop seeing George.'

Violet knew he wasn't joking, but it was so unexpected, so preposterous, that she laughed. Then Frank whacked the chair arm and she righted her face.

'I've been very patient, Violet.'

'I didn't know you were being patient.'

'I've supported you for years,' he was saying. 'Not questioned. Not minded. Now I do. I want this all stopped before you die. I want this dying to be just you and I.'

Seeing George

Violet frowned, plucking at the waddle of loose flesh that hung from her upper arm. 'I'm not going to die, as you so delicately put it, in a hurry. I plan on annoying you for another couple of years yet.'

Frank pulled a handkerchief from his pocket and wiped around his mouth.

'Why are you bringing this up now?' She tried again. 'We made this decision years ago.'

He stood and walked over to the door.

'Frank?'

'I don't want to debate this. I'm asking and I want you to answer. You can sleep on it and let me know tomorrow.'

She laid back and stared at the ceiling.

· 8 ·

Violet and Frank spent Saturday afternoon digging over the vegetable garden. The carrots were stringy and weedy, but after removing the chicken-wire that shielded the strawberry patch from the sparrows, Frank plucked thirty-odd red berries from in between the dark green leaves.

Violet flipped the square lounge room rugs over the washing line and beat them with the broom, while Frank larked about pretending to die from a coughing fit brought on by the billowing dust. Laughing, she sank onto the grass.

'Didn't you ever pretend to be a pirate or explorer?' she asked. They were reminiscing about growing up.

Frank chewed some grass, thinking. He'd been at work from the age of twelve. Although his mother had seen to it that the family always celebrated birthdays and

Seeing George

Christmas, his family didn't truck with fantasy.

'It clogs up the mind like leaves do spouting, my father used to say,' said Frank. 'Not much patience with the imagination, my old man. He thought it was what you used when you were getting up to no good. It's probably true when you think about it; our treehouses and cubbyhuts were really just ammunition bunkers.'

Violet watched as her husband picked up clods of dirt and hurled them against their back brick wall.

'But what about adventure? What if there really is a man on the moon?' Her voice took on an urgent tone.

'That's for poetry and girls. The kind of stuff you would have done, wasn't it?'

'No, I didn't. Maybe that's the problem.'

'It's not a problem. It just means we're honest folks. Dealing with the real world.'

She scrambled to her knees, grabbing his hand and pressing it to her chest. 'But Frank, I believe now.'

'Believe what?'

'I don't know. In things. In the creatures at the bottom of the garden.'

His teeth were stark white against the early evening light as he smiled. 'Just so long as you don't invite them inside, love.'

She moved to stand behind his chair, pressing her lips together so she wouldn't go on. But the problem of seeing George nagged at her for the rest of the weekend and she reluctantly made another attempt to talk to her husband on Sunday night, when he was lying beside her, face relaxed in sleep.

'Frank.'

She repeated his name until he stirred.

'Hello,' he said. It was the voice of someone trying to struggle awake in case he had an emergency on his hands. She nearly didn't go on.

'I can't sleep.'

'Go and have a glass of hot milk.' The tension in his voice gave way to the sleepiness. This wasn't the first of Violet's late-night conversations. Sometimes it was spiders, or wind causing the back door to rattle, or a dream, or any of a million other things that she used to test his devotion.

'That's no use.'

'Then you talk and I'll listen,' his voice dragged.

'I don't know how.'

He turned so he was facing her, eyes still shut.

'I mean, yes, but I can't,' she added.

Frank said nothing, idly scratched at his upper lip which was a bit irritated from his recent shave. If she weren't careful he'd go back to sleep. It wouldn't be the first time for that either.

'Frank.'

Silence.

She gave a little cough.

'Mmmmm?'

'Do you keep things from me. Things you think I don't need to know? Or –.'

Seeing George

He blinked his eyes open, found her and frowned. But didn't speak.

'Frank?'

'I thought we agreed to leave it for now.' His voice was tense.

They looked at each other in the dark, then she said, 'What if I had a secret?'

At that he closed his eyes and let his shoulders sink back to the mattress. 'Do you?'

She sat bolt upright. 'Yes. Do you want to know what it is?'

'Tomorrow,' he mumbled and promptly fell back asleep. Violet wrenched the bedclothes closer up her chest and coughed loudly. Frank startled, but his breathing settled down again in a matter of seconds.

She didn't feel the slightest bit sleepy however; the problem with George eclipsed tiredness. She turned onto her side to watch her husband's face and tried to dismiss the question of insanity. After all, the insane were just as likely to think themselves as normal as the sane – so how could she judge?

Maybe George's features reminded her of dragon features and she had just been mentally exaggerating for fun. While Frank was out of town. She shifted about restlessly. Or maybe George was tricking her somehow. Maybe he had hypnotised her. It suited her to think that George might be arranging things a certain way.

By this time her feet were hopelessly twisted in the

bottom of the sheet and Violet could barely move. It didn't matter how she saw the dragon, the point was that she did see one. And Frank wouldn't like her seeing a dragon. Neither would anyone else. No one would believe her.

Violet suddenly relaxed, then sat up and gently disengaged the sheet from underneath the mattress, freeing her feet. Propping herself up on her elbow, she leaned over to kiss Frank's partially open lips. All at once she felt deliciously tired.

Next morning Violet sashayed over to George's station and, placing both hands palm down on his desk, asked him how his weekend was. He rolled back a little way in his chair, face brightening.

'We're speaking, then?'

'Definitely.'

'That's terrific, Violet. We have a lot to talk about.'

She straightened up. 'That won't be necessary. I've figured out how to put things right.'

George frowned, his tail twitching; Violet studiously avoided looking at it while she spoke. 'Me seeing you the way I do is a problem if anyone knows, because they won't believe it. But if I pretend to see you the way everyone else does, no one will know I don't.'

George's large eyes were very solemn.

'What do you think?'

'I think that's the wrong problem.'

Seeing George

But Violet was already turning back to her own desk to remove the cover from her typewriter, and for the next week or so, whenever George spoke to her, she shut her eyes and imagined a dark-haired man with a square-shaped face.

She ignored his tail getting caught in his chair legs and shifted out of his way when it swung around unexpectedly; she didn't react to the cold feel of his nails on her skin when he handed her some files; and she held a blank face when his ears rotated around so he could hear something that wasn't being said in close range.

It took quite a deal of concentration, but she managed very well. She even made allowances for the fact that all this deliberate ignoring infuriated George, who couldn't stand having conversations with a woman who shut her eyes every time he spoke.

'Are you going to stop this?'

But Violet, who was repinning her dark hair, just laughed and complimented him on his complexion. Her ruse might have gone on indefinitely if George hadn't taken matters into his own hands.

Mr Spatler had installed a new light fixture in the office to help him decide whether to sell it in his stores or not. It was an electric chandelier with looping white branches ending in small globes that mimicked candle flame. There was even a special dial that allowed the light voltage to be heightened or dimmed. Violet couldn't decide whether she liked it or despised it.

Either way, on the day of its installation, for reasons that soon became clear, George found it necessary to walk to and from the central office partitioning, each time hitting his head on the chandelier. And each time he hit his head he breathed fire in aggravation – great orange and red flames shooting from his mouth and nostrils.

The first time Violet saw the flames she shouted at everyone to watch out, but they looked at her instead of at George. She recovered quickly and pointed at him, pretending to be distressed at the bruising she imagined on his forehead. Betsy and Lila rushed to his aid, suggesting a cold compress and some headache powder.

After the third rush of flames Violet understood that this was no accident. George was drawing her attention to his ability to breathe fire; his essence of dragon-ness. So despite the whoosh of heat setting her nerves on edge, she pretended not to notice.

George immediately came and sat himself on the corner of her desk – standing again because he was in danger of tipping it – and said, 'Let's take an early lunch. I'm sick of hitting my head on that damned contraption and you look like you're procrastinating.'

'Go away, George.' She refused to look up at the tall figure holding a wet handkerchief to his forehead.

'Oh, come on, admit it. You haven't done a lick of work.'

She fished around for some paper, a letter, anything to demonstrate that this was not true. But it was true. It had taken all morning to ignore him.

Seeing George

'See you in the cafeteria. I'll be the one wearing a tail.'

By the time Violet looked around to see whether anyone had heard, he was back at his desk. Whistling.

The cafeteria was just starting to get noisy with queues and dinging cash registers when they arrived. It was a favourite trick of most of the employees to take lunch as late as possible: thus shortening the remaining working day after eating.

George and Violet placed bowls of lamb casserole on wooden trays, then he led the way to a table near the windows. It was another beautiful day outside and the sunlight seemed to dissolve the glass as it streamed indoors.

After watching her take a few silent mouthfuls, George held his head in mock-agony. 'Oh, the pain.'

'Are you quite finished?'

'Teach you to think you can ignore me.'

'I just want to see you like everyone else does.'

George propped up his snout with a hand. 'You really want to be like Betsy or Lila?'

Putting down her fork, Violet replied, 'Maybe I do. Maybe I want to be just like all the other women I know. Is there something wrong with that?'

He was silent.

'Don't you ever want to be what you're not? Have something you don't have? Even some of the time?'

He looked at the yearning eyes a moment. 'I suppose I do, Violet.'

Gratified, she picked up her cutlery. 'If you only knew how tired I am of being different. First, the only one with no siblings, then the only one with a sister sixteen years younger, then the only one –.' She looked away. 'Sometimes I feel very lonely.'

George cleared his throat. 'What about your husband?'

She averted her gaze. 'Well, he doesn't see you, does he? Apparently, I'm the only one to do that too.'

'Oh, you're not the only one.' George stabbed some meat with his fork.

Violet's eyes fixed on him.

'I just mean, it's improbable.' George's facial scales were deep purple and he was having difficulty swallowing.

Violet sat back and crossed her arms. Waited as he took a long drink and wiped carefully around his tray.

'You said no one could see you the way I did.'

George sighed. 'No one in the office.'

'But someone else somewhere else, right?' She held a hand to her chest, delighted. This was much better than having to pretend she didn't see him. 'I want to meet them.'

'It's not possible.'

'I just want to meet them, then I'll be fine, George. It would make such a difference to me. You have no idea. Please? Please, introduce me to –.' She waved her hands around.

'Him,' said George.

'Please introduce me to him.'

George's snout was almost resting on the table, so low was his head hanging.

Seeing George

'When?' she asked, excited now.

'I can't arrange it so easily. Next month, perhaps.'

'What about tomorrow? After work?'

'I'm not –.'

She reached across the table and touched his arm. 'Please, George.'

He watched her hand as it grazed his skin, and when she removed it he placed his fingers just where she'd had them.

'All right, Violet.'

9

Violet plucked at a feather-end that was scratching its way through the doona cover. This morning, there had been a shared pretence that all was normal. The breakfast and shower routine unbroken. And now Frank was getting about as usual – mucking out the spouting or giving Gretel a bath. Leaving her to mull over what was going through his mind. It made no sense.

She couldn't simply cleave George off from the rest of her life. Not this late. She pulled the grey and white feather tuft through the doona's cotton weave until it was completely free, and then sat it on her open palm and blew.

As it drifted in lazy semi-circles to the floor, the glint of her emerald ring caught her eye. Perhaps this was about money. Always cautious with money, as Frank aged and

Seeing George

grew more brittle and susceptible to wind and frost, he'd become miserly.

But he couldn't be concerned about her will; they'd already agreed that everything would go to each other in the first instance, and then to Charlotte. The house was in his name, besides which, George had more money than they did so wasn't needing an inheritance. All she had to leave was her mother's jewellery, a painting or two, clothes headed straight for the goodwill bin, and the diaries.

The diaries.

Violet gave herself a mental slap. Once upon a time, Frank had made a rash of secrecy jokes – trying to provoke her to reveal her diary – but she hadn't relented. When he finally did pry, he'd found things he hadn't expected. Was Frank concerned about what she'd written?

She looked across to the shelves.

The small black books held various images of him between the pages. A bit about their sexual life; what a thrill of discovery that had been. Also the stretch of monotony when they moved to the suburbs. Then the reality of him in middle age.

And something of George. Quite a bit about George.

That's why she kept them looking as inconspicuous as possible. Not against Frank – he was welcome to them now – but as a lack of temptation for anyone else who might be wandering through the house. At the kitchen table of their first home, she and Frank had decided that George really wasn't anyone else's business. But by that stage Violet was well into the habit of keeping a diary and she hadn't stopped.

She swung back the bedclothes and sat up. Slid on her reading glasses and walked over to the bookshelf. The ten black books weren't in any order. She selected one. 1955.

> *It's not enough that I see him; he wants some evidence of how well. It's as though a mirror isn't enough for him – not when the rest of the world can't confirm what he is. And Frank knows something is wrong.*

Violet's finger held the page as she turned back towards the bed. She'd forgotten how annoyed she could get with George. How much he needed her. How, once they'd sorted everything out, he kept *insisting* that he needed her. And then there were his incessant visits after work, even though they sat only a few metres apart all day.

It wasn't much different now, if she was truthful. Not knowing when to expect him made the visits seem random, but they weren't. They'd never discussed her illness but he must know because he batted around her like a winter fly at a windowpane.

He brought blueberry jams and salty broths; lifted the corner chair so the legs wouldn't scrape along the floor when he wanted to sit by the window; and he read to her – in the kitchen, lounge room, bedroom – from a list of notes he made about the outside world. Little tales about lonely overcoats and shared umbrellas. His invitations to walk or attend a football match were simply a harmless way of keeping her connected with the real world.

It was George's generous make-believe.

Frank was blind to subtlety, that's all. Couldn't appreciate that George saw keenly, understood *silently*.

She shut the diary and hid it underneath the top few books on the bedside pile.

Being direct was Frank's gift. He liked the obvious. If the back step was rotting through, he'd measure, saw and nail a piece of pine. When she could no longer manage the stove, he sat down and studied her recipe books from cover to cover, garnering enough of the science of cooking – the different applications of heat and timing and ingredients – to produce duck with crispy skin, shortbread pastry and even sugared mint as garnish.

He liked the destination. And if he was abrupt, then so be it. None of his employees would ever have claimed not to know what he valued. It's just that sizing up a situation was not always what the situation called for.

Violet looked up at the ceiling. It was dull without reflected sunlight stippling through the windows. She plucked at the bedclothes. Damn Frank's insistence that she lay her cancer out for George like new clothing. He knew how confounded George was by mortality.

Whenever she had tried to talk with George, even remotely, about death, he shuddered and changed the subject. She didn't think it frightened him so much as confused him. The blackness of it. The unendingness of it.

So why on earth would Frank demand she give up seeing George *now*? It didn't make sense to be prudish about her written thoughts — not after fifty years of friendship and not when she had so little time left anyway? Must be something else. Her brow collapsed into an intense frown.

Once upon a time, she'd have had a stoush with her husband about this little request. They'd learnt after their first few years of wordless fights that black moods didn't simply disperse; they needed prodding. But age had worn down her larynx and she would have to find other means.

She set her chin, listening. There was only the metallic click of the front flywire door not quite snibbing as it shuddered in the breeze. She swung her legs down to the floor and began the well-versed amble to the bathroom, her fingertips running along the wall.

A book held the bathroom window open, and she could hear the lawnmower puttering away in the top corner of their yard, marking Frank's presence. Lost in the task at hand. That was his new form of anger; the remarkable ability to be thought-less. Violet could never have managed that. Her mind was one of the few bodily instruments she could still command.

Tucking her matted hair behind her ears, Violet realised she'd not even considered what George might say about Frank's request. 'In the grand scheme of things'— an

Seeing George

expression Thelma was overly fond of using — surely anger, jealousy and joy were the same irrespective of whether you were a human or a dragon? He would be crushed and reasonably so because he assumed Frank liked him and had done so for years.

She hunted in the second drawer of the vanity for a pair of scissors, then watched her clumsy movements in the mirror as she opened the metal blades. Frank thought her long hair elegant. She used to be able to wind it high on top of her head in a ballet dancer's bun. The most she could manage these days was to plait it.

She closed the blades around her hair.

Then hacked again and again at the same place because the scissors acted bluntly unless she persisted. She sheared it to just above her shoulders. The brown strands riddled with grey fell stark against the light green linoleum. She put the scissors down and slowly swung her head. It wasn't even.

Bending to the floor — gradually so as not to drop blood pressure — she swept the chopped lengths into her hand to deposit in the bin. It was nice to have it kick about her ears instead of trail down the front of her chest—even if it did frame her face in a very lopsided fashion. It better covered the section of baldness too.

Back in the bedroom, her fingertips worried the hewn ends. Perhaps she should shave it all off. Lots of women did that now. She poked about for the silver hand mirror, propped it up against her bent knees and held her hair back — picturing herself shorn. But a tightly stretched pate with sagging jowls didn't appeal: not even for the sake of annoying Frank.

Hearing his footsteps in the kitchen, she snatched up a knitted cap and pushed her hair into it.

'Lunch, yet?' His head poked around the bedroom door.

She nodded.

'Here or there?'

'There.'

He left.

She raised the small circle of reflective glass again to check, but no hairs strayed. It was so short now she could do a neat job easily.

Frank had propped the kitchen door open, letting in the watery autumn sunlight, but also a chill breeze. He shut the door when she pointed at it on her way to sit.

'What are we having?'

'Scrambled eggs.' He whisked yolk and milk in a small Tupperware bowl. Gretel lounged, if not on his feet, then as close to them as possible.

'I forgot to tell you your sister rang earlier. While you were in the shower.'

Violet sucked on her teeth.

The yellow mixture sizzled in the hot pan. Frank wheeled it about, then set it down. 'She wanted to come over for dinner sometime. Mentioned you thanking her for sending Charlotte over.'

Violet looked down at the Formica table top, tracing the fake-marbled lines with her fingernail. That's what

Seeing George

happened whenever she was nice to her sister: Thelma took it too literally. And of course, Frank would be pleased she had made an overture to Thelma. He liked her sister. Liked her great horsy teeth when she laughed, which was constant around him and otherwise never. He and she huddled together on the couch at parties and talked seriously about zoning regulations. Thelma served on the local council's Heritage Planning Board and understood building codes, which meant that she Frank had the language of the rational in common.

When Frank explained an element of construction to Violet, he always spoke slowly and carefully as though enunciating clearly would assist the tangle of acrow-props, skip bins and drive pins in her mind. But with Thelma the words galloped along and by the time he'd finished they were both shaking their heads or nodding in agreement. Thelma made a to-do about him retiring.

'Is she still dying her hair?' asked Violet.

Frank shrugged, scraping the pan.

Violet waited until the browned scramble was cooling on the plate in front of her before she asked what he'd told Thelma.

'I told her you were feeling poorly.' Her husband's skin moved over his knucklebones as he cut the bread. He scooped mushy egg onto his fork and lifted it toward his mouth, pausing only to sprinkle salt on it. Then he drove his fork around the plate to begin again. 'She can wait,' he said.

Violet looked down at her plate. There were very few people Frank considered company. He'd just given one up for a bit because he knew his wife would see her sister only in her own sweet time. 'Thank you.'

'Just taking care of my wife, as I like to do.'

Violet's expression darkened. If he thought giving Thelma the flick was any sort of tit-for-tat for George, he could think again. She pulled off her cap and let her hair dangle.

Frank was dropping the remains of his eggs into Gretel's inside scrap bowl, then turning to light the gas under the kettle. He didn't notice his wife's hair until he was sitting back at the table. Then his eyes widened, dramatically.

'Bit of a change,' she said tartly.

He nodded and reached forward to pin the straggling hair behind her ears.

'Well?'

'Makes it look thicker. Suits you.'

The kettle started carrying on and he rose to lift it from the flame. Violet pushed her plate away. She'd been expecting a comment she could get her teeth into.

'I wasn't sure you'd appreciate it.'

'Didn't want me to, more like it,' he said and sat back down again.

She watched as he put two heaped teaspoons of sugar into his tea, avoiding his eyes for as long as possible. But when she finally looked up he was grinning at her and even

Seeing George

though she didn't want to, she laughed. The old bugger knew her too well.

His eyes softened. 'Perhaps you should get Lottie to trim it a bit further. Even out the edges.'

That was the comment she'd been waiting for, only now it was too late. She closed her eyes and waited to work up the courage.

'Why, Frank?' She pushed the words into the silence.

When she opened her eyes, he was swilling the dregs of his tea and he didn't answer.

· 10 ·

Violet rose early to cook Frank breakfast, flipping the syrupy pikelets and enjoying the look of pleasure on his face. They even held hands a while, after they licked the sugar and lemon from their fingers, although they didn't speak of anything more than shopping lists and his habit of not putting the dirty clothes in the laundry trough.

When he opened the door to leave, Violet felt a surge of guilt at not confiding in him about seeing George. She gripped him tightly, and Frank laughed, kissing each finger as he unhooked it from his lapels. Violet wanted to shake him, to ask whether he couldn't see that she was hiding something. Surely, it was obvious?

It didn't occur to her that Frank might wonder the same thing, and by the time she was at the Spatler & Smith

Seeing George

office, her only thought was about the person George was going to introduce her to that afternoon.

She typed diligently through lunch to catch up on what should have been seen to in the previous few days and only when the clock finally wound up the working day and she had hat and coat in hand, did she admit to real nervousness. She did want confirmation, but at the same time confirmation would make George more real, if that were possible.

George took her to a respectable Victorian terrace with bluestone walls and wisteria plunging from the upstairs wrought-iron balcony. She used her tongue to check for lipstick on her teeth, wanting to make a favourable impression. Violet was hoping this other man would put her at ease about seeing George, would share how unnerving it had been for him too, and, most importantly, make her laugh about it all.

These hopes were dashed the moment the door opened.

'Peter,' said George. 'This is Violet. The woman I told you about.'

'Hello, my dear,' said Peter. He removed his dark glasses to stare with milky blue eyes at a point just above her head. 'It's an absolute pleasure to meet you.'

Ordinarily Violet would have been intimidated by the stately furniture and jewel-like oil paintings in Peter's front parlour, but she immediately took to pacing back and forth on a rug, while twisting at her wedding ring.

After greeting each other, Peter and George seated

themselves on a crimson velveteen couch. They let Violet pace for a while. Then Peter twice used his cane to motion to a petite oak table that held a walnut-fig loaf and three saucers. The third time Violet didn't respond, George tried to assist.

'Violet, don't you think –.'

She held up her hand for silence. This was not helpful. Not at all. Why was George pretending that a blind man could see him? To please her?

Peter hitched up his trousers at the knees and sat forward in his seat. 'As I understand it,' he said in a gravelly voice, 'the point was that someone else could see George?'

Violet's shoes stopped so quickly she almost fell. 'Have you always, were you always –?'

'Born this way.' Peter nodded.

'Then this makes no sense.'

'If I wasn't blind I would have been able to see him as a child. All children can see him.'

'Children can see George?' asked Violet.

They nodded in unison.

She strode out of the room and back into the antechamber where Peter had directed them to hang their coats and hats. When she returned she was frocked up for outside.

'It's no good, Violet,' said George with a sigh to his voice. 'She's ready to go and find one,' he added for Peter's benefit.

'My dear girl, they're only infants,' Peter said. 'They're barely old enough to babble about it a bit and as soon as

Seeing George

they do, adults convince them they can't see him because he doesn't exist, and after a while they can't.'

'It's the damndest thing,' said George.

Violet finally sank into a low chair without unbuttoning her coat. 'I want to meet someone else who can see you the way I do, George.'

'Violet, it's not possible —.'

Peter spoke over the top of him, stretching out a hand toward her voice. 'I do see him, dear. Give me your hand.'

She leaned forward on the chair and let Peter's papery skin enfold her fingers.

'You're married. No children. A worker, but not in a trade. Young. Plump.'

Violet pulled away. 'George told you.'

The old man laughed and tiny wrinkles splintered around the corners of his pale eyes. He looked strangely beautiful and Violet couldn't help staring.

'Not quite. You have no calluses, but not the hands of a lady who has a life of leisure. No chipped nails or grazes or spots of food, which means no children. A ring, hence married or engaged, and I can tell by your voice that you're quite young.' He politely refrained from explaining the observation about her weight.

'So you can feel George's scales?'

'No.'

'You can't see him then,' she retorted. 'How did you even meet?'

Peter didn't answer her question. 'Although I detect

difference between light and dark, I see him best when I shut my eyes.'

'I can see blue elephants when I shut my eyes.' Violet spoke a little more harshly than she'd intended.

But Peter simply chuckled. 'Marvellous. Blue elephants, why didn't I think of that? She's a find, this girl.'

'George, this doesn't help.'

But George barely raised his head to look at her. Clearly disappointed at her disappointment.

Peter stood. 'How about a cup of tea?'

'She doesn't want tea,' George said.

'Goodness, are we all in a bad mood now?' Peter smiled and gestured for his cane, which George tapped against his knuckles. 'Violet, I *believe* that George is a dragon. Doesn't that amount to the same thing as seeing him?'

'No.'

'Why not?'

Violet clasped her hands in her lap and tucked her legs underneath the chair. 'I don't know,' she said stiffly, 'but it doesn't.'

'I have to take you on faith just as much as I have to him.' Peter began walking away to the kitchen, staying precisely in the centre of the floor-runner.

'It's not the same at all,' reiterated Violet to George. 'He's blind and I'm mad.'

'Be quiet,' hissed George angrily. His tail twitched for a moment and then curled itself under the couch and Violet didn't dare look at him until she sensed him relax slightly.

Seeing George

'I think it's very exciting,' he said finally.

Violet covered her face with her hands and her shoulders started shaking. George straightened, ready to comfort her, but then she dropped her hands and he saw she wasn't crying, but laughing.

'I'm exciting?' She shook her head. 'A dragon thinks I'm exciting.'

George's gave a slight smile. 'Peter accepted me as a dragon the first time we met but you're right, he doesn't actually see me. You do, and you have no idea what it's like to live in a world where people can't see you for who you really are. To me, you feel like sunlight – illuminating me.' His eyes softened. '*You* make *me* not alone, Violet.'

'Steady on, George,' interrupted Peter, padding his way back into the room. 'We've got a long way to go to find out about Violet's gift. No point getting ahead of ourselves.'

George sat back in his chair, averting his eyes, and Violet blushed.

Four weeks later and the unravelling of her 'gift' was taking too long for Violet. It had been helpful that Peter could converse with her about George being a dragon. But it wasn't enough.

That first evening Peter had asked her to return to his place once a week, so they could peel away the mystery behind her ability. She honestly hadn't considered that being able to see George was an 'ability' — only a distressing fact she wanted kept from others. Especially Frank. Newly convinced that there might be a *reason* for it, she had agreed to the meetings.

She and Frank didn't have an extensive social life, so it wouldn't make things hectic. On the weekends they occasionally visited Frank's brother and sister-in-law for a game of cards, or Violet might run over to her mother's to help wash nappies for baby Thelma — which was sometimes upsetting, so her mother rarely asked her. But the week nights were free.

However, she could hardly just explain to Frank what she would be doing: she would have to lie to him.

Just thinking about it had made her hands sweat. It was the first real, black lie since their wedding. But when she considered the alternative — telling her husband about George — it seemed far more appealing.

So, one morning while still in bed, Violet mentioned joining a knitting club. She was facing away from her husband and although her voice was sleepy, her eyes were wide open and the blood rushed in her ears.

'Come again?' Frank forced his heel down into his workboot. Thumping about.

'You heard me.'

He stood and looked down at her with a gentle smirk about his mouth. 'Yes, but I don't quite believe it.'

'You don't?'

'I would have said you were as likely to pick up knitting

needles as Menzies. Just don't expect me to tell you I like it if you make me something.'

Violet rolled over and pitched a pillow at him, laughing.

But a moment after their pretend tussle, she thought she might be sick. Had to sit very still so as not to yell that he was right: she had two left hands, she wasn't knitting. This was about a dragon. She could see a dragon and couldn't he please help her? But she didn't say anything so Frank left the bedroom to go and fill his thermos, and she sank back onto the bed. Relieved. Wretched.

It was awful to lie to him. The only way to feel better about it was to stick as close to the truth as possible; the following Wednesday night a skein of emerald wool poked out of her bag when she arrived home, and every Wednesday night since she had pulled out her knotty piece to inspect at the kitchen table.

Not that Frank showed much interest. He seemed to have his own preoccupations lately and she might have been more attentive to this had she not been distracted herself. But she was distracted because after *four weeks* of this knitting and purling ruse at Peter's, the discussions were revealing nothing.

Peter always opened their Wednesday gathering with the same observation: 'Clearly we all originally had the ability to perceive dragons or our knowledge wouldn't have been transplanted into picture books.'

Violet didn't reply now, just checked in her bag for another ball of green wool. Whether or not everyone once saw dragons didn't have much bearing on no one seeing them now as far as she was concerned.

'And we've been overlooking something critical.' Peter slowly walked the floor-runner swigging from a Spanish bota filled with port.

The other two barely gave him a second glance. Peter was fond of making pronouncements of that sort. But over the click of her needles, Violet made an encouraging sort of noise.

'We've not thought about whether this runs in her family at all.'

'Yes, we have,' said George, sitting at the centre table and peering uselessly at his thousand-piece-puzzle of Egyptian hieroglyphics. 'She can't remember having a conversation with either parent about dragons or elves or anything of the sort.'

Violet nodded. Her mother and father were very practical people. Her birthday presents were woollen tights, new school satchels or a set of paintbrushes for art class. No jewellery. No tickets to theatre. Definitely no mythic or legendary bedtime books. After her father had died when she was seventeen, there was an even greater emphasis on facing reality.

'Isn't that the point?' said Peter. His costume monocle swung from a delicate piece of chain hinged to his waistcoat. 'At some stage or another we're told that what we formerly accepted as real, isn't. Surely it's damned near impossible to sustain a belief in something which everyone

Seeing George

else insists is simply a figment of your imagination? I don't think belief has anything to do with it anymore, because belief suggests choice. Violet's ability is involuntary.' Peter sipped at his port. 'You don't have a choice.'

'Of course I don't have a choice,' said Violet. 'If I had a choice —.' But she didn't complete the sentence because George had abandoned his jigsaw and swung to face her.

'Would you give it up?'

'I can't give it up.'

'No, you can't.' He smiled at her and she smiled in return. George never made rash pronouncements like Peter. And he didn't seem to expect anything of her.

'Can you remember your age when someone told you dragons didn't exist?' Peter's voice intruded.

She barely shook her head, turning back to her knitting pattern. Even if Frank wasn't paying much attention, sooner or later he would notice that the mangy piece she'd been working on wasn't getting any closer to becoming a jumper.

'Violet, dear girl, try to remember your own history.'

She slumped in her chair, letting the needles and wool slip down her lap. 'Peter, I don't think we ever spoke about such things at all.'

He shook his head. 'Well, forgive me if I fail to understand why you, who had never had a conversation about dragons, who doesn't believe children can see George, who didn't even *want* to see George, are here at all.'

'Why are you here?' Violet lifted her chin. 'It's you who can't see him at all.'

'I see him more clearly than you do.'

George clapped his hands on the table. 'Peter, she's doing the best she can.'

'In your eyes, all she has to do is sneeze to be doing the best she can.'

Violet bundled up her knitting and squashed it down into her handbag. 'I think I'll be going.'

'You've a great deal more thinking to do, dear,' said Peter, hands clasped behind his back.

George accompanied her to the door. 'Never mind him,' he said. 'You know how he gets whenever we can't find evidence for one of his insights.'

'I just don't think I'm any help.'

George looked down at the pale face. 'Violet, until you, I didn't know if it was even still possible.'

Despite George's placations, on her way home Violet decided she was fed up. They enjoyed having her as audience for their intricate arguments about the importance of ability versus belief and knowledge versus perception – that's all. She had been very patient, but the old, blind man and the dragon seemed reluctant to conclude anything. Her temper frayed further recollecting Peter's rebuke and she tossed her notebook, thick with arrows and dog-eared corners from tracking through her own history, into a garbage bin.

Words were useless. What she really needed was a means of testing whether anyone else might be able to see George. It was at that moment, in a burst of inspiration over

Seeing George

George's phrase about her seeing him '*still* being possible', that Violet suddenly had a plan.

Nervous and excited, she barely spoke as she dithered about in the kitchen when she returned home, and, not for the first time, she apologised as she set a plate of inedible food in front of her husband.

Frank took one look at the charcoaled lamb cutlet and hardened potatoes and slathered tomato chutney all over it, grimacing at the first mouthful.

'Why don't I make some toast?'

He pushed the plate of neglected food toward her and she scraped it into the bin. After a hasty dinner of tinned sardines, Violet walked into the lounge room trying to remember where they'd shoved the boardgames.

But Frank took her hand and deposited her on the couch. He fetched her a weak dry ginger and Pimm's, and a long neck and glass for himself, before tuning their secondhand radiogram to a symphonic. Then he sat himself beside her. 'Talk.'

Violet's heart raced at her husband's insistent tone, but at the same time she felt a great relief wash over her. This would be it then. 'I don't know if you can help, love.'

'Come on, Vi. You're not the only one this affects.'

'I suppose not.'

'Well, I'm not made of stone.'

She swung around to face him. 'It's just that I try and keep work at work and —.'

'This is about your work?'

'Well, my work colleague. George. Yes.'

Frank's face altered gears. 'What work colleague George?'

At his tone, Violet found she couldn't speak and she swished the brown liquid around in her glass. She *had* tried to confide in her husband a month ago – although he was sleeping at the time.

'You've been carrying on like a two-bob watch, Violet. Moody, and I don't know, as though you're not here. I thought it was about us and all the time it's a fellow who's interested in your work. Is that why you're so eager not to move to the suburbs?'

'That's not fair, Frank. And George is not exactly interested in my work anyway.' Violet could have bitten her tongue off.

'What in hell is that supposed to mean? He's not interested in your work, he's interested in you?' Frank was holding his beer across his chest. He always defended himself by protecting his chest, so the gesture upset her. She put a hand on his knee.

'No, love, that's not what I meant. And of course our situation is –.'

'Don't change the subject.'

'I just mean it's not what it sounds like.'

'I find you attractive. It's not so hard to think someone else might, is it?' Frank's fingers were restless on the back of the couch and he took a long swig of his beer. When Violet failed to answer he continued, 'Well, if it's not what I think, tell me what it is.'

Seeing George

She looked away, her mind racing. Moments ago she had thought she would tell him. Now the idea seemed remote. What would he say? How would he look at her?

'Violet?'

She shut her eyes. 'I can't.'

'Meaning what? It's not work, it is work, you don't want to say?'

She didn't answer.

'There's not going to be any trouble, is there?'

Her eyes were bright when she finally faced him. 'Not like you're suggesting.'

'But you can't talk about it?'

'I want to, Frank. Just give me some time.'

He gripped his glass and stood. 'Well, this was pointless. Perhaps I'll try again at a later date – when my wife actually wants to speak to me.'

Violet's cheeks flushed.

'I'm going for a walk.'

When he left the room, she laid her head against the back of the couch and closed her eyes.

· 11 ·

Violet sat with Frank while he ate an early dinner in the kitchen. She'd napped all afternoon and didn't feel like eating just yet.

A cool breeze flowed in through the flywire door and the sound of late season crickets rubbing their legs lessened the need for conversation. Which was just as well, because there was only one thing Violet wanted to ask and only one thing Frank didn't wish to speak about.

She sipped daintily at a glass of Riesling while he helped himself to a second serving of the lasagne.

'You're looking well, Frank,' she said. 'Colour in your cheeks.'

'Wine's gone to your head, love.'

Gretel's tail thumped a chair leg for a while, expressing her pleasure at having Frank sit still with her.

Seeing George

'Charlotte's looking older now, isn't she?'

'She's always been old.'

'What do you mean?'

Frank picked up a bit of crust and waved it over Gretel's nose. The hound watched for a moment then snatched at it. Frank laughed, wiped his fingers on his trousers and picked up his knife again. 'I mean what I said. She gets about as though she's a hundred. She's got no sense of wonder. No awe.'

'She likes me.'

'That she does.'

Violet smiled.

After the table was cleared away, Violet stroked Gretel's long ears when the dog put its head in her lap. Radio National was broadcasting a lecture about colonialism that her husband was listening to, but halfway through she felt cold, so told him she was getting ready for bed.

While squeezing out the toothpaste, she used her tongue to dislodge her false teeth. They chattered into her hand. Teeth were much easier to clean when out of your head. She avoided the mirrored image of her caved-in lips and cheeks – her hair had never been her real vanity – and sucked on her minty teeth when she popped them back.

Frank was sitting in the chair in the corner of her room. Waiting. She lifted the bedclothes and slipped in, smiling as her cold-whitened feet reached the waterbottle he'd prepared.

'Are you going to stay with me tonight?'

He shook his head, arms tightly folded. The house was weatherboard and not terribly well insulated. 'I'm waiting until I hear what you've decided.'

'And if I decide against giving him up, you'll never sleep in this bed again?'

'I didn't say that, but there might be consequences, yes.'

'Like what? Putting me in a home?'

Frank didn't answer and she crossly tucked all the exposed bits of herself under the doona.

'Well?' he said.

'Well yourself. I need more time.'

He squinted at her. 'How much more time?'

'Can't we talk about this?'

He smacked his knees and stood up. 'How much more time?'

'Frank, you're a stubborn old fool. I can't believe you're asking me to do this.' Violet's voice was tremulous with emotion.

'I'll do whatever I like. How much more time?'

'I don't know. A couple of days,' she said. 'Now get out.'

Frank walked over to her and kissed her forehead. As his large hands cupped her face, she felt as though her heart would break.

He walked from the room, pulling the door closed behind him, and small tears trickled down the side of her face and into her ears. She opened her eyes wide and waited until they adjusted to the faint line of light that crept

Seeing George

under the door, before plucking a tissue from the box and wiping at the cold streaks.

In the morning, she didn't wait for him to bring in the breakfast tray. Although her head was pounding, she sat up and let her feet feel their way into her slippers, then shuffled down to the kitchen. If Frank was surprised to see her, he didn't let on. He dropped an extra piece of bread into the toaster, but she sat and poured some cereal into a bowl and then sliced up a banana.

'Bit of an appetite this morning,' he said.

'There's a lot to do.'

He buttered his toast. Then with his plate in one hand, unlocked the back door and kicked open the screen door to sit on the top step. Gretel lounged beside him and the three of them ate breakfast in silence, not quite together.

Violet wiped her mouth then stood and placed her hands on the table edge – pushing – trying to stretch her back a little. Years ago Frank gave her back massages, but now she was too tender. She waited until she heard her husband unclip the leash from the trellis, signalling the morning walk to Gretel, then she retreated to her bedroom.

She poked about in the bottom drawer of her dresser, her junk drawer, until she found the unfinished diary. She'd stopped writing regularly sometime in her early sixties. Around the time when Charlotte was born. She took it and her favourite Mont Blanc fountain pen and walked over to lie on the bed.

The notebook had worn beautifully around the edges, the soft black calfskin almost coming away under her fingers. As always though, her interest in the cover lasted only as long as it remained closed.

Truth is better than goodness.
I could have –

Violet skipped over reading what she could have done. It was only one of her endless excursions into how she might have behaved differently when younger. Besides, that particular wisdom seemed obvious now.

Turning to a fresh page and uncapping the pen, she wrote:

Reasons to give up seeing George

Titles were the easy part. A simple declaration that needed no explanation. But thinking about the possible answer, her gaze drifted out the window. It was another perfect autumnal day. The leaves tripping along the footpath under a gentle sun. Crisp air. There was a faint scent of smoking wood.

She felt a twinge of envy that she wasn't out walking Gretel with Frank and turned back to the blank page. After half an hour or so she had not come up with even one idea as to why she should stop seeing George.

Seeing George

She decided to come at it from the opposite angle.

Reasons to keep seeing George:

I've been seeing him for fifty years
He'll be upset if I don't
I'll be upset if I don't
Who else will see him?

It was a very simple list. Elegant in its sparsity. But as soon as she wrote the final thought, her mouth turned down and she had to shut the notebook. There was no one else. This made her doubly angry with Frank. She was already leaving George; there was no reason to do so before time. Frank was worse than stubborn, he was cruel.

She stood up from the bed and bent over to pull open her junk drawer, stuffing the notebook and pen back inside. She tried to kick the drawer shut but hadn't the strength, so folded herself over again to do it properly. Her vision blacked out and she grabbed at an upper handle, only just keeping her balance as the world righted itself.

After this little episode, she had a further rush of anger that wasn't appeased until she picked up one of her black diaries and smacked it loudly on the dresser surface, the noise and exertion a good substitute for the slam of a drawer.

She wandered back into the kitchen and looked at the clock. She was wearing a marcasite watch that Frank had given her for her fortieth birthday, but even if it had been working she doubted she'd have looked at it. Quarter to nine. That wasn't right. Blasted clock.

Dragging a chair from the kitchen behind her, she walked awkwardly into the entranceway. She and Frank had kept the original placement of the phone line. They liked to leave things the way they were; the less bother the better – even though they both complained about the draught. But knowing she wouldn't be able to stand for long, Violet needed the chair. Its legs made the carpet runner curl over, but she kept pulling until something gave way and eventually she found herself seated in front of the phone.

Waiting a moment until her chest stopped wheezing, she tapped in the number.

'Hello, George speaking.'

'You and Frank always sound like schoolteachers when you answer the phone.'

'Nice to hear you too, Violet.' Then a pause. 'You all right?'

'Does there have to be something wrong for me to call you?'

George snorted. 'Well, actually,' he said, 'you haven't called me since –.'

'Yes, don't go on about it. When are you next coming over?'

Seeing George

'Last time I was around it didn't seem genial.'

Violet looked at the faux-wood panelling of the dado. Refusing to speak.

'Is something the matter?'

'Stop being ridiculous. Just answer the question.'

'I don't know.'

Violet sighed. 'I have to get off this stupid contraption or else I'll get pneumonia, George. Just name a day.'

'Well, I'm having the car washed tomorrow, and Tuesday *I'm* washing. Wednesday. I don't know about –.'

'Oh, for goodness sake, come on Wednesday.' Violet hung up. She immediately realised that she'd arranged for Charlotte to come on Wednesday and she didn't want to share time between them. Had managed to keep them apart for years. She was on the verge of calling George back when she heard Frank shutting the side gate.

She stood to drag the chair back into the kitchen. One of the legs caught on the carpet again and she had to untangle the fringe with her foot, but she was sitting back on the chair at the kitchen table when Frank wandered inside.

'You haven't moved an inch.'

She waved at him. Too tired to speak.

He put his hands on her shoulders. 'Let's get you back to bed, love.'

She nodded, welcoming the arm around her. They walked in small, slow steps back to her bedroom and he tucked her in, pulled the curtains shut and said he'd be back in an hour or so. It was wonderfully warm in bed.

When Frank came in to wake her with the habitual sandwich, biscuit and tea, she was smiling. She waited patiently as he eased a cushion behind her back and opened the curtains. Clouds had come over outside, so the room was barely any brighter.

'I dreamt I was a bird,' she said.

Frank picked at one of his nostrils a bit and sat down on the chair in the corner of the room.

'Didn't you get a cup for yourself?'

'Had one earlier.'

Violet blew across her tea, then said, 'Tell me about your walk. The patch of sky I could see earlier looked so blue–.'

'Every time you go to sleep,' Frank spoke over the top of her, 'I wonder whether you'll wake again.'

'So do I,' she said, forcing herself to sound cheerful.

'That's not good enough.' He bent forward, his hands clasped and his elbows sitting on his knees.

'I can't give you any guarantees, Frank. What do you want me to say?'

He cleared his throat. 'You know what I want you to say.'

'Why?'

'There aren't reasons for everything.'

'There are for this.'

Unexpectedly Frank put his face in his hands, his shoulders shaking. Her heart swelled fit to burst.

'Come here, love,' she said urgently, and put down her cup of tea.

Seeing George

He stood and walked over to the bed, not taking his hands away from his face. She tried to pull them away but he wouldn't let her and he wouldn't sit. So she hugged his legs fiercely, looking up at him every now and again to see whether he'd show his face. But in the end he pulled away from her and left the room.

Violet pushed back the doona and walked over to open the junk drawer. She fetched out the diary and pen, splayed the book open on top of the dresser and wrote a reason under the lonely title as to why she should give up George.

· 12 ·

Tuesday morning, almost a week after she had conceived her plan, Violet was in the office thumbtacking yellow streamers from the electric candelabra to the doorframe. In her nervousness she'd already pricked herself three times.

Lila had stopped chewing gum long enough to blow up some red and blue balloons, and Edward was busy scotch-taping one each to the chair backs. Near the office pinboard sat a small, round chocolate cake – its frosting slightly melted as it had been applied while the cake was still warm. Betsy carried in tearoom saucers to sit beside it.

Each time the elevator doors rang, everyone looked around nervously to see whether George was stepping out – and by the time he did they were grouped together, grinning stupidly.

Seeing George

'Happy Birthday!'

He laughed and tucked his briefcase under his arm, brushing his way through the drifting streamers. 'Who told you?'

'Guess,' said Lila, mischievously.

George smiled delightedly and looked straight at Violet, who couldn't help the corners of her mouth turning up too. Edward ushered him forward, shaking his hand and clapping him on the back, while Betsy wheeled a chair out for him, but George sat his briefcase on it — preferring to stand as he grinned at the unexpectedness of it all.

'How old are you?' called out Sam.

George let his gaze fall on Violet's quick fingers as they struck a match and worked their way from candle to candle. He tugged at his collar and shrugged. But his colleagues laughed at his silence.

'Mum's the word, old chap.'

He leaned against the chair while they sang and then obligingly bent forward to blow out the tiny flames. Violet wielded the knife and Betsy handed around saucers with triangles of the chocolate dessert. George almost declined because he didn't like chocolate, but a glance at Violet's strained face made him change his mind. He carried his piece over to her and told her she had a good memory.

'I suppose you weren't even thinking about what you were saying, George. Just trying to smooth over one of Peter's questions.'

He nodded. 'No one's ever done anything like this for me.

And it's not a significant birthday. You really didn't –.'

'I did,' said Violet, moving away from him. Something in her tone made him straighten his back, and from that moment he kept her in his sight line. But it didn't do him any good.

Just as the office was settling down again – cups of tea transferred to desks, a phone ringing, and idle glances at the in-tray paperwork – Violet knelt up on her chair and clapped her hands together. Heads swivelled immediately and several people raised their cups, thinking this an extension of the cheer.

'Now we're all together, I wonder if you might look at George,' she said.

George frowned slightly.

'Speech!' called Barney.

'George,' said Violet, her face reddening, 'is a dragon.'

There was a hoot of laughter from Sam, and some puzzled looks on other faces as people tried to work out how to fit this with birthday celebrations.

Violet put her hands on her hips. 'I mean it. Look at him.'

Brows creased but they did look, and those who couldn't see moved to get a better view.

Violet continued, 'He has green and purple skin and a snout, and he can breathe fire.'

Now there were chuckles and murmurs of disbelief.

'Please stop,' said George.

'What can you do, Violet?' Edward teased. 'Fly?'

Seeing George

Everyone looked from George, who had closed his eyes, to Violet whose knuckles were turning white from clasping her chair so hard.

Lila sat back down and began to type.

'Please,' said Violet, raising her voice. 'Look at him and try to see him.'

Sam and Edward and Barney were all trying. Sort of squinting as though to bring George into focus. But Violet's female colleagues were tapping their heads and exchanging derisive glances. She watched as they turned their backs, flicked through internal memos and began other conversations — ignoring her as usual.

She clung to the back of the chair. 'He really is a dragon. Tell them, George. Tell them what you are.'

George opened his eyes and shook his head at her.

'Please, please, George. I don't want to be the only one.' Her voice quavered and she looked at him a long minute. Willing him.

The room fell silent as George put down his saucer. 'I have no idea what you're talking about,' he said, then he strode over to the hat-rack to hang up his coat.

Violet looked at the floor.

She could vaguely sense the others milling about, murmuring, and she hopped down from the chair, trying to be dignified as she slowly walked from the office to the women's restroom.

Her eyes were dry and glazed, and once she was inside a locked cubicle, she put down the toilet lid and sat, leaning heavily into her hands. She knew why George had pretended not to know what she was talking about, but that didn't help right now. Right now she just wanted someone else – anyone else – to know what was going on. She froze when she heard a door hinge, then pulled out several leaves of toilet paper and blew her nose.

Knuckles rapped on the cubicle door. 'Are you all right, Violet?' Lila's blue pumps were in view. 'We didn't know about the joke, George only just explained.'

'I'm fine.'

'He said to tell you he's sorry.'

Violet's neck and cheeks were suddenly hot. She pulled away more toilet paper and wiped her nose.

'I brought your purse. Do you want it?'

Violet put a hand to her chest, stunned at how much the gesture meant. 'Please.'

Lila bent to push it under the door. 'I'll see you back in the office then.' Her shoes clacked away.

Violet sat the plump object on her lap. After a minute of staring at the back of the door, she dug out her compact and, using the small circle of mirror, tried to salvage her composure with powder and lipstick. It didn't work. She kept seeing George turning his back and hanging up his hat; kept imagining the mouths gabbing in the office.

She opened the cubicle door and walked to the window to look out over the tin rooves of the neighbouring factories. She recalled sitting with her mother a few years ago, trying to comfort her over the death of her husband,

Seeing George

Violet's father. But her mother had remained unresponsive and simply said that each person was all alone in the world. Violet hadn't understood what she meant until this moment. Now she felt shut out. Shut out from everyone else.

At a sudden murmur of voices, she scooted back inside the cubicle.

Two pairs of shoes entered the restroom.

'Violet?' said Betsy.

Violet closed her eyes.

'Are you all right in there?' asked Lila.

No answer.

The two whispered to each other and Violet couldn't make it out.

'Honey, you've got to come out sooner or later.'

One of them tried the door. 'Can we do anything, dear?' asked Betsy.

'Get Frank.'

More whispering.

'Aren't you coming out?'

Finally, at her lack of response they hurried away, only to swing the bathroom door open again.

'Violet?' It was Lila. 'Sam's going to get Frank. We know he's working in Caulfield, but we need the street name.'

'Mayrose Crescent.'

'Okay.' Lila hesitated, holding open the bathroom door with her foot. 'Are you sure you don't want to come out? It's really all right. We know it was just a joke.'

Silence.

Lila left.

Violet sat without moving for a good hour, only bending to rest her handbag on the floor when it started sliding from her thighs. No one came in to use the toilets. They must have put up a sign. It was very quiet in the bathroom. Occasionally a pipe cranked or water sloshed through from upstairs, but other than that there were only white tiles and cream walls and porcelain basins, and none of it made any noise. Sometimes the hum of traffic rose, or a bird gave a fluted call, but mostly Violet sat listening to her own breath. She wasn't thinking about anything now — just waiting.

Then the door opened, admitting Frank's workboots. She unlocked her cubicle door just as he was about to call to her. Betsy, Lila and Edward were crowding behind him, so he shut the bathroom door and reached out his hand to her. They held each other for a few moments.

'Let's go home.'

She nodded, sniffling a little.

'Do you need anything from your desk?'

'My hat and coat.'

'Let's leave them, hey? I'll buy you a new one if you get cold on the way home.'

Violet tried to smile and he squeezed her hand. When he opened the door, she expected to see Lila or Betsy or someone else waiting around. But they'd all retreated to the office and she and Frank walked to the elevators. Now she wasn't cocooned anymore, she had a flood of thoughts

Seeing George

about George and Mr Spatler — but she still didn't feel anything. It was as though all the pent-up frustration and worry of the last few days had been muted.

Frank drove her home, taking the long way, winding up through the jasmine-scented Northcote backstreets. She kept waiting for him to ask what had happened at the office, but he said nothing and when they arrived home he bent down to take off her shoes and pulled back the bed covers.

'I'm not sick,' she said, but when she looked around he was shucking his boots too. So she stripped off her blouse and skirt, unclipped her barrette and slipped into the bed, anticipating the roll to the middle when he lay down. Then she curled across his arm and chest, surprised at how loud his heart sounded, and how motionless the house was this time of day.

Frank gently stroked the dark hair from her forehead for what seemed like hours, and finally said, 'I think this might be our weekend talk.'

'Did they say anything in the office about —?'

'They didn't need to, love. You've been tense, we've both been a bit crazy, these last few months.'

Violet sighed. Her fingertips brushed over her husband's warm skin and she found she was crying. He rolled towards her and enfolded her more tightly against his body, resting his chin on the top of her head. She wept silently, until strands of brown hair were plastered to her hot face and she had to push away to breathe.

'I'm sorry,' he said.

A short hiccup caught in the back of her throat. 'It's not your fault.'

He closed his eyes.

'Everything is such a mess.'

Frank tried to quieten her.

'Don't shush me, Frank. We keep avoiding it. Not talking about it. We can't have children and it hurts. It makes me ache and it makes me want to scream.'

He moved away from her, his forearm over his eyes.

'That's what women do, Frank. I'm supposed to have children. I don't know what else to do if I can't do that.' Suddenly she was angry. 'Why don't you say something?' She pulled herself up on her elbows, looking over his leanly muscled limbs, watching his ribcage rise and fall. 'Frank?'

He didn't respond.

'Frank, I'm talking to you!'

He balled a fist and smacked the mattress with it.

Violet flinched and lay back again. Watched the shadow of the tree leaves slapping the ceiling.

She didn't want to believe she couldn't have children, she didn't want to believe about George. Perhaps Peter was wrong and it was *belief* you couldn't choose.

She started laughing. And at the harsh sounds, her husband roughly pulled her to him and wound his limbs around her. Violet wanted to tell him he was hurting her, but she could feel his heart knocking. Feel the heavy grief in his body. So she lay still. Silent and uncomfortable for the rest of the afternoon.

Seeing George

Climbing out of bed they were groggy and tender. Violet slopped about in her dressing gown, pulling a rabbit pie from the fridge and trying not to clang the oven door and crockery about too much since everything seemed especially loud.

Frank sat at the kitchen table with a beer, and poured one for her, softening it with lemonade. She sipped at it, although the lemonade was flat. They left the back door open to encourage the afternoon air in as the house was stifling.

After the pie, Frank wiped his knife across his bread and finally asked her what had happened at work — what had triggered things?

Violet leaned against the sink, her arms folded. The morning's events seemed like weeks ago now and she hadn't the strength to be honest, so she tousled his hair and bent to kiss him.

'It doesn't matter.'

'It wasn't that George fellow, was it?'

'Please, Frank.'

He let it go. Just as eager to consider the day's emotion spent. He took another beer and the newspaper into the lounge room to listen to the news, and Violet had a soak in the bath, then snuck into the passageway to use the phone.

'Hello, George speaking.'

'It's me.'

There was a long silence. Then: 'Please don't ever do that again, Violet.'

She looked down at her bare feet. 'I rang to apologise.'

'Did you tell your husband?'

'No.'

'Good. We'll have to tell Peter tomorrow night.'

'Why?'

'Because it's all changed.'

Violet wasn't sure why it had all changed, except that facing Betsy and Lila and everyone would be awful. 'I'm not coming in to work tomorrow.'

'Then I'll meet you at Peter's at the usual time.'

Violet heard the shudder of water pipes in the wall: Frank must be back in the kitchen rinsing out his glass. 'George,' she whispered. 'The birthday party – I meant it.'

A long pause. 'Did you?'

'Yes.'

'Thank you, Violet,' he said, and hung up.

· 13 ·

Violet pulled at the liver-spotted skin on the back of her hand, watching it take a good minute to settle its way back down. It was amusing to see how time had stretched her skin. And her understanding of herself.

When younger, she'd thought the lists in the diaries assisted her to make decisions. She now knew they were mere justification for what she had already decided to do; which is why her morning's list about not seeing George rankled.

She half-heartedly thought about crossing it out. But Violet didn't like to throw things out. The diaries were an historical marker, without which her past might not have happened. Isn't that what some philosophers said was the case? Besides, the written words reined in her memory; wouldn't let her stray into more pleasing versions.

She sighed.

Frank said history was constructed by the present; the fantasy always existing in the present. That way, remembering was just an echo of the lies and make-believes created earlier.

Frank. Frank. Frank. He would bring in a dinner tray soon, and he would want her to say nothing about this afternoon. About his tears.

Violet looked at the shimmering patterns of light reflecting from the hand mirror onto the ceiling. The glow was getting fainter with each minute and she decided she wanted a sunset vigil. Her dressing gown clung to her shoulders as she walked to the bedroom door. Saucepans were clanging in the kitchen, and Gretel was giving a low, pleading whine that meant Frank was handling food.

In the lounge room, Violet made her way to the bar stools, rounding the box of books Frank had dragged in yesterday. Charlotte had left all the Dickens behind.

Using the metal rung that ran around the stool's four legs, Violet hoisted herself onto the orange seat. One of her slippers fell in the effort, but she eventually sat facing the windows. The gauzy white curtains filtered the view to the garden. Never mind. She let her legs swing, and took pleasure in holding out her arm on the bar top, basking in the fading glow. The moment seemed to go on for a long while.

'Violet?' Frank was looking for her.

She smiled and stayed where she was, even though her

backside and legs were aching with her immobile weight. After a visit to the bathroom and back calling her name, he stuck his head into the lounge, looked around and withdrew — then popped back again, something having caught his eye.

'What on earth?'

'I wanted to see the sun.'

'You'll get cold.'

A magpie warbled just outside the window and Violet smiled at her husband. He came into the lounge to stand at the bar.

'Would you like a drink, Madam?'

'Sir.'

He elbowed through the wooden saloon doors adorning the bar and pretended to take down several bottles from a high shelf and splash the contents — rather liberally — into an imaginary glass. He picked a sprig of mint and, dropping it into the glass, set to muddling it with a teaspoon. She could almost smell the fruity scent. A non-existent cube of sugar was daintily added with tiny tongs, then it was up with the miniature pink umbrella and the concoction was complete. She took it, sipped and pronounced it perfect.

'Care to dance?'

Violet checked the dance card on her wrist, then nodded, finding this mazurka free.

Frank shouldered back through the saloon doors, making sure they were swinging wildly, and came around to hold out a hand to her. It was difficult to get down from the bar stool – he had to grab her around the waist and she lost her other slipper – but he immediately invited her to stand on his feet.

She curled her hand into his palm and put one foot and then the other on top of his large brown boots, refraining from remarking that they needed a polish. He held her tightly around the waist and she tilted her head back the better to see him, smiling at a small patch of black and grey whiskers beneath his chin missed in the morning shave.

'What is the orchestra playing?'

'Blue Danube,' he answered, and lifting his foot, started to swing her around. They spun in slow, loose circles until reaching the coffee table, which he had to navigate more carefully, and then back toward the bar again.

Around and around they swept, her polyester dressing gown floating behind like a bridal veil. Her mouth open in pleasure. Then she laid her head on his chest and heard his heart bullying his chest.

'I feel dizzy,' she said, knowing he wouldn't stop for himself.

He halted and she stepped from his shoes, giving a tiny curtsy. Picking up her slippers, he followed her as she made her way back to the bedroom. Then he sat, her slippers in one of his hands as she took her time getting into bed and tucked up ready for dinner. He was open-mouthed breathing, all sweaty around his neck and torso.

'No more foxtrots for you, love.'

Seeing George

He lifted his legs one at a time feigning pain. 'You've put on weight.'

'Perhaps,' she said, content to continue the deception. In the last two months she'd dropped a stone or more. She still billowed disproportionately at the breasts and hips, but her arms, legs and neck looked scrawny. Her arms were so bony that some days she took off her watch because the face kept dropping to the underside of her wrist, and she couldn't be bothered with it. When she was in better humour she pushed it right up her arm, but that never lasted long because she thought it inelegant.

Frank fanned himself with her slippers and mumbled something about having to put dinner in the microwave after all that horsing about. She rested against the pillows, saying nothing. She was hungry but didn't need to rush him.

They breathed together for a while in the cold room and then the slippers dropped in soft slaps to the floor. Violet sat upright, but saw it was only sleep that claimed him. In the next moment quiet snores came from his slack-jawed mouth.

She looked at the way his trouser cuffs sat above his ankles, and at the twitch that made his right thumb jump, then she poked around on the bedside table and fetched half of her dry cheese sandwich from lunch. She opened it up to turn the triangles of bread inside out – peeling off the cheese to lie it back down and moisten the dry insides. It tasted delicious after the little bit of exercise.

She was pleased he was napping. He would wake disoriented and hungry, ready for a cup of tea and bed. They wouldn't have any further chats this evening.

Pushing back the doona, she quietly wandered up to the bathroom, resting against the wall to counter the dizziness. After using the toilet, she noticed a towel on the floor near the dirty clothesbasket. She bent to retrieve it — and watched as the floor came rushing up to meet her.

When Violet properly woke, she was back in bed with a headache and sunlight was streaming in through the window. Late morning. Had she lost a night? She tried to move and a shape leapt across the room from the chair: Frank. His clothes were creased and his face quite grey — from sitting there all evening, she guessed. As soon as he saw she was all right, he let his limbs sag and sat on the edge of her bed, patting her hand.

'Would you like some Panadol?'

Suddenly aware of where the pain concentrated, she gently stroked the bump at her temple, marvelling at its apparent size, although she suspected if she looked in the mirror there'd be hardly anything to show for it.

'I'm fine, love.'

He scoffed at her and let his tired eyes travel over her face.

'Why don't you go and lie down?' Now that she was

concentrating, a hazy recollection of the night before came to mind. Frank lifting her into bed; trying to get her to wake up; eat something.

He pulled at the waistband of his trousers — hated anything too tight — and shook his head. 'Why do we have to go over the same ground every time this happens? You know you can't be left alone for forty-eight hours after a fall.'

She put a hand up to her temple again, compelled to pet the swelling. 'You could nap here.'

He ignored her and pointed to the bedside table. 'Eat something. It's past your usual time for lunch.'

She craned her neck and saw a gluggy bowl of porridge and a glass of cranberry juice. Always cranberry juice. Didn't he have any imagination? She shrugged her shoulders at first, but found that she did feel hungry, so nodded. He handed her the bowl. Cinnamon was sprinkled across the oats.

'Couldn't you have left the towel where it was?' His voice finally gave in to the irritation he must have been feeling all evening.

'Don't pretend to know what I was doing.'

He returned to sit on the chair in the corner. 'I don't know what you were doing, but I do know you can't bend that low anymore because the tumour — because you can't get back up.'

She blinked at him and ate more of the half-set glue. 'What day is it?'

'Tuesday.'

'It's not.'

'Okay,' he said, tiredly.

'Please go and have a sleep. It's just a bump.'

'Dr Kearsley's been.'

'I'm surprised that between the two of you I'm not wearing a straitjacket.'

Frank's mouth soured. 'I'd like to get you in one of those cots where the sides can be raised to stop you getting out.'

Violet put the partially emptied bowl back on the bedside table. 'What are you going to do Frank? Guard me right up until the moment I die? You can't stop me from dying, you know?'

He snorted. 'I can't stop you from doing anything.'

She felt all teary at that.

He looked at her a minute. 'I think I will go and have a nap.'

She kept her mouth shut, knowing that if she tried to encourage it, he'd dig in his heels like the mule he was. So she closed her eyes just to speed him along, and sure enough, five minutes later he was trying to tiptoe from the room. She heard his bedroom door groan and swung her legs out of the bed. But hearing footsteps in the hallway, she lifted her legs back up again and closed her eyes against the race of her heart. Not long afterwards he peered into the room – making sure she wasn't out of bed. She grinned when he left for the second time; it wasn't like Frank to be so clever about getting around her.

Seeing George

She waited a good long while and then swung her legs out of the bed. But she stayed sitting there because without Frank to be getting around behind, she really didn't have any reason to be up.

· 14 ·

Violet wished she had asked George more about what to expect when they told Peter about the office party, because for five whole minutes the old man didn't speak. Was unable to speak. His face mottled and he sat his hot cup of tea on top of the lacquered Chinese writing desk. Violet quietly rescued it as she and George followed him through to the parlour.

'This will affect everything. It's not good at all, George,' Peter finally said.

'Don't blame him,' said Violet. 'He knew nothing about it.'

But the elderly man put his fingers to his lips for silence, then walked to the corner of the room where a circular staircase took him up to a private library. He returned holding an enormous book and without specifying who, he said, 'Read this. Aloud.'

Seeing George

Since George appeared reluctant, Violet took the heavy book from Peter and cleared her throat.

1431. Who-so that kan may rede hem as they write.

She stammered, not understanding the sounds that came from her mouth.

'Phonetically,' instructed Peter, pulling his sky-blue cardigan tighter. Violet took a deep breath and began again.

I bidde my lady close hyre eye and telle me as I am.
At ffirst she seyde, 'I kan see a stomak whit, lyke marble,
yt eyes widewes habit blak.
I kan see two sharppe ere lyke bestialite.
Your tail is like the foule netle, rough and thikke.'
'Al true,' quod I, 'here bygynneth game.'

'She's describing a unicorn,' confirmed Peter.
Violet continued,

Then I seye 'Open thow eye to see me
the same as the imagenynge.'
Hyre look som tyme she caste –
than waillynge, poyntynge, then feynte!
Yt 'No' was al she seyde with pitous vois.

'Someone else saw a unicorn,' said Violet, astounded. 'A unicorn tried to make someone see him. Not the same thing.' Peter held his hands out for the book and then, locating the centre table with his foot, laid the heavy tome on it.

'Perhaps I should have told you there were previous attempts. Perhaps I should have told you about the others.' George shook his snout, weary.

'A little late for "perhaps",' said Peter.

'It's against the rules.'

Violet looked from one to the other. 'What rules?'

Peter pushed his dark glasses further up his nose. He only wore them inside when he was upset. 'There are hundreds of examples of failed attempts to have people see dragons, if you'd care to read, Violet. Very unfortunate, all this involving your colleagues.'

Violet shrugged off his criticism. 'You said children can see George, so I thought adults might simply need reminding.'

'Dear, don't manipulate my words to justify standing on top of your desk —.'

'I did not stand on my desk.'

He took off his glasses and pointed them at her, his milky eyes opening wide. 'What you did was the height of ridiculousness. You paid no attention to my question about your family, did you? I was asking about your ancestors, Violet. The only link between the tiny number of individuals over thousands of years who have been able to see dragons is heritage. Someone else, somewhere along your line, will have been able to see a dragon as well.' He put his glasses back on. 'I don't like this. I don't like this at all.'

Seeing George

Violet glanced at George. 'No one at the office believed me, did they? There's no harm.'

'No harm? For goodness sake, George, read her some of what happens when people don't believe.'

George stood to retrieve the book, barely glancing at Violet, and then sat to read aloud.

The Examination of Bridget Byshop at Salem Village 19. Apr. 1692
By John Hauthorn & Jonath: Corwin Esq'rs

Why you seem to act witchcraft before us, by the motion of your body, which seems to have influence upon the afflicted?
— I know nothing of it. I am innocent to a Witch. I know not what a Witch is.
How do you know then that you are not a Witch?
— I do not know what you say.
How can you know you are no Witch, & yet not know what a Witch is?
— I am clear: if I were any such person you should know it.

'That was hundreds of years ago,' interrupted Violet.

'All right,' Peter agreed. 'But just ten years ago, in 1944, an English woman was tried under the Witchcraft Act for summoning spirits. And no one supposed that she was flying about on a broomstick wearing a pointy hat, Violet.

But she was still imprisoned for nine months.'

'I don't believe you.' Violet's pallor belied her words. Suddenly she realised how cocooned the weekly meetings had been: discussing the existence of a dragon safe from the incredulousness of the outside world.

'You have a gift, Violet. But you *must* keep quiet about it. In earlier centuries, you might have been burned at a stake. This century people will decide you are mad and you run the risk of being shut away. Is that what you want?'

Violet's jaw clenched. 'You don't understand, Peter. I'm tired of being quiet about it. I'm tired of being alone. And I'm tired of being the only one to see him.'

Peter pounded a fist against his open palm. 'Gracious girl, what does being the only one matter if it's the truth?'

'It matters!'

Peter thrust his hand out for her to take. She reluctantly obeyed and he carefully led her into the antechamber off the entranceway. Navigating them past the coat rack, he let go of her, and under his breath said angrily, 'How long do you think George was alone before you came along?'

Violet's mouth went dry. She had no idea. It had never occurred to her to ask. How long had he been alone?

When she didn't answer, Peter edged forward and tapped against a large floor-to-ceiling mirror that loomed in front of them. 'Look in there and describe me.'

Flustered, she couldn't think where to begin.

'Long legs, white eyes –,' he said, impatiently.

'Ginger hair,' added Violet.

Seeing George

'Enough. Now, describe me as a dragon.'

She looked into the mirror, then shut her eyes. 'I think you'd have large claws and –.'

'Are you closing your eyes?'

She didn't answer.

'Look in the mirror and describe me as a dragon.'

'I can't.'

'What?'

'I can't. I don't see you that way.'

He turned to face her. 'So it makes absolutely no sense for me to ask you to, does it?'

'My mother says that most of what we see comes from what we think everyone else sees.'

'All you mean is that you're afraid.'

She looked away. Was this the same Peter she'd been seeing every Wednesday night? Such a doddering old man, yet now his voice was like steel.

Peter clasped his hands over his stomach. 'Tell me, Violet, how do I know what you are?'

She wanted to say he knew because George would corroborate it. Or because she wouldn't lie. Because he had read her hand. But none of those reasons were right. Violet looked at her solid figure reflected in the mirror. The scarf Frank had bought her, the wedding ring glinting on her finger.

'But it's not just about what I believe. How can Frank believe me if he can't see George?'

Peter shook his head. 'You and George make the same

mistake, confusing love and belief. They're not the one thing.'

Violet's chest heaved, but before Peter had the chance to elaborate, George suddenly filled the doorway, a letter in hand. 'I've been summonsed to a Council meeting.'

'Well, that's done it,' said Peter.

'What's a Council meeting?' asked Violet, watching as George's ears flicked nervously. Neither Peter nor George answered and she took Peter's arm to help him back into the front parlour. George then sat heavily on the velveteen couch, but she remained standing.

'Why don't you answer my questions?'

'Keeping quiet about George is only one half of the equation, Violet. Keeping quiet about you, is the other.' Peter picked up his cane and kept on to the kitchen.

George patted the seat beside him, but Violet refused to sit, too nervous at the sudden tension, and he sighed. 'A long time ago I made a decision to live with humans, Violet, and I'm allowed to be friends with Peter, even though they don't like it. It's because he's male. I haven't wanted to tell you this,' he said, 'but I knew if they found out about you, there would be trouble.'

Violet heard him perfectly well, but none of it meant anything to her. Who allowed him to be friends with Peter? She did come to sit down now, but George leaned forward, resting his elbow joints on his knees, and looked at the floor instead of at her.

'Most of our kind have died out. When I say "our kind" I mean all the different species; unicorn, phoenix and so

Seeing George

on. Peter will have a book if you're interested. The point is that they all exist, we all exist, but we're decreasing in number.' He paused for a moment, as though it might be difficult to go on and Violet put her hand on his arm. He shivered slightly.

'We have a Council of Elders to guard the relationships between ourselves and human beings, Violet, because the demise of a species is due to interaction with humans. That's why what happened in the office —.'

'What do humans, what do we do, that ends —?'

'A little less information is probably the go.' Peter was walking down the floor-runner holding a plate of fudge in his free hand.

'She'll have to know sooner or later. I want her to see my world.'

The plate shook as Peter settled it on the table. 'Isn't it enough that you're prancing around in clothing and adopting meaningless names? Enough that you're altering your physiology and psychology to fit in here? Don't ask her to do the same there, old boy.'

Violet didn't understand what Peter meant, so she looked at George; he had closed his eyes. She squeezed his arm. 'Could you please tell me what humans do —.'

'I want you to come with me, Violet.'

'Come where?'

He opened his eyes. 'To the Council meeting next Saturday.'

'Oh dear,' said Peter.

· 15 ·

Frank stood in her bedroom doorway, pulling his fingers through his hair as he yawned. He looked more tired after his nap.

'Perhaps we should get someone in,' she said.

He screwed up his nose.

'If I'm going to start falling –.'

'They'd only muck up my new cupboard arrangements.'

'She wouldn't touch your precious cupboards.'

Frank hitched his trousers up by the belt. '*She*?' he said. 'By all means then, bring her in.'

Violet wadded up her tissues to hurl at him, but her vision swam and she held very still. Frank moved into the room, looking at her. Waiting. Her fingers tentatively touched the bump again. Satisfied she wasn't going to be sick, she smiled. 'I'll just have to get used to a lower standard of cleaning,' she said.

Frank didn't laugh.

She pointed at her plastic medication bottles and he came over to unscrew the lids and shake out the pills. He cupped the brown, green and white capsules in his palm for her to inspect. She picked up the large brown one and licked it — laughing at the surprise on her husband's face. Then she placed it on the back of her tongue and swallowed half a glass of water to get it down.

'Why don't they make them smaller and just have us take two?' She sighed. 'I don't know if I'm going to be able to get up to use the toilet.'

Frank nodded and tipped the remaining pills onto the sheet covering her chest. She put the green tablets in her mouth and watched as he scooted the bedpan out from underneath the bed.

'I should have had a daughter.'

He glanced sharply at her then.

'I just meant that you're my husband, not a nursemaid.'

'And a daughter would have been?'

Violet's cheeks went scarlet and Frank looked away. His best means of apology.

'You know that's not what I meant.'

He nodded.

'It's your sensibilities I'm trying to save.'

Frank gave a sly grin. 'I thought I was as rough as guts.'

'You've worn down nicely.'

He chuckled and accidentally kicked the bedpan again,

sending it clanking over the floorboards. 'You want this now?'

'No.'

'You yell out, then.' He shepherded the metal bowl out of the way and headed towards the door. 'I'm going to cut up some vegetables in here.'

And to her delight he did. He wheeled the butcher's block, complete with capsicum, asparagus and pumpkin jolting about on top, down the hallway and into the bedroom. Placed it near the window. Then he rigged up the radio – using a coat-hanger as antennae – and started chopping to the strains of Chopin. His fingers were so agile. He held the point of the knife still, raising and dropping the back end of the blade over the medley of red, green and orange.

'What are we having?'

He shrugged. 'I haven't started concocting yet.'

'Do you miss building things?'

'You haven't seen the pergola in the backyard.'

Violet's brow lifted before she realised he was having her on. 'Seriously, do you miss it?'

'I've retired. I like to pin butterflies against balsa wood now.'

'Can we have a proper conversation?'

The knife made a satisfying smacking sound against the wood, and he nodded.

'Why do you think Thelma and Doug had Charlotte so late?'

Seeing George

Frank appraised her, before picking up speed with the knife again.

'Perhaps they couldn't stand being alone with each other,' she said.

One side of his mouth turned upwards.

'I want your opinion,' she prodded.

'Do you?'

She nodded, pleased to find her head wasn't tumbling.

He scraped the crudités of vegetable to one side of the board, and fished his handkerchief from his back pocket to wipe his nose. 'I think it was because they became unselfish.'

Violet looked as though she had been slapped. 'Surely it's the opposite?'

He stuffed his handkerchief back into his pocket.

'Frank?'

'You're too old to be jealous of your sister.' He started manoeuvring the block toward the door, unplugging the radio at the last minute.

Violet watched him push, and thought his legs and arms mean with lack of flesh. 'Are you coming back?'

'In a minute.'

She relaxed into her mood at that. It was a luxury to be annoyed when he was nearby, but it was awful to work up to it when he wasn't about.

Gretel's nails scratched along the hallway floorboards and into the bedroom.

'Hello.' Violet dropped a hand over the edge of the bed.

A wet, cold nose nudged her fingers, followed by an insistent, rough tongue. She petted the dog she couldn't see, then wiped her sticky fingers on the sheets; they'd be due for a change with the way her body sweated now anyway. She heard Gretel clipping around the room, turning in tight circles before dropping near the chair.

'She up with you?' Frank's voice rang along the passage walls.

'Yes.'

Gretel panted loudly. Violet tried to raise her head to glimpse the dog, but couldn't get very far without her temples pounding. She looked up at the ceiling again, glad for the distraction when Frank returned.

'What did you decide on?' she asked as he sat down.

'Risotto.' He put his hand down to Gretel, who crawled along the floor to sit on his feet, her tail whacking the wall. 'Dopey mutt. You know they've started the election campaign already?'

'Which party are you barracking for?'

He smiled at her. 'George doesn't get sport, does he?'

'He tries hard. Speaking of which, are you going to tell me what your request is all about?'

Frank shut his eyes and sighed heavily.

She waited.

Finally, he said, 'No.'

'Why not?'

'Let it go, Violet. You asked for another couple of days and you got them.'

Seeing George

She tried to think of more subtle verbal approaches, but didn't have the patience. Wanted to prod his eyes open. 'What if I refuse?'

'We'll cross that bridge when we come to it.'

'Knowing why might help me.'

He opened his eyes wide and tapped the side of his nose. 'That's where you're wrong.'

'At least I wouldn't be cursing you under my breath every two seconds,' she said.

He started laughing at that, and she had to laugh too — from sheer frustration. She wiped her eyes and said, 'I've never known you to be so stubborn.'

He nodded. 'I've got to go and stir the pot.'

He started humming as he walked back down toward the kitchen.

· 16 ·

After the visit to Peter's, Violet had come down with a cold so took the rest of the week off. Returning to work on Monday, she deliberately wore a new rose-patterned frock with several layers of petticoat she'd starched in sugar and water. It was a little too dressy for the office and she hoped it might divert talk from last week's surprise party for George. Lila did comment on it and Betsy wished her a good morning and Sam put a cup of tea on her desk.

It seemed as though it would be fine until she noticed Edward and Barney taking the longer route to the filing shelves, avoiding her desk. Then she realised they were all just handling her with kid gloves.

She ignored the cup of tea and concentrated on the invoicing instead, hoping that if she was quiet enough from now on, she might just blend into the furnishings.

Seeing George

Even George understood not to ask her to lunch. With all that had happened at Peter's neither of them wanted more trouble.

But in the late afternoon, just as Violet was feeling confident one part of her life was manageable, Mr Spatler invited her to his office.

He was sitting behind his highly polished oak desk when she knocked to see him and he gestured for her to shut the door. She settled herself on a low wing-backed chair, trying not to notice as he sucked on his teeth.

'Are you satisfied with your job, Mrs Rolden?'

She nodded.

'Do you dislike any of your colleagues? George, for instance?' He waved his hand about, as though it was a casual question.

She shook her head, nervously touching her bun of dark hair.

'So what possessed you to get up on a chair and address the entire office in that manner?'

'I wanted people to see him.'

'I assume they are perfectly capable of that all by themselves.'

She swallowed. He must have heard. 'I wanted them to see him as a dragon.'

Mr Spatler swivelled a bit on his chair — not taking his eyes from her. Violet waited. But he just tucked his chin into his neck and continued looking at her.

'I said, I wanted —.'

'I heard you; I'm ignoring you.'

Unsure what it was that her employer wanted to hear then, she said, 'Perhaps it was a joke for George's birthday.'

'All right,' Mr Spatler said. 'Perhaps it was a joke. A very poor joke that won't be repeated.'

'Yes, Mr Spatler.' She stood.

'And may I suggest that in future you handle things more traditionally.'

'Pardon?'

He spread his hands. 'Why not just play a little music and leave it at that?'

'Music?'

Mr Spatler nodded. 'I'm sure George likes music better than he does being called a dragon.'

Violet struggled not to laugh and sniffed instead. Mr Spatler patted his breast pocket to locate his handkerchief, then pushed the neat white square across the desk. She delicately patted around her nose.

'He said I could bring the handkerchief back to him tomorrow,' she told George as he walked her home. 'He was very polite, but I wanted to say you'd rather have me see you, than play you "Happy Birthday".'

George adjusted his large steps down to a stride more manageable for her. Didn't answer.

'George?'

'Yes.'

Seeing George

'You would rather me —.'

'Much.'

They walked another block in silence. It was an enchanting idea to walk home under the sunlit leaves of the plane trees. The train was always so stuffy. She didn't know why she hadn't done this before now: it wasn't as though she had to hurry home.

A brightly painted object wedged in a drain catchment caught her eye and Violet bent to retrieve it. The wheels were off-kilter, but she held up the little metal train so George could see it too.

'It's a dear thing. Someone will miss it.' She glanced towards the houses as though expecting a young boy to come crashing out a gate, hand outstretched.

'Leave it on the footpath then,' suggested George.

But she hugged it to herself instead. 'What am I going to tell Frank about Saturday?'

'Nothing.'

In order to go and see the Council, Violet and George would have to spend Saturday in Warrnambool. Chamber meetings were held in the late morning at a small town called Port Fairy. Violet had laughed when she heard the name, it seemed too perfect. George told her it was originally called Belfast, but they had renamed it to be less conspicuous.

She delicately propped the toy train on a brick fence, and couldn't help looking back a couple of times as they walked on.

'I have to say something to Frank, George. I can't just go away for the whole day.'

'Those who can't see us can never accept those who do.'

'You don't really like people who can't see you, do you? You only like –.'

She stopped talking, aware of how the sentence was ending. Her hands felt hot and she kept her face turned away from him. They walked in total, almost breathless silence for five or six blocks. All sensible thought was gone from her head. And by the time the two of them were standing in front of her garden gate, George looking down at her and she looking up at him, she realised she didn't want to stop walking and talking with him.

'George, what do humans do that – you know?'

'I can't tell you yet.'

'Why not?'

But he only shook his head. His ears twirling.

And they stood there, looking at each other.

Violet remembered that Frank was probably inside –he'd offered to try and cook a mince tonight. Should she introduce them? It might make things worse. In her hesitation, George lifted his hand and waved, backing away.

The gate squealed when she pushed it and Violet walked slowly up the front path, but before she could lift her key Frank had swung the door open.

'Who was that?'

'You saw?' That wasn't the best thing to have said. 'George.'

Seeing George

'That bloke with the poncy looking hair is the same bloke who was upsetting you? Looked mighty friendly to me.'

She swept past him, dropping her clutch on the entranceway table and walking on into the kitchen.

'I should have asked him in for a cup of tea. You'd like him, I think,' she called out as Frank shut the front door. She was shaking some tea leaves into the pot. Putting the kettle on to boil. Wondering if she could ask Frank more about what George looked like.

'Now you're saying I'd get along with him? It was a different story a couple of weeks ago, wasn't it?' Frank stood in the kitchen doorframe, his arms crossed. 'On top of which, I don't like my wife walking home with another man.'

'He's a perfect gentleman.'

'A perfect *married* gentleman?'

She took the jug of milk from the fridge and the sugar from the pantry. 'We have to get a new bowl for the sugar – this one's chipped. No.'

'I didn't think so.'

'Have you started dinner?' She bent down to the saucepan rack and pulled at a skillet, making metal clang.

'What's going on, Violet? You were going to talk to me about all this, remember?'

She dropped the pan on the stove and turned on the tap to wash a potato. Keeping her hands busy. She definitely couldn't tell Frank about George. Couldn't. He'd say she was crazy and probably try to stop her seeing him.

Frank tried again. 'Every time you and I argue lately we end up discussing your work.'

She didn't turn. 'Isn't it as important as yours?'

'Maybe it is. For the wrong reasons.'

She fetched another potato. Rummaged around in the cutlery for the peeler. 'Why don't you go to the Ham & Beef? We can have sausage for dinner since you've done nothing.'

When he'd stormed out, she leaned her palms against the sink, her legs shaking. She couldn't keep this up much longer.

In the living area she fished out a small diary beside the photo albums, replacing a piece of paper that fluttered to the floor. She sat at the card table and used her hand to flatten out the middle section of the notebook, then wrote:

Reasons to lie to Frank:

I've already been keeping a secret
He won't believe me about George
He already doesn't trust me
If he doesn't trust me how can he love me?

That was enough.

By the time Frank was back and sitting at the table waiting for the sausages – in complete silence – she had a strategy all settled. Sprinkling salt and pepper over her potato salad, Violet told him she was going away Friday

Seeing George

night to visit one of Spatler & Smith's country stores. She kept her voice very even. Had already phoned George and asked him to make the necessary arrangements and he'd been very pleased.

'We need to make sure that their book-keeping system is in line with ours, since some of the accounts aren't right. Lila's had difficulties reconciling and —.' She made herself stop talking. There *was* a Spatler & Smith store in Warrnambool. Very close. Since she would make every effort to step inside it, it shouldn't technically count as a lie.

Frank hadn't picked up his knife or fork. 'Another thing you haven't mentioned.'

'I only met with Mr Spatler today.'

'Is this part of what you still won't speak about?'

She tried to look him in the face. 'There's nothing to speak about, Frank. I was having a problem at work and now I'm not.'

'Was it to do with that George character?'

'I suppose so.' She looked down at the hot food.

'You suppose so? For crying out loud.'

She watched him push away from the table, and the blood ran from her face. Why was she hurting him this way? 'It'll be over soon, Frank. I'll make it finish.'

He stopped retreating and turned to skulk in the doorway between the kitchen and living room, long limbs crowding the doorframe. 'You'll make what finish?'

She forked at some potato. 'This work stuff. Everything.'

'I don't like what's happening to us.'

'Nothing's happening to us.'

'Is that man going with you to Warrnambool?'

Violet tucked stray hair behind her ear. 'No man is going with me,' she answered.

On Friday Violet didn't want to come home before leaving for the train, in case Frank offered to drive her to the station. So she and George had planned to attend Friday night drinks with the others and store their overnight bags at the railway station before work.

That afternoon at Clancy's Hotel Violet was in the ladies' powder room with the other office women, staring at the tiny movement of her pulse jumping just where her neck met her jaw. She couldn't make it stop, and Joan, who had finished rouging her lips, was leaning into a corner watching her.

Feeling her redheaded colleague's cat-like stare, Violet took extra time to wash her hands, but she finally had to swing around to use the paper towelling. She finished up and looked at Joan, saying, 'Shall we?'

Joan pushed off from the wall with the heel of her shoe and inspected Violet more closely. 'Who are you getting dolled up for?'

Violet blanched. 'Frank's taking me away for the night.' She bent to scratch at some imaginary stain on her skirt, silently cursing her colleague. But when she looked up again she saw that the answer had bored Joan, who was rummaging through her handbag.

Seeing George

'That's darling of him, isn't it?' said Lila through lips stretched over teeth so she could better apply her lipstick. 'Get away a bit after —.' She stopped, and looked at Violet.

But Violet was more flustered by the realisation that everyone had heard her lie.

'Where are you going, dear?' Betsy asked. She didn't ever preen in the mirror, but waited in the bathroom until everyone was ready because she wasn't at all comfortable being in a Public Bar.

'It's a surprise.'

'Well you could at least sound excited about it,' mock-scolded Lila. 'Wayne never takes me away.'

'Perhaps she isn't excited,' said Joan, her gaze flicking over to Violet again.

Violet forced herself to laugh. 'Oh, I'm just nervous because I don't like surprises.'

Joan walked from the room and Violet locked herself inside a toilet cubicle. She quietly put the lid down and sat with her head in her hands. Tears rose in the back of her throat. It took a minute or two to fight them down and another minute of blowing her nose so that it wouldn't turn red with the emotion. She hoped George wouldn't notice.

He was at the bar with Edward. Sitting on his tail. He hated having to do that, but in crowded spaces people tripped over it, always mystified as to how they could have fallen. He most often held out a foot and said they'd come a cropper on that. But his tail ended up quite bruised.

Violet bought herself a Pimm's — which was a mistake

because it reminded her of Frank – and wiggled onto the seat between the edge of the booth and the rest of the office girls. Lila was leafing through the pages of a magazine, pointing out desirable clothes. She particularly liked a low-cut, mauve blouse with bolero sleeves.

'Strictly for singles,' said Joan.

Lila pouted and hugged the picture to her chest.

'Come on Lila, once you've made a catch there's no need to keep putting out the bait.'

Betsy laughed. 'Nonsense, Joan. You young things have got your work cut out for you in that department, unless you want your men to get a roving eye.'

'Thank you very much.'

'You could wear it if you wanted, Lila,' said Violet.

Lila nodded and lifted a glass to salute her.

Joan twirled the straw in her cocktail. 'What's the colour of your favourite piece of clothing, Violet?'

She shrugged. 'Something black probably.'

'To help create a slimmer silhouette?'

Lila immediately put a hand on Violet's knee. 'Like we all need, love.'

Violet sat stunned. She wore black because it made her skin seem creamy. She wasn't thin like Lila by any means, or as well-proportioned as Joan, but she didn't mind her curves. Frank said her hips and breasts were 'generous'.

Feeling agitated again, she finished her drink. Wouldn't stay for another round. There was plenty of time but her nerves were a mess and now she felt awkward. She put her

Seeing George

glass on the table and stood, wishing everyone a pleasant weekend.

After a surreptitious glance at George, she was pleased to get outside Clancy's. The early night air soothed her flushed face and the slow walk to the train station was just the lift she needed. Now that she hadn't any eyes on her, it was easy to pretend that she *was* going away for work. That Mr Spatler *was* sending her down to the Warrnambool store to see that the new office book-keeping system was in sympathy with that at headquarters.

By the time George showed up she was settled in the lounge area of Spencer St Station, devouring a ha'penny novel and a small packet of Sunshine biscuits. She smiled to see him, then reflexively checked around to make sure no one from the office was about. They laughed nervously and when he went to fetch his suitcase from the lockers, she walked in the opposite direction, checking on her ticket.

· 17 ·

Perhaps she could manage a shower before breakfast. She didn't have to wash her hair today, so Frank wasn't needed. Just as she was pushing back the bedclothes, he opened the door with the tray. After setting it down, he walked over to the curtains and flung them open. Violet watched him pick up the tray again and patiently wait for her to smooth down the doona.

'Don't you ever get sick of this routine?' she asked.

He took the newspaper from the tray and went to sit in the chair. Unfolding it, he told her it would be twenty-one degrees today. She looked down at the bowl of cereal with sliced banana and wheat germ.

'Birdseed,' she said, pleased.

He turned a page.

'Charlotte's coming today. After school.'

Seeing George

He looked over at her. He hadn't remembered. Or hadn't known. Violet couldn't remember whether she'd told him.

'And George,' she added.

'George, what?' he asked, still looking at her.

She deliberately took a large spoonful of cereal and chewed slowly. But Frank didn't move a muscle, until she swallowed – then he rattled the paper; possibly wishing it was her neck.

'George said he was dropping by today.'

'What time?'

'Which reminds me, the clock's playing up. Slow or fast. I don't know which.'

He continued looking at her.

'Oh, for goodness sake Frank, I don't know what time George is coming. Whatever time he gets here.'

He snapped the paper again and raised it to cover his face. That suited Violet because she was blushing before she could help herself. This was ridiculous.

'Does this mean you've made a decision?'

She shook her head, but he couldn't see, so she said, 'No.'

'When he gets here, tell him I want to see him too.'

'Well, I dare say you'll be letting him in the front door.'

'No, I won't.'

She glared at the newspaper. 'Sometimes, Frank Rolden, you are the most disagreeable man I have ever met.'

He stood, walking over to whip away the tray, leaving the

spoon dangling in her hand. Marching out into the corridor, he banged it down before opening the back door and calling to Gretel. The dog bounded up the back steps and Frank led her through the house – as he knew Violet didn't like – before pulling the front door firmly shut after them.

Violet pushed back the doona cover, doubly determined to have a shower without him now. Her legs were weak today, so she used her arms to take some weight and leaned heavily on the bed, the door handle, and then the wall to get to the bathroom.

She was able to shed her nightgown by forcing it downwards. It was far too large around the neck and the smocking buttons were undone anyway. It took a moment to work the taps on, the spray of cold water shocking her. Her teeth were working loose by the time the hot water came good. And it was only once sitting there that she noticed there wasn't any lemon soap. All in all, it was a very unpleasant shower. Not the same without Frank, which annoyed her even more, because that was the whole point of doing it.

Her short hair made a nice change though. Standing in front of the mirror she didn't have to worry about patting great knots of it dry. She just shook it and let it be. Then she worked on as much of her body as possible without bending down – which wasn't a great deal – so she improvised: holding the velvety green towel against the wall and rubbing herself against it. But one part of the towel quickly

Seeing George

saturated, while the rest remained dry. In the end she decided on a naked walk down the corridor.

The small breeze against her wet flesh felt divine. Lying back down on her bed she was able to dry all the creases and pockets of her flesh that aerating missed. She was quite pleased with herself and by the time Frank was whistling his return, she was sitting at the kitchen table, newspaper spread in front of her.

He went straight to the sink to fill up the kettle.

'Aren't you using rain water in that?'

He pulled a face, but dutifully tipped out the tap water and disappeared down the back steps to the tank-stand. Rainwater was softer than tap water so the kettle wouldn't corrode as quickly, and the few wriggly worms it contained died in the boiling.

When he'd lit the flame, she said, 'While I am making my decision I'll ask you to be polite to George.'

'When have I ever not been polite to him?'

'Just you open the door when he knocks.'

'If I hear him knock I'll let him in. But my hearing's not very good these days. You've said so yourself.'

Violet let her gaze fall back to the newspaper. He had pretty much always been polite to George, it was true, but there was a recklessness about him these last few days that was very uncharacteristic.

'Is he why you're up and showered?' Frank asked, looking pointedly at her wet hair.

'I wanted to impress you.'

They looked at one another. Then he came close and kissed the top of her head – the balding patch where she could feel his lips on her skin. She automatically reached for a cap, and because there wasn't one about, plucked out a sheet of newspaper and let it float there instead.

'I don't know why you bother,' he said, turning back to the throaty kettle.

She went to sit in the lounge room after the cup of tea, tilting the Jason-recliner all the way back like a bed. It was almost as good, except there was something about being in bed that allowed the muscles to fully relax. Still it was nice to be up. Not 'invaliding about' as Frank called it.

He waltzed in and pottered around, pretending to see to things. He liked to check up on her whereabouts. Make sure she wasn't keeled over somewhere while he was picking tomatoes. When he saw where she was, he adjusted the footrest higher and fetched a blanket to throw over her knees.

She patted the side of his neck, where the wrinkles were all latticed, as he tucked the knit underneath her. He really was splendid when he wasn't speaking.

18

Frank pushed open the door of the Ladies' Lounge, a yellow rose in hand. His forehead was sweaty because he'd half-run the last three blocks. One of the men on site had taken sick and the foundations had to be finished as there was a forecast of rain, so Frank finished up later than usual. It was a spur of the moment thing, the yellow rose. Violet was the romantic one. But it would show that he regretted last night's argument, regretted that his fears were getting the best of him.

It had taken ages to purchase the flower and then there were no parking spaces, but seeing Violet's office colleagues seated on the couch, he smiled; it would be worthwhile after all.

Lila looked at the opening yellow petals and squealed. 'How romantic.'

'Aren't you dressed up like a sore toe,' said Joan.

The red staining Frank's neck deepened. He grinned.

'But she left for the train station about fifteen minutes ago, love,' said Betsy.

Frank nudged the brim of his hat with his thumb, trying to hide his disappointment.

'Where are you going?' asked Lila. 'We won't see her to spoil the surprise, so you can tell us.'

Frank's face dropped into a frown as he tried to work out what she meant. 'No, I've missed her.'

At this obvious confusion Joan suddenly stood, taking time to smell the rose and insinuate herself closer to him.

'Don't you mean you're late?'

Frank looked at her. 'I think that's what, Miss,' he looked down at Lila, 'I'm sorry I don't remember your name, what she was just trying to tell me. That I've missed her. Thanks anyway.'

Joan cocked her head to one side. 'But how could you have missed her when you're taking her away for the night?'

Frank blinked, looking down at his feet then back up the sinuous body of Violet's colleague. Although he scarcely knew what he was saying, he instinctively attempted to protect his wife. 'That's right, I was supposed to meet her at the train station. Bit of a mix up.'

Joan smirked. She fiddled with the straw in her empty glass while looking around. 'You could always ask George about her plans,' she said. 'He and she are as thick as thieves at the moment.'

Seeing George

Frank's youthful face pinched and he followed Joan's gaze, through to the front bar.

'He came down with us, but I didn't actually see when he left.' Joan swung towards Lila and Betsy. 'You girls don't happen to know what George was doing this weekend, do you?'

Frank's mouth set in a thin line. 'Like I said, I'd better get going. Thanks for your help.'

Joan smiled, and gave a small wave.

Frank pushed his way back through the crowd.

Back in his utility, he threw the limp rose on the passenger seat and leaned on the steering wheel. He wouldn't go to the train station. But the fact that Violet had only mentioned the work trip yesterday and evidently told her colleagues he was taking her away for the night snagged any clear thoughts. When he finally started off for home he sat on his horn the whole way.

He could see that Joan tested other people's relationship mettle because she didn't have the courage to maintain her own intimacies. But the mention of George reverberated painfully around his chest.

At home he threw his car keys onto the hook and shrugged off the jacket he'd worn over his work shirt to impress his wife. He poured himself a scotch and wandered into the kitchen, leaving the lights off and rolling his shoulders a couple of times to push away the feeling of being watched. The clock tick irritated. He rinsed out the amber liquid so the ants wouldn't come and hunted for a small chore he might turn his hand to. But finally, spying nothing, he shoved himself away from the sink.

She'd promised to phone later in the evening, but he couldn't wait. He'd have put a call through to this George fellow if he knew the number, just to check his whereabouts. Failing that, there was one other option.

Frank crouched down in front of the bookshelf. Pulled out Violet's diary. Flicking through, he found his wife had been making lists. Lists about reasons to lie to him.

Three hours or so into the journey to Warrnambool, Violet had lain aside the novel, preferring to lose herself in the pleasing jerk of the carriage. Out the train window she could make out the flat, green countryside dotted with spindly trees that thrive in salt-drenched air and soil. Beyond that was the sea, the white tips of wave illuminated by the moon.

George sat over a crossword puzzle, angling the paper toward one of the small cabin lights. Occasionally he looked up to ask whether she knew a five-letter word for cartoon-strip, or a six-letter word for mould. Violet shrugged and smiled and they spent the rest of the journey in silence. By the time they arrived at the seaport of Warrnambool, there were a few more stars sprinkled up high and the air was cold.

They caught a taxi to the hotel, which sat squat on a hill

Seeing George

in front of the ocean. And in the cold foyer, George fiddled with his suitcase and room key, wondering aloud whether she wanted a nightcap.

'I don't know if a drink is a good idea, George.'

He scratched at his skin and nodded. Beneath his eyes, his scales were smudged and red, which Violet supposed was due to fatigue.

'Besides, we have to get up early.'

He nodded again, forlornly.

'Oh, all right then, but not for long.'

He ushered her into the bar area and they settled themselves into overstuffed chairs flanking a low table.

'There'll be quite an array of species present tomorrow,' said George after ordering their drinks from the lonely barman. 'Gorgon, Pooka, mermen and merwomen.'

'Really?'

'It won't be alarming for you, I hope?'

'You'll know when I scream.'

George started to protest, then realised she was teasing.

'Anyway,' she continued, rubbing at her eyes, 'it's you they want to see. I expect they're only going to ask me to keep quiet.'

'Perhaps.'

The bartender slid a small glass of hot chocolate frappe in front of her, and placed a brandy tumbler on a coaster for George. Violet spooned a marshmallow into her chocolate and stifled a yawn. 'You're worried about it, aren't you? I imagine they'll just be asking about my lamb-brained idea of trying to get others to see you.'

'What's lamb-brained?'

'It's one of Frank's words. Speaking of which, I'd best get upstairs and phone him.'

George dropped his snout to nudge the lip of his glass.

Violet knew she was being jumpy, but now everything seemed to remind her of Frank. It had been easy to forget about him during the train journey. Trains always felt outside time, somehow. But sitting in the hotel bar with the cold sea air at her ankles, it all became too real again.

'They might want to know about the time we've spent together, Violet.'

'Working?'

'And out of work.'

She drank quickly, pretending not to hear.

'I don't know that they'll be too pleased with the way things have been going.'

She pushed away her glass, the remaining chocolate streaking down one side to pool in dregs at the bottom. 'I'm tired of having to explain things.'

George's smile flashed. 'Perhaps after this is done we won't have to.'

'That'd be nice.' She looked at him. Flushed. 'I'd like to tell Frank about you soon.' Her breath caught and she couldn't read his expression. She wasn't sure how she felt about it either. Wasn't sure why her stomach felt so fluttery.

She stood and picked up her overnight bag. He reached for her free hand. 'Good night.'

Seeing George

Looking down at him, she said, 'Good night, George.' It was the first time she had seen him from that angle and he looked vulnerable. And she noticed that he sat staring at a fixed point in her chair as she climbed the stairs.

Her room was cramped, but immaculate. Several layers of quilt draped over the high bed, matching the floral curtains. She dropped her bag on the bedside chair and startled as a sea wind knocked at the window's metal sashes.

After brushing her teeth, then combing out the long, dark sheets of her hair, she climbed into bed. Propping herself up against three pillows, she sat the heavy phone on her lap, and the hotel operator cleared a line with the exchange.

When it rang a couple of times she bit her lip because Frank had obviously fallen asleep. He knew she'd be ringing late – the train journey took four hours – but he'd insisted that she call. When it rang out, she thanked the operator and asked her to try again in a couple of minutes. Ten minutes later, it rang out a second time and the lady from the exchange suggested that the party was probably asleep.

Violet sat the phone on the nightstand and pushed two of the pillows onto the floor, reminding herself that Frank boasted of sleeping through thunderstorms. But her eyes wouldn't close. The fight she and Frank had last evening flooded her chest and then she made herself nervous by trying to picture all the creatures George had mentioned.

It was a little after one o'clock by the time she drifted into an uneasy sleep and when she finally woke to the sound of shoes in the corridor and a newspaper being shoved under the door, she avoided looking at herself in the bathroom mirror, reluctant to see the bruised skin beneath her eyes.

Outside the hotel window, tree branches whipped in the wind even though the sun was out, so she zipped up a heavy, woollen, off-white dress. Her pallor wouldn't be helped by the colour, but she didn't want to be cold as well as nervous. By the time George rapped on her door, she was dressed and again cradling the phone receiver.

'Frank didn't answer last night or this morning. That's not like him.'

'How do you know? Have you ever done this before?'

'Of course not. But we had a fight before I came away.'

George looked at his shoes. 'Let's get going and you can sort Frank out later.'

They left their luggage at the reception area and walked out onto the street. Although there was time for breakfast before the Spatler & Smith store opened at nine o'clock, they decided to just walk around a bit as neither of them felt like eating.

They made their way along the boardwalk – a sandy sweep of concrete that curled the foreshore – and looked out at the murky blue sea. A chill wind picked up the sand and stung their faces. But this small irritation scoured away other thoughts so Violet leant her head forward to enjoy the struggle until they turned onto the main strip of shops and she saw her reflection in a window. Quickly, she pulled

Seeing George

out a scarf from her purse and fixed it around her tangled mess of hair.

Shortly after nine o'clock, they went into Spatler & Smith's and walked each of the store aisles – much to the amusement of the serving lad who said he rarely had customers in this early, unless it was a plumbing or farming emergency, and especially not city folk. Violet looked for a screwdriver for Frank, but it didn't seem nearly enough, so she bought a tape measure as well.

'Present, is it?' asked the fifteen-year-old, and Violet asked him how he knew.

'Well, it isn't for you and he doesn't seem to be the type.' The boy cocked his head in George's direction and she turned to see him trying to soften his shoes with a hammer. She smiled and asked the boy about the store business. He told her a few things about the turnover on different days of the week and the local community of men and the hardware they wanted – the details of which she planned to impress upon Frank and Mr Spatler.

Back at the hotel, while George picked up the hire-car, she made another attempt to reach Frank. Nothing. So she put down the phone and took a deep breath, telling herself he'd worked so hard he slept through the phone last night and then this morning he had to get back on site early.

· 19 ·

It was getting on for half past three by the time Violet decided she'd better dress for George's visit; she didn't want him to see her moping about in a housecoat. She sat on the edge of the bed, trying to ease a stocking up her leg. The thin material was so slippery she couldn't get a good grasp on it, and her toes had forgotten how to curl. Frank stood in the doorway with his arms folded.

'Help me, then.'

He shook his head.

'What's wrong with you these days?'

He scratched his nose and sniffed.

'Frank?'

'Why don't you hop back into bed?'

Violet stood and with her back stiffly bent, walked over to the dresser – the stocking trailing behind along the

Seeing George

floor. She opened the top left-hand drawer and shuffled through the undergarments. Pulling out the leather-bound photo album she'd located for Charlotte, she pressed it open to two sepiaed photographs: a suited gentleman with a large moustache and light-coloured eyes, and one of a woman wearing a soft stole, looking past the photographer, a slight smile playing on her mouth. Violet turned to Frank, her finger arching towards the images.

'They're dead,' she said.

'Your parents?'

'I'm not.'

Frank uncrossed his arms. 'I'm well aware of the fact.'

She slapped the album shut. 'Then stop trying to get me to lie down and act as though I am.'

'For pity's sake.'

'Don't —.'

'Do you even accept your bloody illness?'

Violet stamped a foot. 'Frank, I don't know what's up or down with you anymore. I refused chemotherapy because I didn't think it would help. What's that tell you about how ill I think I am?'

'You refused it because you'd hate to have more of your hair fall out. You didn't want George to see —.'

Violet placed her fingers in her ears and shut her eyes.

Frank waited, but couldn't help grinning at the stupid sight of her. Eventually, she opened her eyes and noticing his smile, dropped her fingers, trying to glare at him. But she half-smiled too. Then sighed. It was all too silly.

'We haven't fought this much since I don't know when,' she said.

'Honeymoon. Get back to bed.'

She stayed leaning against the dresser. 'We did not argue on our honeymoon.'

'Like hell we didn't. That's why we didn't dare argue again for a full year. Shocked the pants off me. Little pin like you railing at me.'

'Well, what on earth were we fighting about?'

Frank hesitated. 'Contraception.'

'Well, that was a waste of energy.'

'Wouldn't be the first time. Hop back into bed, Vi.'

'Hop back to bed. Hop back to bed.'

'You're barely able to stand.'

'What are you going to do if I refuse to give him up, Frank?'

'You already guessed, I'm going to lock you away.'

'I'm being serious. What are you going to do?'

Frank shook his head. 'It's not about what *I'm* going to do, is it? Shit Violet, you're as blind as a bat.'

He left the room.

Wasn't about what he was going to do. Well, what was it about then? Violet sat heavily on the edge of the bed, and continued to dress. But she could see it wasn't going to work so she lay back, lifting her leg slightly to draw on the stocking that way. It kept snagging on her toenails, leaving tiny pockmarks. She dropped her leg and looked at the ceiling. Ceilings, she thought briefly, were very unattended

Seeing George

features of a room. Then she rolled sideways and pushed herself upright again. Charlotte could help her with the stockings.

She inched into the corset. It smelt a bit after the other evening, but would have to do. Frank refused to wash her dress-ups. She had the stays at the front which was ugly, but ease of use more than compensated.

At the wardrobe, she rifled through the skirts and yanked the blue satin one from its clipping. She zipped it on, but Charlotte would have to fasten the hook and eye. Leaving the choice of blouse for later, she moved into the bathroom, pulling the plastic chair in front of the vanity.

She put on her face: pressing the foundation into the wrinkles, ringing her eyes with kohl, pushing her teeth loose to stretch out her lips – giving a tighter surface on which to dab the lipstick.

Her hair was difficult: too short to be wound into a bun. She tried to neaten it up with bobby pins, but the whole lot sagged like flowerbeds after a storm. Her arms tired trying to reach up, so she plucked out the pins and fired hair-spray at it.

'Did you cut it all off?' asked a little voice.

'Is it obvious that I did it, pet?' Violet held out her hand, indicating that Charlotte should come closer because her aunt couldn't turn toward her, seated as she was.

But although Charlotte stepped eagerly into the room, she blanched at the sight of her aunt's face.

'What happened?'

Her niece's voice was so serious, Violet laughed. But this seemed to only further frighten the child. 'It's make-up,' she snapped. Perhaps her cheeks were too rouged against the black outlining of her eyes. 'Doesn't your mother ever let you try lipstick?'

'I like eye shadow.'

'Nonsense eye shadow. Your mother shouldn't wear it during the day either. You get around here and learn about lipstick. A Depression standard: lipstick on the cheeks and rub in.'

Charlotte backed against the wall, her hands tucked behind her.

Violet continued fossicking through her make-up case, trying to find something suitable for the girl. Her perfumes were too cloying and eye shadow on children made them look older, not dressed up. Inappropriate. 'Why don't you put these on?' She gave Charlotte a set of gold and silver bangles. Frank had taken them off her arm after the other night's dinner party and shoved them in here with her vanishing creams.

Charlotte came away from the wall, but kept her distance by stretching out her arm, hand folded shut like a miniature umbrella.

'You didn't say what you thought about my hair.'

Charlotte let the bracelets jangle to her elbow, and then glanced again at her aunt's haircut. 'Yes. I like it.'

'Good. Now let's pop back to the bedroom because I need you to help me get my stockings on for George.'

Seeing George

'Who's George?'

'He's a dear friend of your aunt's.'

But when Violet was seated on the edge of the bed, watching Charlotte's reluctant hands trying to wind the stocking higher, she changed her mind and had her niece fetch a long pair of black socks from the dresser instead.

'Now what about a blouse? And stop staring at me.'

Charlotte dropped her head, her fringe shaking with embarrassment.

'You're as bad as Frank. What's the matter with the pair of you? Can't stand to see me up and about.' She couldn't seem to help snipping and the young girl didn't reply.

As Violet used a tissue to blot her make-up, she tried another tack with Charlotte. 'You pick me out some shoes, darling. Ones to match my grand blue skirt.'

Charlotte turned and buried her head in the bottom of the wardrobe, her little fingers lifting then rejecting various items of footwear. Finally she presented a pair of white sandshoes. Very comfortable and completely wrong. Violet crooked a finger and beckoned her niece closer. She snatched the proffered shoes and flung them out the bedroom door.

'High heels,' she said.

But Charlotte backed away into the dresser, her gaze fixed to the floor.

Violet began to feel weepy. It was infuriating to find there was nothing she could do if the young girl decided to be wilful. She hadn't any physical strength.

She got up from the bed, but when Charlotte retreated further, sank back down again. She put a hand up to her cheek – and the back of it came away caked with sweaty beige and red.

'You've helped me get dressed before, Charlotte. Into my dressing-gown and slippers. What's wrong today?'

The child shrugged.

'Don't you like dress-ups? The make-up?'

Charlotte shook her head.

'Well, it's not for you anyway.'

Her niece's hands stayed hidden behind her back.

'Look at me.'

The child lifted her chin and stared at her aunt, who immediately wanted to tell her not to look.

'Come here.'

Charlotte took one step, then shook her head.

'Do you want me to take it off?'

'What?'

'The clothes. The make-up.'

The small girl nodded.

Violet's face scrunched. 'Why?'

But Charlotte refused to answer.

In a pique, Violet stood and violently unzipped her skirt. She balanced a hand against the bed then kicked the blue folds of material across the floorboards. Still standing, she unlaced the stays – eventually just wrenching at the ties to rip it off and push it down over her hips. She kicked that away too. Panting hard, she forced out the elastic band on

Seeing George

her petticoat and pulled it up her chest; when it popped tighter once over her shoulders, she used it to roughly smudge away the lipstick, rouge and eyeliner. Then, blinking from particles trapped in her eyes, she pushed the silky material over her head and let it drop. Charlotte was watching through her long fringe.

Unsatisfied, Violet sat on the bed and bent over as far as she could to unhook her bra. It took several attempts before her shoulders and upper arms were loose enough to allow the movement. Sweat dripped from her forehead and she finally freed her drooping breasts and threw the contraption to the end of the bed.

'Happy?' She barely had breath enough to speak.

Charlotte turned her face away. Teary.

'Come and help me.' Violet had to pause. 'Damned socks. Only wore them – you wouldn't do the stockings.'

Her niece didn't move.

'Charlotte.' Violet was hot and highly coloured.

The girl came forward a step, but at the sound of Frank's boots in the hallway ran to the door to meet him and hugged at his legs in a way she hadn't since a toddler. Frank reached down to the shaking child and looked quizzically at Violet.

Violet put her face in her hands.

Frank would have gone to her, but when he tried to walk forward, Charlotte gripped him tightly, forbidding it. He put a hand on her small head and told her to get down to the kitchen. She ran.

He came into the room to sit beside his wife, but she turned away from him. When he touched her, she shrugged his hand off, so he stood and began to gather up the strewn skirt and stays.

Violet fetched a tissue to wipe her nose and eyes. Then put a hand on her chest until she was able to speak properly. 'She was frightened of me.'

Frank stopped bunching up clothes and leaned on the dresser.

Holding the sodden tissue, Violet gestured to the clothes. 'Is it that awful?'

'You tend not to do things by halves.'

'Do you think the same?'

'Love —.'

'I need to know what you think, Frank.' Her voice was angry.

'Why? It's not for me.'

She scowled.

Seeing this Frank pitched the clothes at the wardrobe. 'Even a child sees it clearly, Violet, but not you. You only want bite-sized versions of the truth. Everything's got to be on your bloody terms or not at all.'

He strode out — slamming the bedroom door shut behind him.

Violet pulled back the bedclothes and got into bed. Underneath the covers she curled into a ball as best she was able.

· 20 ·

Frank nosed his ute into a parking space in front of one of Warrnambool's four hotels.

After reading Violet's diary last night he had gone for a long walk. Paced the blocks surrounding their house under the bright moon, his breath coming in chilled white bursts as he tried to make sense of what he'd read. He might have waited to receive the phone call she'd promised to make, or he could have rung to find out which hotel she was staying at, but — and he hated to admit it — he didn't want her to have warning that he knew something was up before he found out what it was.

He was exhausted by the time he put the key in the front door, but he hadn't slept. And at five o'clock in the morning he finally made himself a strong cup of tea: he wouldn't wait out this situation any longer.

A cold five-hour drive later, he was starting his search at the hotel closest to Warrnambool's main road, reasoning that since she got seasick she'd not be at one near the water. But George had booked the hotel, not Violet. So it was only after George and Violet were on the road to Port Fairy that Frank's ute turned towards their hotel.

At reception, he asked whether there was a Violet Rolden registered for the night. The clerk ran a finger down the signatures, then nodded.

'But she and her gentleman friend have already checked out.'

Frank paled and the clerk asked whether he would like to sit down. Frank shook his head. 'It's very important that I find her. Do you know where she went?'

'We arranged a car for them last night, sir.'

Frank nodded, trying to appear as though this was expected.

'If you like, I can ask the company whether they mentioned where they were going?'

The young man walked into a back room and when he returned to the counter he was smiling. 'They're on their way to Port Fairy.' When Frank didn't respond, he said, 'We know because they asked for a map.'

After finding that the route was quite direct, Violet tried to put away the map so she could look at the countryside. The road wound inland with drifts of wild daffodils

Seeing George

blanketing the paddocks. But the concertinaed paper refused to fold.

'Can you wind down your window a little?' asked George. 'I can't stand moving at such a high speed without the feeling of wind.' He pulled at his collar. 'Damn cars, I get lost using them.'

'I didn't know you didn't like driving.'

He glanced at her. 'I always walk home.'

'You do too. I forgot.'

'You want to know what else I don't like? Shoes: impediments to moving. Ties: impediments to breathing. And why shave off facial hair when the whole point of it is to protect you?' He paused. 'I don't like a lot of things.'

Violet stopped trying to force the mismatched rectangles. 'You seem at home.'

'Not with machines. Useless, useless contraptions.'

'The telephone?'

'All of it.' George warmed to the topic, waving his hands around, then grabbing the steering wheel again. 'More and more replacements for essential activities — washing, cleaning, cooking, travelling. It's all about getting there faster. Cooking faster? As though cooking is a chore.'

Violet laughed and looked out at the dark fold of crows crowding a telephone line. 'Cooking is a chore for me.'

'How awful,' snapped George.

'For goodness sake, slow down!'

George just pulled at his collar again and in a fit of

temper Violet wound up the window and tossed the splayed map onto the back seat.

They sat in angry silence until rounding the bend into Port Fairy, where George parked the car in front of an unadorned grey façade. It was a nineteenth century building right on the street, with a prominent sign reading 'Civic Chambers'. Violet shivered slightly.

Out of the car, she tugged at her dress to smooth out the wrinkles and George came around to her, scratching behind his ear.

'Bloody cars,' he said.

'Bloody maps.' She smiled.

They regarded each other a moment.

Then George said, 'I'll go in first.'

Her face fell. 'Aren't we doing this together?'

George smiled so warmly, she almost forgot her fear. 'Of course we are,' he said. 'But I need to prepare them.'

'Well, what am I supposed to do?'

He held out his hand and they walked up the steps to a covered entranceway. 'I'll come and get you soon.'

'I could just stand quietly up the back,' she pleaded, looking at the large and ominous doors, trying to imagine what was behind them.

George shook his head and let go of her hand. She stood watching as he pushed open one of the heavy doors and slipped behind it. There was a brief surge of noise, a cacophony of voices, and then nothing.

Violet decided to give him five minutes before peeking

Seeing George

into the hall. She sat down on the stiff-backed wooden benches that faced away from the main street.

It was only when Frank headed into the small town of Port Fairy that he realised he wasn't sure what on earth to look for beyond a white car — and there were five currently in view. All parked. Only an FJ Holden had someone sitting inside: a young man with his legs out the door, smoking.

Frank pulled up beside him and wound down the window. 'Do you know where the nearest hotel is, mate?'

The young man flipped the hair out of his eyes and pointed his cigarette in several directions.

'Well, is there some sort of occasion on here today?'

The man shrugged and exhaled. 'Go on up the general store. Gertie'll know.'

Frank accelerated up the street and parked in front of a weatherboard building which had a small, dirty 'General Store' sign stuck in the window. Pushing open the door sounded a little bell, but he had to wait patiently while Gertie, in her late fifties and wearing a hessian bag over-locked into an apron, weighed some spuds for a woman with three youngsters. They were enjoying a conversation about the demands of children.

Holding his hat in his hand and rocking on his boot heels, Frank looked around at the jars of tuppenny and ha'penny sweets and brown bags of flour, sugar and unwashed potatoes on display. He had no taste for food at that moment; actually he couldn't ever imagine eating again.

Finally Gertie turned to him. 'What can I do for you, love?'

'I need to know if there's anything happening in town today. Anything that might interest some visitors.'

The elderly woman bent to rub her hand against a tired calf muscle. 'Time on your hands then?'

'Anything,' repeated Frank.

'Well, there's a girl guides ceremony on. There'll be all of six of them got up in the brown uniform. The local's nearly open but you'll be drinking with flies at this time of day. And there's a special Councillors' meeting in the hall, but that's not for the public.'

Frank looked away, setting his mouth.

'Would you like a cup of tea?'

Although he didn't answer, she padded away from the counter to an area out the back, giving him a moment to compose himself. When she returned she had two full cups of tea and a small plate of biscuits.

'You only in town for the day?' Gertie sipped the boiling liquid, her lips and tongue immured to scalding.

'I'm looking for someone.'

'And you think she's doing something in Port Fairy?'

Frank raised his eyebrows at the assumption, then nodded.

Gertie broke off one half of a Scotch Finger biscuit and

Seeing George

popped it in her mouth, softening it into mush with another gulp of hot tea. Neither of them spoke again until Frank was swishing around the dregs in his cup. Gertie held out her hand for it. 'It's never quite as bad as you think it will be, love.'

Frank nodded and walked back through the door with its little singing bell. He buttoned up his coat and shoved his hands into his pockets, deciding to at least walk the main street.

Shivering, Violet edged open one of the heavy doors separating her from the Council meeting. She glanced at a spectacle of rich colour and rapid movement before George's large shape eclipsed everything and forced her backwards.

'I'm cold,' she said, by way of excuse, trying to make sense of what she'd glimpsed at ceiling level.

'We're just finishing.'

Violet twisted her purse strap. 'Am I coming in?'

George ushered her back toward the bench. 'They don't want to see you, Violet. It's all gotten very complicated. They're going to hand down a judgement in seven days.'

'A judgement about what?'

'Our relations.'

'I don't understand. Without even meeting me?'

George put a hand to his forehead in an uncharacteristically human gesture. 'They don't need to meet you, Violet. You're not one of us, that's all that matters.'

She threw her hands up in the air. 'I've come all this way, risked God knows what with Frank and —.'

'I'm sorry. I hoped they might see you differently if they just met you.'

'See me differently to what?'

'Differently to other human beings. So they wouldn't be afraid of our friendship.' He looked away, then sighed. 'Violet, when humans and dragons form a union, the children are human beings.'

'Pardon?'

'That's what humans do to us. The children of a union display no characteristics of our kind whatsoever, so naturally choose to marry another human being,' he said. 'We disappear, Violet.'

She laid her hand on his arm. 'George, I know this is important but I don't understand.'

'Violet, Peter thinks you can see me because you have a dragon as an ancestor.'

She put a hand to her chest. 'I have dragon's blood?'

George smiled gently at her. 'Maybe. That's why he kept on about your family lineage.'

At first Violet smiled too. It had an elegant logic: one of her ancestors had loved a dragon. But then she put her free hand to her mouth. 'Could that be why I can't have children?'

The view from the street was of a distraught couple. The woman, dressed in white, was wringing her hands while the tall man tried to comfort her.

Seeing George

As Frank ran up the steps, his chest hammered at the sight of them together, at the bare fact of her lies. And the colour drained from his face as he watched George embrace his sobbing wife and say, 'Perhaps you need to marry into our bloodline.'

Frank's heart nearly left his chest. 'She's already married, you bloody bastard!'

· 21 ·

Violet's head throbbed when she woke to the knock at her bedroom door. She decided to stay still, looking at the faint tree-leaved shadows on the wall.

'You awake?' asked Frank.

She mumbled something unintelligible and shivered. Her skin was goosepimpled; it'd been years since she slept naked. And on top of it all, her chilblains were acting up because she'd left the damnable black socks on.

'Scared the hell out of Lottie.' He moved further into the room.

'Thank you, Frank.'

She shifted restlessly. The sheets no longer had the lavender smell from three days ago; they emitted a slight but sour body odour. 'Please pass me my dressing gown.'

Seeing George

He waited patiently while she wrapped the faded red gown around herself as best she was able.

'I want to know how you're feeling.'

'Ill. Clearly.'

She watched him try to determine how serious she was.

'I lost my temper, Frank. I misbehaved. I'm a rotten old woman who has nothing better to do than frighten nieces.' She sniffed. 'I'll apologise.'

'I've sent her home until later.'

Violet's eyes were panicked. 'You shouldn't have done that. If she's upset, Thelma might not let her come back.'

'Thelma would never do that.'

'You don't know. You don't know that, Frank.'

'Violet, this is just —.'

'Leave me.'

He did and she sat back against the bedhead, feeling utterly helpless. How would Frank like it if it were she preparing menus and deciding when Charlotte should go home? If it were she leaving the house for walks whenever she felt like it, leaving him bed-bound and helpless? What was wrong with everything lately?

A knock rattled the front door. George. She looked at the wig drooping in the corner and tucked her shorn locks behind her ears. They strayed, so she pulled a cap from her dressing gown pocket. A striking dark blue and pink one Thelma had knitted, that Frank said made her eyes stand out. By the time she'd pushed her hair into it she was expecting to hear footsteps treading the floorboards;

instead there was another knock.

Frank wasn't going to answer it.

Her hands shook as she swung off the doona and retied the dressing gown. Walking down the hallway, she heard Frank out the backyard singing at the top of his voice so he couldn't be accused of ignoring George.

She leaned heavily against the door when she'd opened it and George, who had been about to thrust some red geraniums at her, froze. She waved for him to enter, and he did – but gingerly.

She shooed him down the passage, but stopped off in the bathroom before she followed. Her reflection ruined her composure: hiding under a hot facewasher she let some tears smear into the clown-like run of eyeliner and the blotch of lipstick around her mouth. It was difficult to get the make-up off without cleanser and she couldn't be bothered. George would have to see her 'as is' for once.

By the time she got back to the bedroom, the stalky flowers were wilting on the dresser. Her scalp prickled with irritation as George followed her every slow and jerky movement. When she was tucked in, he took a seat in the chair in the corner and asked, 'Where's Frank?'

Violet flapped her hand about, indicating that she didn't want to talk about it. She didn't have the breath. Which meant they were both forced to listen to Frank's carrying on in the yard. First the singing, then the whippersnipper. Meanwhile, George looked solemnly at her.

Seeing George

'He only did the lawns two days ago,' she said.

'Bit of rain and they're growing again,' said George, tugging at his collar.

'What have you been up to since you were last here?'

'Crossword puzzles.'

'How's the writing going?'

He fidgeted. 'I've started about a hundred times.'

'Well, you'd want to get on with it. It'll make a change from all those failed experiments in that great tome Peter was fond of lugging about. Besides, I'd like to read it.'

'You'd like to correct it, you mean.'

She smiled faintly at that.

His tail tapped nervously on the floor. 'Should I get Frank?'

Her frown deepened. 'Go and put the kettle on. The herbals are on the left-hand side now. Frank keeps changing things around. I just want a normal tea.'

George strode eagerly from the room. Violet didn't know whether she was pleased or not to hear him open the back flywire door and yell to ask whether Frank wanted a cup too. The whipper-snipper was promptly shut off and soon Frank's boots were thumping around the kitchen. They made some sort of small talk. Violet couldn't pick up the actual conversation, but she felt smug that Frank had to be sociable with George.

Another tray came into the bedroom. Just cups of tea. 'Out of biscuits,' Frank said to her. 'I'll pick some up from the shops later.'

'How long was I asleep before?'

'Barely half an hour. Just long enough for me to tidy things up.' He looked pointedly at her. 'I rang Thelma and Charlotte's coming around again later. For a quick visit.'

'You didn't tell my sister – ?'

Frank shook his head.

'Thank you.' Violet had difficulty with the words.

George dug out some fruitcake from his pockets. He hated sultanas, but knew they both liked them, so bought the cake from the 'birdseed' shop on the way over. He didn't think about presentation like Frank did though, so when he unwrapped the glad-wrap, the cake fell into small bits. It tasted of nuts and alcohol. Very rich.

Frank remained standing in the doorway – wouldn't go and fetch a chair no matter how they entreated him. 'Got to get back to the yard,' he said. 'Needs a proper going over. Nice to see you, George.' He wiped his hand on his overalls and reached over to shake George's hand. George furrowed his brow, but took Frank's outstretched hand, balancing his cup and saucer on his leg.

Sure that this was her husband's subtle way of reminding her about giving up George, Violet said, 'Next time you get around here George, bring a whole cake. Frank loves a fruitcake.'

Her husband shot her a look and left the room, carrying his still half-full cup.

Violet frowned.

George waited as the footsteps retreated, then turned his insistent stare back to Violet.

Seeing George

'What?'

His gaze travelled about the room as he tried to find the words. 'You look a bit –.'

'Old?'

'Perhaps it's your hair. I haven't ever seen it in a hat.' His cup rattled slightly on its saucer.

'It's a cap and I put it on because my hair is falling out in big clumps now.'

'Really? It'll grow back though.' He seemed bewildered.

'Nonsense.' Now George was going to be trying as well. She didn't look at him.

He tried to grin. 'You're in a mood.'

'Black as the ace of spades,' she replied. 'I upset Charlotte. Behaved terribly, and now she's gone home.'

'Lost your temper?'

'Lost my temper. Yes.' Violet blinked back her emotions. 'A horrid day so far and it's only going to get worse.' She paused while trying to find courage. 'George, I have to tell you something.' Her hands were trembling. 'I can't see you anymore.'

George laid his cup and saucer on the floor, out of harm's way. Then sat up straight again.

Violet didn't want to go on. 'I can't –. It's just –.'

No, no. She couldn't do it. George's ears were back, wary. Then suddenly, she put her hand to her chest, flooded with an idea. 'I can't see you as a dragon anymore. Do you understand? You look like a man to me now. It's been that way for the past few visits and I didn't want to say anything, but I have to. For the sake of our friendship.' She exhaled. 'It might be the illness. Perhaps our theories were wrong, I don't know. But I can't see you as a dragon anymore.' She reached for some Kleenex – Frank had brought her a fresh box – and wiped around her nose. She had to stop herself from smiling: this was so very clever.

George squinted at her.

'I was hoping things would get back to normal. But they haven't. That's why I want you to get on with writing me up.'

'This is peculiar. I don't know of any other case where –.'

Violet waved her hands about. 'Stop worrying about other cases. Not everything is the same. I don't need you to analyse this.'

'It's just so unlikely, don't you think? Perhaps you hit your head or –.'

Violet purposefully widened her eyes and struggled to sit up higher. 'I did hit my head. Quite hard. I was knocked unconscious for ten minutes or so. Dr Kearsley said I was going to be admitted if I hadn't come around.'

George stood and walked to the window. 'That was a cheap shot on my part and the fact that you took it up is flabbergasting.'

She sank back down into the pillows. George should just mind his own business. He didn't have anyone in his life telling him she wasn't a human being. Telling him to get rid of her.

Her thoughts arrested. That wasn't true. Is this what it

Seeing George

had been like for George all those years ago? Choosing like this? Her temper boiled again. Damned Frank.

'George, look, it doesn't matter how it happened. The important thing is that it happened and now it's done and that's that.'

'Well, what are we going to do about it?'

'I've been able to see you for more than fifty years.' She neatened the sheet edge over the doona cover. 'Let's leave it at that.'

He looked around the room and she could see this was the last thing he wanted, but didn't quite know how to say so.

'For me,' she added.

'For you, what?'

'For me, just let this rest.'

George looked at her for a long minute. Then he nodded his head and closed his eyes.

Violet clasped her hands together. Good. She could no longer see George; it was decided. Now, perhaps that might ease things with that fool of a husband and she wouldn't have to give up George altogether.

· 22 ·

Violet's heart seized when she heard Frank crying out from the steps of the Civic Chambers. It was only after a couple of seconds that his words about her already being married made sense and she freed herself from George's arms. But it was too late.

'This isn't what you think, Frank.'

'It isn't a lie to me about work? About him not being here?' Frank could barely control his anger.

'You wouldn't have understood, but I can explain.'

'*Now* I'll understand, will I?' He smacked his hat onto his head and turned back toward his ute.

Violet lifted up her skirt, moving as quickly as she could down the steps – only realising the horrid coincidence of the white dress when she tried to run. By the time she got to him, Frank was already inside his ute. Leaning over the

Seeing George

steering wheel. Stunned.

She opened the door and crouched beside him. 'It's not what you think, whatever you think, I promise. It's something else entirely.'

'You were talking about marrying him.'

She pulled on his sleeve, trying to get him to look at her. 'I'll get George to explain.'

'Don't bring him anywhere near me.'

'It's not his fault.'

Frank slammed his fist onto the horn, causing her to jump. She stood to lean against the ute door. She didn't know how to put it more delicately, how to make sense of what she knew, so she just said, 'George is a dragon.'

Her husband didn't respond. Didn't even blink. Didn't see that George had begun to walk down the steps, his tail curled in the air.

'He and all the others I was down here to see are not actually people. They're unicorns. Among other things.'

'Violet.' Frank's loudness startled her. 'All these lies. You've come away for the night with another man, for crying out loud. You could at least try to make sense. Say it doesn't mean anything. That this was all a coincidence. Or even, that you and he – that your affection is for him and not me. But stop lying.' He raised his voice even further. 'It's damned insulting.'

'Please, Frank. I know I didn't tell you before but I have to now. Please give me a chance. Please, love, get out of the ute.'

As Violet pulled Frank's arm she saw that George was now only metres from them. She took a moment to wave him away, watched him retreat back up and into the hall.

Frank reluctantly swung his legs around until they rested on the bitumen and then he stood, leaning heavily against the car. His face was hard and he didn't quite seem to know what he was doing.

'When I realised I was the only one to see him as a dragon –.'

Frank grabbed her and shook her. 'Stop it! Stop it! What's wrong with you?'

She started sobbing, her nose and cheeks reddening as she tried to twist from his hands. 'Frank, if you love me, please believe me. George is a dragon.'

Frank looked at her long and hard. 'You believe it, and that's enough malarkey for one day.'

He let her go and walked around the open ute door towards the hall. Violet ran after him, clutching at his jacket. 'Don't go in there angry, Frank. It's not George's fault. If you're angry, be angry with me.'

He let her catch him a few times, pulling on his arm and belt, then he wheeled round and slapped her on the face. Violet reached to cup her cheek, her mouth open in shock, but when she held out her other hand to him, his shame and anger only propelled him more forcefully and he strode up the steps and wrenched open the hall doors.

George was pacing just inside and immediately put up his hands, trying to calm Frank down. But Frank wasn't

Seeing George

capable of it. He picked up a chair and brandished it in front of him.

'You've brainwashed Violet and I want to know why!'

'No one has brainwashed anyone,' George said, backing away.

Slipping inside the doors, Violet immediately ran to stand between them. 'Frank, please don't fight!'

Frank looked at his wife's wan face and smacked the chair down in frustration. He paced a moment, then pointed a finger at George. 'You've been causing her problems at work for a couple of months, and the next thing I know she's come away with you for an evening – lying to me, telling me it's for work when her colleagues know nothing about it.'

Violet looked up. She hadn't thought about why Frank was here. But it made sense that the women from work had helped somehow.

'And the next thing I know,' Frank continued, yelling now, 'you've got your arms around her. Do you understand? I saw it. But instead of just dealing with me, she's telling me you're a dragon. Now you and I know better, but for some reason she doesn't seem to and I want an explanation.'

'I am a dragon.'

'For Christ's sake!' Frank shook his head in disgust. 'Just tell me the truth or you'll wish you never met me.'

'It is the truth.'

Frank dragged the chair away from both George and Violet. He was walking awkwardly, as though someone had kicked the backs of his knees in. Suddenly, he planted it down and sat on it, hands across his chest and shoved up under his armpits.

'Frank –' began Violet.

'Shut up, Violet.' Frank's voice rolled over hers. 'I'm sick of this dragon rubbish.'

'I'm from Ireland. A sea-dragon.' George was beginning to smirk.

'He has purple and greeen scales.' Violet choked on her words in her hurry to draw the atttention to herself. 'And he's taller than how you see him.'

Frank jeered at her. 'Can you even *hear* yourself? How is that possible, Violet? How can someone be taller than what they are?'

'I don't know. The same way you can't see his tail.'

Frank looked at George. 'I don't know what you've done to her, but you won't convince me of this bullshit.'

'I didn't convince her of anything. She saw me.'

'As a dragon?'

George nodded. Smiling.

Frank clenched his fists, but Violet held a hand out to her husband – beseechingly. 'I tried to tell you months ago. I just didn't know how. Didn't think you'd believe me. But I only learnt today about having dragon blood, I swear.' She walked hesitantly toward him. 'I only just found out that's possibly why we can't have children.'

As Frank looked at her, as he took in these words, the rage dropped from his face and he crumpled. 'Oh God,

Seeing George

that's what this is.' He covered his face with his hands.

Violet crouched in front of him.

'I wanted to talk to you about it,' Frank whispered hoarsely.

She put her hand on his knee, too concerned about his sudden deflation to try and make sense of what he was saying. 'I'm so sorry —.'

He lifted his head. 'No, Violet, listen. I'm the one who can't have children. Not you. We got a letter. That's why I took the job in Adelaide — to try and think things through. It's me who can't have children.'

The blood ran from her face.

'I'm the one who's sorry.' Frank lifted her hand to his cheek, crushing her fingers.

Violet stood. She couldn't breathe, felt as though she'd been punched in the chest. She pulled her hand from Frank's, but he grabbed her around the legs.

'But the hospital said they didn't know who —.'

He rose and tried to embrace her. 'They found something. I couldn't stand to tell you straight away, Vi. I just couldn't. I think I even hoped you'd see the letter yourself. And now I've caused this mess.'

She pushed away from him. 'No, this is different, Frank. What you're saying —. What you're saying is separate from George.'

'Not, it's not,' said George, startling them both.

'You shut up,' shouted Frank. 'You've preyed on her long enough.'

'Frank!'

'Love, he can see the connection himself; we can't have children and to cope you've invented some fantasy.'

'That's not what I meant at all,' said George, quietly. 'I meant perhaps she can have children – just not with you.'

Frank covered his eyes with a trembling hand, and Violet, after looking from one to the other, turned and ran out of the hall.

Frank went after her and when he saw her faltering at the bottom of the steps, led her to the ute. She resisted at first, but then collapsed into the passenger seat. He ran around to his side – as though afraid she might change her mind if left alone too long.

Violet stared blankly out the side window at George, who was walking down the steps. And as the engine started, he sat suddenly and wound his tail tightly around himself, looking at her.

That image took up all the room in her mind and by six o'clock, when the ute pulled into their driveway, she was exhausted.

Frank carried her straight into the bedroom. While she slipped into a nightgown, he fetched a hot-water bottle and a cup of tea. She could have screamed when she saw it. A blasted cup of tea. Still, she drank it because his hands shook with shame. Frank: her honest husband.

'I need to sleep.'

'Do you want me to stay on the couch?'

She shook her head. 'I need you to hold me.'

Seeing George

He grabbed her to him, bowing his head to her hair, and she felt his body shake. She'd always thought he was the strong one. Being older, being a man. But perhaps strength meant something else. She was too exhausted to support him and pulled away to unzip her dress.

He took off his clothes too. Padded around the bedroom, kicking away his boots, shutting the door. She was quiet by the time his cold body clambered in beside hers and although reluctant to touch him, allowed herself to be enfolded.

As he rubbed her back, his breath rasped gently in her ear, telling her how sorry he was, how this was going to be all right.

Somewhere in this nest of body heat Violet fell into a heavy, dreamless sleep, only disturbed when the early rays of sun hit her face. The curtains weren't pulled across all the way and she put a hand up to her eyes to shade them, but her mind was already racing.

'Frank.'

His breathing quickened as he roused himself to respond. Wrapping an arm around her, he pulled her closer, but as he properly woke, she felt him tense.

'Are you all right?'

The concern in his voice made her tremble. 'I'm worried about you.'

'Stuff and nonsense, me.' He wiped at his eyes and propped himself up on an elbow to better look at her. 'Now I know what you've been carrying around all this time on top of our —.'

She turned to him and they held each other.

'How about breakfast?' Suddenly Violet wanted to delay their talking and maintain this simpler feeling of closeness.

'First explain to me why you've been lying.'

His change in tone was such a shock that her temper flared. 'You lied to me!'

'We both know we can't have kids.'

'I *can.*'

He abruptly let her go and laid back, staring at the ceiling. She reached out to touch his cheek.

'I didn't mean that.'

He didn't reply.

'Why didn't you just show me the letter, Frank?'

'Why didn't you just tell me about him? I lied about something between us — you lied about another man.'

'I didn't lie about another *man.*'

He restrained himself from retorting.

She sat up, arms folded. 'I didn't know what to do. What was I going to say? I can see a dragon? I'm telling you now. Are you reacting any differently than you would have a couple of months ago?'

'If you hadn't gone away with him, yes.'

She briefly shut her eyes. 'I've already told you that nothing happened. I was trying to clear things up and I didn't think you would believe me.'

'Good. Because I won't believe what isn't true.'

'Even if you reckon there are no dragons, Frank, the problem is that I can see one.'

Seeing George

'Violet —.'

'Don't "Violet" me.'

Her husband looked at the soft skin on her face and neck. 'I think your dragon is just a way of avoiding the truth. I've seen the guy and he's in love with you and I need to know whether you're in love with him.'

She looked at him. 'I really see him as a dragon, Frank. I really do.'

He shut his eyes.

'Frank —?'

'This is insane, Violet. What else can you expect me to say?'

This was it then. The beginning of the world deciding she was mad. She tried to calm herself. Perhaps it would be best if she didn't fight it? She waited until he opened his eyes. 'I'll see a doctor.'

His thumb made small circles on her shoulder.

'If that's what you want, Frank, I'll see a doctor.'

Silence.

'Well, isn't that what you're suggesting?'

'No. We can fix it another way.'

'Like we'll fix you?'

He pushed her away in disbelief.

Her face reddened. 'We're not going to get anywhere by ourselves.'

23

George's coat, which had been flung over the back of the corner chair, smelled of the air outside. He'd been walking near a fire and the bitter smoke pierced the bedroom and left a woody residue on the chair cushion. Much nicer than body odours. Violet was in a far better mood now that she had her stratagem about not seeing George as a dragon. Evidently, she had learnt a few tricks over the years.

'Do you remember that doctor I saw?'

They had been silent for fifteen minutes or so and George turned toward her from the bedroom window, where he was standing with a saucer of leftover cake. 'Which doctor?'

'Very funny. The psychiatrist, Dr Fornet. Remember?'

'As much as I can remember someone I've never met.' He grinned at her. 'I read recently that in the 1950s, more

Australians spent time in a mental asylum than went to university.'

'Thank you very much for sharing that with me.' Violet shut her eyes. George and his mind for endless facts. Thank goodness he wasn't the type to press anything upon you, unless you asked first. Actually, he and Frank were similar in that way: capable of letting their thoughts remain thoughts. It was strange to consider how Frank and George were alike rather than different.

'Are you going to consult Dr Fornet about not being able to see me?' George plucked a few more sultanas from his now dried piece of fruitcake. His fingers were far too large for such a delicate activity, but he managed with considerable grace.

'Lord, no. He was eighty if he was a day back then. And I don't need any more doctors.'

'Good. I thought I might have the wrong Violet for a moment. Why did you cut your hair?'

She opened her eyes. The blue and pink cap had come loose, trailing down one side of her head onto the pillow and revealing knotted curls of frowsy brown and grey. She put a hand up and tried to poke the hair back into the knit. But it wouldn't go, so finally she threw the cap onto the bedside table.

'I got sick of it.'

George looked at her a moment and then turning back to his mangled piece of cake said, 'Of everything I think.'

Violet gave a harsh laugh. She didn't like the way he kept

inspecting her, making her self-conscious. If he didn't stop she'd get very peevish.

'Are you happy, George?'

He grinned, bits of cake stuck to his teeth.

'I mean without a wife? Or "partner" as they sadly call it these days?'

He returned to playing with the sultanas on the saucer.

'I can't imagine how you've gone all these years without —. Then again, Frank drives me barmy.'

George arranged the dried grapes into a small pile in the centre of the saucer, then knocked them over. Set them up. Flicked them over. Didn't answer.

There you go, thought Violet. George doesn't want to discuss his personal business so he stays silent. Doesn't have to demand from me that I stop asking, doesn't have to lay down any reasons why he doesn't want to get into it. Just remains silent. Sensitive. Frank doesn't understand the way George works at all.

She resumed looking at the ceiling and they stayed in the room together, without speaking, for half an hour. The sunlight moved across as it always did. George sat and read a bit from a small leather-bound book he carried in his shirt pocket, and Violet dozed, sleepy from the warmth.

The peace was ruptured when the back kitchen door slammed and Gretel's claws scraped on the floorboards.

George stood. 'I'll get going.'

'Stay.'

He fidgeted, brushing his coat, scratching his head.

Seeing George

Then he stopped suddenly. Stricken. 'What do I look like now?'

'Pardon?'

'What do you see if I'm not a dragon anymore?'

Violet put a hand up into her hair. 'Just a man, George.'

'You still here?' Frank appeared in the doorway.

'Which one of us?' asked Violet.

Frank rolled his eyes.

'George wants to know what he looks like.'

'Mirror's in the bathroom.' Frank pointed as though George hadn't been coming to the house for years.

'No, no, tell him what *you* see,' corrected Violet.

Frank leaned against the doorframe, his spine not as straight as it used to be, inspecting George. 'You're barely starting to get grey hair.'

'Just a touch here and there,' Violet added.

George looked over at her, inviting her to continue, but when she didn't speak, Frank said, 'You've still got good skin. Unweathered. You're a bit like that Dorian Gray, for my books.'

Violet slapped the doona cover. 'Stop speaking rot, Frank. You haven't aged much, George, that's all. Anyway, we're not interested in the exterior around here, are we Frank?'

'Not unless I have a corn that needs attention.'

Violet saw that he was waiting for a laugh, but George had stopped speaking and she knew her face was strained with emotion, so she shook her head.

Then, in a manner typical of him, Frank clapped his

hands together. 'May as well come and help out with dinner then, George,' he said, before leaving the bedroom.

Violet managed a smile.

24

George didn't think a doctor was a good idea either. Violet was eating lunch with him on Monday, having convinced Frank to let her return to work. She had argued that not fronting up to Spatler & Smith would only make George far more important than he really was. Besides, after what had happened she couldn't rest until she knew he was all right.

She waited for him out the front of the elevators, doing her best to ignore the curious stares and whispers of Betsy, Lila and Edward. She had no idea exactly what they knew — Frank hadn't told her how he'd come to follow her — but from the way they were carrying on, she guessed they knew enough.

George dropped his briefcase when he noticed her, and turned a very pale shade of purple. But he regained some of his colour upon learning that she was fine, although they had to wait until lunchtime to speak properly.

'You have to forgive Frank, George.'

He selected a hot roast beef sandwich from the cafeteria's *bain marie*.

She didn't pay attention to what she picked up, just concentrated on George. 'I'm so sorry. It was unthinkable. But he was very upset.'

George turned his back to walk to a table and waited until Violet sat down. 'I want to know what happened.'

Violet looked down at her hands. 'We're still talking.'

'He doesn't believe you.'

'Of course not.'

George clumsily picked at the cling wrap until she took the sandwich and unpeeled it for him.

'What did he think he was going to accomplish by waving a chair about?'

'I lied to him.'

'The Council hand me their decision this weekend — how's he going to behave if he doesn't like that?'

Realising that George wasn't listening, that he was expecting her to placate him, Violet's tone changed. 'This has to end,' she said firmly.

'I quite agree. We can't be putting up with —.'

'I'm going to see a doctor.'

George stopped stripping the crusts from his sandwich and stared at her.

Seeing George

'I think it will do us both good. All good.' She didn't look at him.

'After everything that's happened? Everything you know? You're not sick, Violet. Don't listen to him.'

She scrunched up her napkin and pushed away her untouched sandwich. 'It was my idea.'

The day she was to visit the doctor, Violet made sure Frank collected her from the office so everyone could see her greet him with a wide smile. But Frank didn't even take his hat off. He put a protective arm about her, kept a solemn face and ushered her to the lift. Then he sat morosely in Dr Buchanan's waiting room during the first part of her consultation.

The doctor gave her a thorough physical examination and she laughed when he pressed the white stick against the back of her tongue. But it was a harsh laugh. It stopped her from gagging and it stopped her from crying. When he removed the stick and asked whether she was all right, Violet wanted to scream that she would be just fine if only everyone would stop asking her that, but she smiled and nodded and hopped down from the examining table.

Frank was called in then, and they held hands while Dr Buchanan asked her a series of questions. She had been unsettled by her husband's insistence that they not use their family doctor; he believed the situation called for more discretion and expertise. Dr Buchanan had a snake of letters after his name and wore a three-piece suit. But she didn't like the way he deferred to Frank rather than herself.

'Do you or have you ever heard voices?' he asked.

Violet looked puzzled.

The doctor brought his fingers together in a point. 'Violet, the voices might instruct you to do things, like call George a dragon, for instance.'

'No,' she said, hotly.

'Have you seen ghosts or other spiritual apparitions?'

'No.'

'When did you first begin to believe that George was a dragon?'

'I didn't begin to believe, he was a dragon from the first moment I saw him.'

Dr Buchanan wrote for a while and Violet glanced at Frank. Although he held her hand, he was looking away — staring at the desk legs. She gave his hand a squeeze and he eventually looked at her, but couldn't meet her eyes.

'So there were no other dragons before George?'

Violet shook her head. 'What about the fact that George considers *himself* to be a dragon?'

'Yes. Very interesting. Now your husband mentioned your father died. What age were you?'

Violet glanced at Frank: he and Dr Buchanan must have had quite a telephone conversation. 'Seventeen. What's that got to do with this?'

Dr Buchanan adjusted his glasses and looked at her a moment before answering. 'Could be nothing, could be significant, Violet. You might be compensating in some way. We're very complex creatures.'

'You're not even entertaining the possibility that I might be right.'

'No one else can corroborate your story.' Dr Buchanan sighed gently.

'George can.'

The doctor smiled at Frank. 'Those aren't odds I'd bet on.'

Frank straightened in his seat. 'What do we do now?'

'Wait and see.'

'Wait and see what?'

'Whether it gets better.'

Violet said, 'You don't know what to do, do you?'

Dr Buchanan looked down at his pad. 'You're not the first, Violet.'

'But, if I'm not the first –.'

'Not the first to see flying saucers, or hear strange commands, or feel hands on you that aren't there, or any manner of things. And in most instances, until there is a sign of danger – to yourself – for example, a failure to function, prepare food, shower and the like – or a danger to others,' he looked at Frank, 'then we'll just keep a close eye on you.'

Violet brought a handkerchief up to her nose and closed her eyes. For the first time in months she wondered about her sanity. Maybe it made no sense that George colluded with her, but Frank had his opinion on that part. If there really were so many other people who had delusions, surely the doctor was right? She began to shake.

Dr Buchanan came around the front of his desk and took one of her hands in his, patting it tenderly. 'I wouldn't worry too much, Violet. Either you'll find this will go away of its own accord – perhaps when you have children –.' At her horrified expression, he stopped.

'We can't have children,' said Frank, flatly.

Dr Buchanan swung around to make a few more notes. 'I wasn't aware. I am sorry. However, I still maintain it will cease of its own accord, or it will progress and we'll assist you with all the marvels of modern medicine. We are beginning to understand the mind, you know.'

'But what am I supposed to do?'

'Well, can you still work when seeing this fellow?'

She nodded.

'And do you still feel happy with Frank and want to continue your marriage?'

She nodded, glancing at her husband. He wasn't looking at her.

'Then let's just keep things as normal as possible,' said Dr Buchanan. 'Unless something else happens.'

'Like what?' asked Violet.

'There you go again,' said the doctor. 'If you're going to follow my advice you'll do better to just relax, not start anticipating what *might* happen. Now why don't you hop out into the waiting area so I can have a quick word with Frank?'

Seeing George

'He's my husband, not my guardian.'

But Dr Buchanan simply smiled and waited until she left the room, then he closed the door behind her.

All the way down in the lift from Dr. Buchanan's, walking to the ute and even for the first five minutes or so of the trip back home, Violet waited. Finally, when she couldn't bear it anymore, she slid sideways in her seat and said, 'Tell me.'

Frank reached across to the glove compartment and hunted out a soft packet of cigarettes without taking his eyes off the road. He motioned for her to pluck one out for him and she did so with wide eyes because she'd never seen him smoke. Clamping it between his lips, he burnt the end with the glowing orange tip of the ute's cigarette lighter and inhaled.

'He thinks you're under some kind of stress. Thinks you should take a holiday.'

'I can't take a holiday.'

Frank nodded and tapped his cigarette out the window — ending up with ash all over his collar because the wind blew it straight back. He handed the cigarette to Violet so he could dust off the ashes and she promptly ground it into the ashtray.

Neither of them spoke another word until the ute was parked outside their house and Frank had cut the engine. 'He thinks you might like a rest in a hospital.'

'That's what he meant by holiday?' Her eyes filmed. 'What do you think?'

'I don't know what to think. Doctors of his sort probably recommend patients to psychiatrists all the time. But on the other hand there's what you say you believe. And he's got years of experience on the both of us. I don't know what to think.' Frank's voice was expressionless.

Violet opened her handbag, took out her damp handkerchief and loudly blew her nose.

'What are you going to do?' asked Frank.

'It's just "me" now, is it?'

'That's not what I meant.'

'We'll talk when you get back.' Frank had to check his site had been locked up for the night: he had left early to collect Violet for the doctor's appointment. She opened the ute door to get out.

'Violet, we have to think this through properly.'

She pulled the door shut again. 'Dr Buchanan says to wait and see whether I can accept things the way they are – in other words get rid of my "vision". Yet George and Peter tell me that accepting things the way they are means seeing George.'

'Peter?'

'My knitting club,' said Violet. 'Don't ask. Just don't ask. I see a dragon, Frank. I know it sounds insane. I can hardly believe the words as they come out of my mouth. I can't begin to imagine what they sound like to you.' She stopped a moment. 'But I do see him.' She cupped a hand to her mouth, fearing that she was about to vomit. It took her several minutes of swallowing to stop panicking. Then she sat back against the car seat.

'Are you asking me to believe you?'

She didn't answer.

Frank twisted the end of his tie. 'I believe that you see him and I believe that something's not right. With you.'

'I should take this "holiday" then?'

He shook his head.

'You can't tell me you think I'm crazy and then tell me not to get help, Frank.' She looked across to him, but he said nothing. 'You think I should just banish George from my life?'

Animated, he turned towards her. 'Now there's an idea.'

'That won't change anything.'

'It might.'

Violet gritted her teeth. 'It'll just mean there's a bloke out there who, if I saw him, would appear like a dragon to me.'

Frank closed his eyes. 'That's not all it would mean.'

'It's settled then,' she said. 'I'm going to the hospital.' In her anger, she suddenly felt much more in control. 'What else did Dr. Buchanan say? Did he have a recommendation for a hospital?'

'Yes.'

She deflated again. Had to muster all her strength to get out of the ute, and once on the curb, she bent down to speak to Frank through the open window. 'I'll bring my holidays forward at work. Take leave as of this Friday, that's only three more days. You arrange things with the doctor.' She looked away. 'The sooner I get this over with, the better.' She pushed herself away from the vehicle and walked up their concrete path.

Frank watched her for a moment, then took a fresh cigarette from the soft pack and lit it before pulling away.

Inside, Violet walked straight to the bathroom mirror to look at her reflection, staring to unmask any physiological signs of madness. All she saw were the beginning of crow's feet and confused, brown eyes.

At lunchtime the next day, George stood in front of Violet's desk and asked whether she would mind eating with him. And she exhaled through her nose and said, 'Listen George, why don't we do nothing for a while? No lunch. Just until everything settles down. All right?'

'Why?'

Violet shoved the typewriter carriage across, 'Because.'

She could feel rather than see that he wanted to ask some more questions but she kept typing and worked straight through lunch. And after work, seeing George in front of the heavy wooden revolving doors, she hurried away. Said that Frank was waiting to pick her up and would he mind please leaving her alone. George stopped trying to keep pace with her and simply stood, briefcase in hand, watching her retreat.

Seeing George

On Friday night after work he invited her to cocktail hour. 'We don't even have to talk,' he said.

Violet tied her chiffon scarf over her hair and waited until everyone was out of the office. 'I'm not coming.' At the look of sadness on his face, she added, 'Things are a mess right now, George. Frank and I —.'

'Are you sure you know what you're doing?'

She looked up at him. 'I'm not sure of anything.'

He smiled a little at that.

'But I have to let things calm down.'

He nodded.

'Go to drinks. The others'll be wondering where you are.'

She walked over to the coat rack and plucked off his hat, tossing it to him in a burst of playfulness. He allowed her to shoo him out of the room.

But when she heard the elevator doors shut, she let her shoulders drop and walked back to her desk to gather her things. She felt so tired.

· 25 ·

Violet swatted away a dozy winter fly and pushed herself into a more upright position in the bed. She had taken the opportunity to get to the bathroom and wash her face while Frank and George made dinner. She still looked a fright; no wonder George had reacted badly.

There had been a lot of unnecessary banging about in the kitchen for the last little while and she'd been tempted to pad up there. But Frank called out that they were only minutes away now, and sure enough she could hear them clopping down the hallway.

She was hungry. But when Frank set the tray down over her legs she pursed her lips in disapproval. Stew. He knew she hated the big chunks of lamb and carrot. It was difficult for her to chew and the meaty smell hung around the room for hours afterwards.

Seeing George

She trailed a spoon of gravy over the rice intending to eat just that. But Frank sat a small bowl of roasted capsicum, corn kernels and peas on the tray as well.

'Thought I'd include meat, just in case you changed your mind which you've a tendency to do. But I did some vegetables too.'

She struggled to contain her emotions as he brushed away some of her stray hair. She wished it was silky under his fingers like it used to be, but he didn't seem to mind.

George took up position in the corner chair, insisting he was fine with just a plate and no tray, and Frank actually hopped into the lounge room to fetch himself a stool. Violet looked at the two of them, embarrassed to feel herself the centre of their attention.

'I should have come down to eat.'

Frank grinned as he placed his stool at the foot of her bed.

'I made a bit of a mess in the kitchen.' George's emerald scales flushed darker. 'I usually have larger pots.'

Frank sat forward, pointing his fork at George. 'The poor sod was only doing a bit of reheating. You should see it, love; Gretel's having a field day working her tongue from one end of the room to the other.'

Violet looked at her husband and raised her eyebrows — letting him know she was tickled he'd had such a good time with George. But he frowned and speared some meat, wiping it in gravy before lifting it to his mouth.

When they'd finished, George collected their plates and

sat them on the floor near his chair and Frank eased back on his stool, hands behind his head. But without the eating there was an awkward silence, broken only by the drone of the fly charging the window.

George suddenly cleared his throat. 'Can I just say, now that we're all sitting here and since Violet can't see me as a dragon anymore and,' he inclined his head towards Frank, 'you never have, can I just say that it doesn't matter. I thought it would. I thought I would feel much worse than I do. But really it's all right.' He nodded his head emphatically.

Frank looked at Violet, but she knew he wouldn't say anything while George was present. Instead he stood and hooked the stool under one arm, then reached his free hand forward to shake George's hand for the second time that day. 'That's terrific, George.'

'Where are you running away to, Frank?'

'Got to fix the kitchen, love. Then pick up Charlotte.'

He left the bedroom.

'I knocked over the saucepan rack in the kitchen and the clock fell off the wall.' George actually looked sheepish.

'Not like you to be clumsy.'

'Lot of strange things today, Violet.'

She didn't want to pursue that observation, so held out her arm, indicating that he should help her up. 'Let's watch the sunset.'

In the lounge room George lifted a cashmere blanket at each corner and as Violet settled into the recliner, tucked it around her knees.

Seeing George

'On with the show.'

He seated himself on the leather couch, the closest seat to her, and any conversation was momentarily halted by the squawk of roosting birds in the trees outside the window.

'They go on, don't they?' George's tail unfurled along the couch. He much preferred them to ordinary seats.

'Don't you like it?'

'I like it when they sing, not when they harp on to each other about enough space and how cold it is and who's responsibility it is to wake them all up.'

Violet pulled the blanket a bit higher and the pair of them didn't say another word. They watched as the fiery orb slipped from their view, leaving behind a feeling of tranquillity. Then they sat in the early dark, drinking in the slightly heavier night air and listening to the sounds of dogs echoing each other.

The room was almost dark before George spoke. 'It must be odd to not see me properly anymore.'

Violet's cheeks pinked. She hid her hands beneath the cashmere and looked at him. The whites of his eyes were beginning to glow faintly, as they did in the dark.

'Anyway,' he said at her silence, 'I enjoyed the sunset.'

'Just pollution in the air making a spectacle.'

He snorted. 'More like natural wonder.'

'Always a silver-lining for you, isn't there, George?'

'There's no point to anything otherwise. I thought it was marvellous.'

'Sometimes marvellous things have a bitterness right at their centre, where you can't see it.'

George stared at her.

She shook her head a little. 'All I meant was that a sunset is just a ball of gas on fire. Nothing special about it.'

To her great surprise, George began laughing. She watched him, puzzled. But it took him quite a while to stop. And even then he kept grinning.

'We've known each other a long time Violet Rolden and even if I entertained the idea that you were unable to see me anymore, you winced when Frank put the stool leg down on my tail.' He paused. 'And you're in a dark mood. I don't know what you're up to, what you've been up to from the first moment I arrived today, but you're not doing a very good job of hiding the fact that you are up to it.'

Violet took a deep breath, inclined to tell him to mind his own business. But her chest weighed with sadness rather than anger. 'I'm in a fix with Frank.'

George nodded.

'And I don't know how to get out of it.'

He nodded again.

'Stop being so agreeable; it involves not seeing you.'

George frowned and Violet could have bitten her tongue for telling. She picked at the beginnings of a hangnail to avoid looking at him. 'If I knew why, I'd have half a chance at talking him through it, but he won't open his mouth.'

'He doesn't want you to see me as a dragon after all this time?'

Seeing George

'He doesn't want me to see you at all. Anymore.'

He sat back and Violet left her finger alone and waited in the black of the room now that she'd managed to tell him the truth. But he said nothing. 'That's your useless advice, then?'

'By George, it is.' His grin was gone.

'Splendid.'

'What do you want me to do, fight about it?' George looked down at his large shoes. 'I guess he wants you all to himself.'

'That's what he says.'

'I didn't think I took up much.'

Violet shut her eyes. She shouldn't have told him about Frank's pettiness. That was a mistake. She yanked at the blanket, untucking it, and tried to wrench the wooden handle that lowered the recliner. George let her go for a while, then reached across to lever it himself. Standing up, he offered his arm and she pulled herself upright. Small repetitions.

'I want us to continue, Violet.'

She couldn't look at him. Watched as his tail snipped the floor.

'Violet —.'

'Don't. Please.' Her voice wavered. 'I don't know what's going on in his stupid mind. But I have to abide by it. He's my husband.'

George let go of her then and took off his hat, playing with the hatband. He took a few steps toward the door and opened his mouth several times, but he ended up shaking his head instead.

Violet leaned her hands against the chair back. 'It's not you. Give me some time to sort it out.' She tried to think of how to soften the blow. 'I'm sure it's just a muddle because of my illness –.'

'I don't want to hear about it.'

'Oh, you never want to hear about it, George.' She scowled. 'You left the country when I had a collapsed lung. And you insisted on getting me walking far too early after my pneumonia. Frank was livid.'

George shook his head, shuffling his hat from one hand to the other.

'Well, this time I had an operation. While you were in Mexico, I had an operation and they found a tumour. This time I can't just walk it off.'

'He's never really liked our friendship, has he?'

Tears flooded Violet's eyes. Her back had started to ache. 'Are you listening? I'm telling you all this because we don't have much time.'

She watched as George dropped his snout, and his ears twirled. But he didn't respond. Why was he avoiding talking about this?

'Frank does like you,' she said, finally. Tired now. 'You'd be wrong to think otherwise.'

'No.' George gave a terrible smile. 'He doesn't. But he sure had me fooled.'

Violet raised a shaking hand to her mouth. She could

Seeing George

barely make him out for the tears, and when she wiped them away she saw that he was on the other side of the doorframe.

'George—.'

'I'll see myself out.' He turned awkwardly and walked down the corridor.

· 26 ·

Dr Buchanan had referred Violet into the care of the psychiatrist, Dr Fornet. But it was a Mrs Staynor who met Frank and Violet at the hospital door just as the sun was setting. She was a middle-aged woman dressed in stark white, whose very gentile manner was at odds with her severely drawn bun of grey hair. She said she'd been looking out for them because she liked to greet people rather than have them come through reception for their first visit. This put all manner of questions into Violet's mind, but her tongue felt like lead.

Mrs Staynor sat with them in a waiting room area furnished with plastic chairs — like those Violet wanted for the kitchen — and asked for some personal history. Violet clutched Frank's hand as she explained that she wasn't allergic to any medications as far as she knew; no

Seeing George

one in her family had a mental illness; and she only had a small compact mirror in her bag.

Mrs Staynor took the completed form and the compact over to a receptionist's window. Violet asked Frank why they took the mirror and why they needed to know about allergies to medications? Dr Buchanan hadn't said she would be taking medicine.

Frank looked down at his shoes, avoiding Violet's strained face, and told her it was probably just standard procedure. Violet wondered how on earth he would know, but she bit her lip as Mrs Staynor returned.

'I've handed over all your details. You're only in here for a week of observation, all right?'

Frank and Violet nodded in unison.

Mrs Staynor picked up Violet's suitcase and wouldn't yield it despite Frank's insistence. She headed off down a corridor. 'If you'll follow me then.'

They walked through a set of double doors along an empty hallway. Everything in the long corridor was very clean. It was as though there were no people at all; only walls and linoleum and small glass windows in doors that remained shut. One of the fluorescent lights kept buzzing on and off and Violet squeezed Frank's hand.

Mrs Staynor unlocked a door on the left of the corridor and held it open. Violet entered first. Everything in the room was a light blue or grey: the linen, the bedside drawers, the walls. And her face, she supposed. Suddenly it all felt very real and Violet had to keep reminding herself that the visit was voluntary; Dr Buchanan said she could leave any time she wanted.

Frank gripped the rim of his hat with both hands, and didn't take his eyes off Mrs Staynor, who sat the suitcase on the bed to unstrap it and pop the catches.

'You can pack your things in these drawers.' The elder woman straightened and looked at her watch. 'Dinner is in half an hour. Keep walking down the corridor until you reach the last door on your right. You'll hear the other girls going. Now, I'll let you say your goodbyes. Mr Rolden, please inform the receptionist when you're leaving. I've signed you in this time, but you'll have to sign out yourself. All right?'

Then she turned and with a rapid kick of her foot released the door catch, leaving it to swing closed behind her.

Violet sank onto her bed beside the open suitcase and put her face in her hands.

Frank shifted the suitcase onto the floor so he could sit beside her. He kissed the top of her forehead, but as she leaned into him a bell sounded. She immediately straightened and tucked her blouse into her skirt.

Frank stood and looked out the window. 'It's quite a garden,' he said, so she stood to look too. Some night lights were on, illuminating the corrugated bark of an old elm spreading high and wide in the centre of a perfectly manicured lawn. Violet could make out the muted colours of flowerbeds further away. It all looked magical under the light.

Seeing George

'I'll get some knitting done.' She began to unpack her clothes into the small drawers. She would have to leave her shoes in the suitcase. 'I wonder why they don't have a closet?'

There didn't seem to be a logical explanation and for some reason this distressed them both.

Frank put on his hat and opened the door. They both started as a young woman walked past, even though she didn't give them a sideways glance. They stuck their heads around the doorframe, watching. She was going to the dining room.

Violet pulled her cardigan tighter. 'I'd better go and eat. I don't want to begin this all wrong.'

'I'm sorry, Violet.'

She looked up at him.

'Sorry that you're in here because of me.'

'Frank. For the last time, me seeing George doesn't have anything to do with that.'

He nodded and jerked forward to kiss her dryly on the mouth. She hugged him, then just as abruptly let him go. Didn't watch as he made his way back through the double doors.

She touched up her lipstick and hair, peering into a square of buffed metal near the door handle before hurrying down to the dining room. This would be all right. She would treat the week as an adventure, that's all.

Pleased to hear the familiar noises of scraping cutlery and murmuring voices as she approached, she relaxed even further as she saw the women all looked quite normal –

different ages, but socialising with each other as though this was a hostel.

No one quite met her eyes, but a few acknowledged her. She chose a seat at a table with the young woman who had walked past her room, and soon a plate of cold ham and hot vegetables was placed in front of her. She picked up her splade, suddenly quite hungry.

'Hello, I'm Gracie.'

Violet looked up with a full mouth to see the young woman looking at her. She wore a heavy-knit blue jumper and had her hands under the table. Violet smiled and gestured with her fork to her mouth. Gracie smiled too.

'The woman who was in your room had to be taken up to the locked ward, North 9.'

Violet looked down at her plate.

'I don't know how serious it was. One night she was there and the next morning she wasn't.'

Violet struggled to swallow the food in her mouth, washing it down with some water. Finally, she said, 'I'm Violet.'

'How long are you here?' her dinner companion asked.

Violet shrugged and pushed the peas around on her plate. 'A week.'

Gracie grinned again and this time Violet noticed her stained yellow teeth. The younger woman leant across the table. 'No one only stays for a week. They told you observation, right?'

Violet nodded.

Seeing George

'There's always some reason for you to stay longer. Gosh, you could put a perfectly normal girl in here and they'd find reason for her to stay longer. I've been on the open ward now for three months.'

Mrs Staynor came up behind Gracie, laying a hand on her shoulder. Gracie flinched slightly, but the older woman was looking at Violet. 'How are you getting on, Violet? People being friendly I hope?'

Violet's eyes were filmed with tears, but she nodded obediently. Gracie watched this with a smirk on her face, and when Mrs Staynor walked away, she whispered, 'Never let them know you're not all right. That's the trick to staying on the open ward.'

Violet turned her attention back to her food. Her stomach was churning with fear but she knew that if she didn't eat she would feel even more tired and emotional. While spooning up the meat and vegetables and avoiding looking at Gracie, she sensed another woman sitting down at the table. The stranger said hello. Violet didn't know whether to answer – not sure she was up to it.

But the woman said, 'I thought I'd introduce myself, now that Gracie has no doubt given you the gothic tour. My name's Kathleen.'

Violet looked up in time to see a mixed expression of anger and admiration cross Gracie's face. Kathleen, a redheaded woman, probably not yet thirty, had a pleasant face. Tired around the eyes.

'I'm Violet.'

'Pleased to meet you. You're in Amelia's old room. She's a psychotic. Gets shunted back to the locked ward when the rooms down here are full.'

Violet held her cutlery still. 'Why are the rest of you – us – in here?'

Kathleen laughed, and suddenly Violet noticed that a few of the women at the other tables were also laughing and talking loudly.

'Oh, nervous breakdowns.' Kathleen sprinkled salt over her ham. 'Or some scandal with money or a baby. Some women here are very highly strung and can't walk outside without getting hysterical. Others are just the opposite, and don't hardly have the energy to get out of bed. And some, like Gracie, don't want to eat. No one seems to know why – least of all Gracie.'

Gracie gave a shy smile from underneath long eyelashes. She'd pulled her hands into her jumper cuffs, stunting them. 'What about you, Violet?' she asked.

Violet looked at the two new faces and took a deep breath. 'I see a dragon.'

'Where?' asked Gracie, looking up at the corners of the ceiling, as though trying to spy it for herself.

'Everyone else sees him as a man.'

Kathleen raised her eyebrows. 'That's difficult. Is he your father or something?'

Violet shook her head. 'I met him at work.'

Gracie put her fingers up to her mouth. 'Does he think you're mad?'

Seeing George

'No.' Violet's eyes welled with tears. 'He thinks he's a dragon too.' Then she looked down at her plate and began to cry in earnest.

Kathleen put an arm around her and waved Gracie away. The two of them took a cup of tea back to Violet's room after dinner. It wasn't allowed, but Kathleen knew how to smuggle the hot liquid without drawing attention.

To take her mind off things, Kathleen told Violet about the others. About Molly's habit of dipping her clothes on her toes six times before putting them on, and about how Amy insisted that one of the day nurses smooth a vanishing cream into her hands each morning but otherwise yelled if someone even accidentally brushed up against her.

The way Kathleen explained it, these were just habits. In the everyday world no one noticed, but in here, against the stark white walls, the mannerisms seemed more frightening than they actually were.

They talked through the bell, which Kathleen explained signalled bed-time, and they were still talking when the lights automatically switched off. The moon and the outside light laid a perfect white frost over all the plants.

It was very peaceful, just the occasional echo in the hallway, until Kathleen suddenly said, 'No.'

Violet looked at her, waiting for an explanation, but the older woman brought her hands up to hold her head, continuing to loudly say, 'No. No, I won't. Go away.'

Violet reached a hand over to rub her back, but Kathleen

sprang from the bed yelling as she ran from the room. Violet was relieved to see that Mildred, one of the senior nurses, was striding up the corridor.

'She's just saying "No" all the time,' said Violet worrying a button on her cardigan. 'But we weren't even having a conversation.'

'Go back to your room.'

'I want to know if she's –.'

'Now.' Mildred barked the instruction and Violet uncertainly shuffled back up the corridor. Mildred entered Kathleen's room and shut the door. Kathleen could be heard yelling for quite a while. Every time it seemed she had stopped it would begin again.

It was impossible to sleep after that. Violet sat upright, blood rushing, every time she heard a strange noise. There were no locks on the inside of their doors and the broken light kept buzzing on and off, casting ghostly shadows through the small square of glass. She had to force herself to stay lying down. But her eyelids kept jumping; so finally she let herself lie awake and alert.

The next morning the dining room was subdued. Everyone was nervous about what had happened with Kathleen, but the nurses weren't allowed to answer questions. Gracie didn't want to talk about it either, so Violet let it go. She ate cereal then eggs, trying not to mind as Gracie watched her every mouthful. In the end Violet pushed the basket of toast towards her, but the younger woman promptly sat on her hands.

Seeing George

'Won't you have to eat before they let you out?'
Gracie shrugged. 'What time is your first appointment?'
'Ten.'
'You'll have to talk about when things first got strange, and whether you think it is strange.'
Violet nodded and gulped at her tea.
Gracie regarded her. 'Do you?'
'I don't know anymore.'
And she said the same thing when Dr Fornet asked the question.
'Well,' he said, 'that sounds to me as though you're avoiding answering.' Violet shrank back into the oversized chair. Dr Fornet had perfect white teeth, which she had only glimpsed twice because he didn't smile very often. He was bald, quite tall and very old. Hundreds of years old, it seemed to Violet. When he shook her hand at the start of the session, she had been amazed at the smoothness of his creased skin.
'Violet?'
'I don't know what I think about seeing George. I honestly don't.'
He put down his pen and sat back in his chair, rocking a little. 'Then this is what we will have to discover because it clearly serves a purpose for you, and we must find out what that purpose is.'
Violet had no idea what that meant.
'Because you are initially here for a week only, I want to see you every day. And every day I'd like us to have more

conversations about how you felt at first seeing George, and how you feel now. For example, when did you decide George would be his name?'

For what felt like the thousandth time, Violet said, 'He was introduced to me that way. And when I first saw him I screamed.'

Dr Fornet leaned over his notepad, writing for a good five minutes. 'Why did you scream?'

'Because I saw a dragon.'

'Does that seem sensible to you?'

Violet looked at her hands. Did he mean seeing the dragon or screaming? 'I don't know,' she said finally.

Dr Fornet had her look at some pictures of strange shapes. A Rorschach test, he said. She was supposed to talk about whatever came into her mind after seeing the ink picture. Perhaps what the shape reminded her of or made her feel.

The first one looked like a hat. He wondered whose hat it looked like. She frowned and said it was Frank's. The next one didn't look like anything much. The only thing she could think of was a meal she had dropped on the floor once, which led her to say that she really wasn't a good cook.

'Does Frank mind?'

Violet squirmed. 'I'm sure he does, but he doesn't say so.'

'And why do you think that is?'

'He doesn't want to hurt my feelings. He knows I try.'

'Do you think he often doesn't express how he feels about things to protect you?'

Seeing George

Violet sat up, surprised. It seemed the usual thing couples did, not a sign of problems. She said she didn't know. Dr Fornet sat back in his chair and nodded. They went through the next few images and each time, to Violet's alarm, she related the picture to Frank in some way.

At the end of their session the doctor said she was making excellent progress. He wanted her to think about her marriage with Frank because it probably had something to do with why she saw George as a dragon. He said she might be allowing herself to imagine any other men as 'beasts' in order to remain faithful. Or she might be viewing the dragon in Frank outside of him, afraid that if she saw his anger or ferocity over things that annoyed him, it would be intolerable.

'Maybe, Violet,' Dr Fornet spoke with his eyes shut, 'Frank is denying his feelings and you are bringing them to the surface for him. Do you think that's possible?'

'I don't know.'

Dr Fornet opened his eyes. 'I also want you to think about the fact that anytime I ask you a difficult question, perhaps a disturbing question, you tell me you don't have an answer. You do have an answer, Violet. And when you tell me you don't, you're not wanting to face it. Can you see this?'

· 27 ·

When Frank's key worked the front lock to let Charlotte in, Violet was sitting high in her bed against some pillows. Her nightie sat askew and her hair was wild: her attempts at toilet depended on hands that betrayed her emotion. Alone in the house for the past half hour, she had cried and yelled at the walls, unable and unwilling to contain her grief at what she had just done to George.

But right now, she had to appear calm. She only had Charlotte for ten minutes or so and wanted to make an apology to her.

Then, after her niece left, she would tell her husband she would *not* stop seeing George. And not for her own sake: but because it was obvious that George simply wouldn't cope. This afternoon he hadn't even been able to discuss it.

She settled her minty teeth back in her mouth. Even

Seeing George

with her preparations she couldn't help her chest pounding at the sound of the young girl struggling down the corridor with her string bag full of goods. It must have been her black mood over Frank's request that made her treat her little darling so badly.

When Charlotte saw her aunt she hung back, unsure about whether to stop with her. Violet held out a hand, obliging the child to move into the room, closer to the bed, but Charlotte hoisted the bag of biscuits up on to the little space Violet had patted.

'Where's Frank, love?'

'Checking for mail.'

'This late? Goodness me.' Despite not feeling disposed toward her husband, Violet was grateful he had sense enough to give her some time alone with the girl. 'Did you pick up some Butternut Snaps?'

Her niece edged back towards the door, unwilling to be drawn into any old banter.

'Do you want to talk about earlier, love?'

Big eyes peered at the floor from under heavy blond locks. 'It's like an accident.'

'Is that what Frank said?'

Her niece nodded.

Violet heard Frank closing the front door. 'Take the bag into the kitchen, poppet. And when you come back, I've got a surprise for you.'

The young girl headed off as Frank waltzed into the bedroom, hands in pockets. 'I take it George is gone?'

Violet had never noticed how large Frank's nose was. Or perhaps his cheeks were looking gaunt. Whatever it was, it wasn't attractive. 'Bring me the photo album so I can go through it with Charlotte.' Frustrated that even when she was furious with him, she still depended on him, the best she could manage was to be civil.

He fetched it out from her dresser drawer and opened it. 'Your cousins were a noisy-looking lot.'

Charlotte came back to the bedroom and ran to her uncle to see the pictures. But Frank carried the album over to Violet and then set up the corner chair beside the bed, so Charlotte could see. He petted his niece's head and reminded them he'd be running her home soon. 'Otherwise your mother'll have a fit, you being out on a school night.'

Violet waited for him to leave, then eased herself up enough to grab the silver hand mirror from the bedside table. She held it up and tapped her bent finger on the silvered glass. 'See the black marks here, pet.'

Charlotte leaned forward as she struggled to separate the black scarification from the reflection of the room's objects.

'Are those marks on your face?'

Charlotte looked again, then shook her head.

'Most things in the world don't have anything to do with you.'

Her niece looked at her blankly.

'When bad things happen, it's not you, love.' The chit still didn't understand a word she was saying. 'I'm trying

Seeing George

to say sorry about what happened today, Lottie. Sometimes I get cranky for no good reason.'

The young girl turned to look at her aunt's face. 'Was your stomach hurting?'

Violet's breath caught at the concern in her niece's voice. Who told her? 'Did you think I was ill this afternoon, Charlotte?'

The young girl looked down at the photo album.

'Oh, darling.' Violet put an arm around the little shoulders and Charlotte turned to hug her aunt. The small body smelt of fruity shampoo and grass. So soft and young. She shouldn't have to think about her aunt not being well. 'I was just playing, sweetheart. But I won't do it again when I know you're visiting, all right?'

'Yes.'

Violet kissed the silky hair. 'Now don't fuss over me or I might miss you too much when you go home.'

'Okay.' Charlotte disentangled herself and sat back properly on the chair.

Violet dabbed at her eyes and then pushed the mirror onto the doona. 'I can't believe I haven't shown you these before, Lottie. It's high-time you saw your mum's side of the family.'

Opening the album she began leading her niece through the photographs of their recent ancestry. Most of the various great aunts and cousins and so forth were dressed in dark colours that appeared black, as portraiture had been considered a formal business. It was a treat to talk about her mother and father again. Violet could barely remember her grandparents on either side, but she pointed out that Charlotte had her great-grandmother's thick, blond hair. Everyone had said Violet took after her grandmother too: same strong spirit. Just different coloured hair.

'They all look stiff.'

'That's the way we took photographs back then. But they danced and sang just like you. My Pa was always singing or whistling. Haven't I ever told you that?'

'No.'

'What have I told you?'

The young girl shrugged.

Violet shuffled the pages of the photo album, then pointed to a sepiaed print of a young girl sitting primly with a porcelain doll. 'Who's that?'

'I don't know.'

'That's me. That's me when —.' Violet prised the photograph from the pages of the album and turned it over to inspect what her mother had written. 'That's me when I was eight years old. One year older than you. I wasn't as pretty as you, was I?'

Charlotte contemplated the young girl a moment, entranced. 'You had really black hair.'

'Dark brown, yes.'

Frank's voice hailed from the kitchen. 'Time to get you home, lass.'

Violet closed the album. 'We'll get to the earlier photo-

Seeing George

graphs next time. Great-grandmother's side of the family came out from Ireland hundreds of years ago and they had very bad teeth.'

Charlotte giggled and blushed.

Violet put a finger to her lips before pointing toward the bookshelf. 'Lottie, one day when I'm not here anymore, those black books will belong to my friend, George. He is very nice. You can meet him when you go to his house to collect the diaries, because I want you to read them. All of them.'

'Did you write them?'

'Yes, and I want you to read about my life and everything in it. I've been lucky, Charlotte. I've had a wonderful life.'

'With secrets?'

Violet laughed and tucked a stray lock of blond hair behind her niece's little ear. 'With plenty of secrets.'

'I've got a pink diary at home.'

'You'll have to remind uncle Frank or your mother that I said you could read them because George will have them, okay?'

Frank's footsteps sounded along the hall.

'We could ask him now,' Charlotte suggested.

Violet shook her head.

'All right.' Her niece kissed her cheek and ran out of the room and collided into Frank's legs. She squealed as her uncle pretended to heave her up and over his shoulders.

'We'll be about quarter of an hour, Vi.'

She turned her face away from him.

· 28 ·

Frank called the hospital later that night. Violet had asked him not to visit unless they arranged it first. It would shake her up too much not to be able to leave with him. His voice was a treat though. She stood as close to the phone as possible and listened as he asked about her session with Dr Fornet.

She wanted to tell him that the open ward called Dr Fornet 'the vulture' because he liked picking over the bones of their failures. Kathleen had said his favourite word was 'why', and Gracie told Violet that all she had to do was keep answering the questions: even if what she said didn't make any sense. Violet had asked them what the signs were of someone getting better, but neither of them seemed to know.

But instead of talking about any of this, Violet told Frank she was getting used to things, that she felt more relaxed

Seeing George

than she had done in ages. This was true. The mess of work and George and lying to Frank and the meeting in Port Fairy were all remote in here.

'The only problem, according to Dr Fornet,' she said, 'is to do with you.'

There was a heavy silence, then Frank calmly asked her to explain. Violet tried, but fumbled her words. Said it had to do with him hiding anger and her shaping a dragon from it.

'I'd hardly call what happened at Port Fairy hiding my anger.'

'No.' The relief in her voice was immediate.

'And what's it got to do with seeing a damned dragon?'

'I don't know.' She felt disappointed because she'd broken the rule about saying 'I don't know,' but she really *didn't* know. It had made sense in Dr Fornet's office and she'd done nothing but think about it all day – winding herself up – and now Frank was pooh-poohing it.

'There's nothing wrong with you and me. Unless you think there is?'

'No. But Dr Fornet said –.'

'Well, he's just starting with you. You might have mixed up his words somehow, or maybe he's just wrong.'

She stared at the seamless wall. 'There are some other women here who think that I'm not crazy.' Too late she realised this was hardly a recommendation.

Frank breathed down the phone line. 'Violet, this wasn't

my idea. I'd hate for you to be spending time in there and end up worse off. Aside from giving you hare-brained ideas about what's wrong with you and I, has he said anything useful?'

'Well —.' But there was nothing to say.

'Have you talked about not being able to have children?'

She heard the fear and tension in his voice.

'Vi?'

'I'm not going crazy, Frank.'

He sighed.

She clutched the receiver to her ear and chin.

'I saw George today,' her husband said.

'You didn't do anything did you?'

Her husband sighed. 'I bloody wanted to take a swing at him, but for your sake I didn't. In the end I told him where you were though.'

'What?'

'He was all worked up, love, hanging around our letterbox, probably hoping you'd turn up.'

'You didn't have to tell him I was here, it's embarrassing,' said Violet hotly.

'I wanted him to know that you're making a concerted effort to sort out this hogwash.'

'Damn it, Frank, this is an awful day. One of the women I made friends with here started yelling last night and didn't stop, I can't get my head around what Dr Fornet's doing, and now this.'

'I thought you were relaxed?'

Seeing George

She stayed silent.

Frank tried to apologise. She let him go on for a good minute and then reminded him that their phonecalls while he was in Adelaide only agitated them both too. So, with some hesitancy, they decided that until he came to collect her on Friday night they wouldn't speak. After hanging up Violet wondered whether this wasn't a mistake.

She wandered down to the dining room and sat with Gracie – watching her pick up a pea and thread it onto her fork, then lick it. She wanted to slap the younger woman, so she returned to her room to knit and in the morning went to her next appointment with Dr Fornet without having any breakfast.

She repeated bits of the conversation she'd had with Frank, explaining that George really wasn't anything to do with her husband. Was quite a separate thing altogether.

Dr Fornet picked up his notepad. 'Let's go back to you and Frank not being able to have children. How long after you found out you couldn't have children did you meet George?'

She took a deep breath. 'Nearly three months, I think.'

'And how long have you been able to see George now?'

'About three months.'

'And at this point, the final trimester, you're debating the consequences of giving him up or keeping him. That's very interesting, don't you think?'

She stared at him.

'What does Frank feel about George, Violet?'

'He wants me to stop having anything to do with him.'

'He wants you all to himself. Very common in the first stages after pregnancy.'

'I'm not pregnant.'

'Not conventionally, no. But what if you gave birth to a vision?'

Violet looked down at her hands.

'I said what if you gave birth to a vision, Violet?'

'It's a vision that talks back and other people can see him.'

'No, they can't.'

Violet wanted to shield her face from this bald man. 'Frank can't have children,' she blurted.

'But you can.'

She hesitantly nodded.

'What does a dragon represent, Violet? Immortality?'

'He really is a dragon.'

Dr Fornet slowly closed his eyes to speak. 'We've reached the sticking point. Part of you is willing to know the truth – hence your decision to come here – but another part of you is resisting.'

Violet watched as his shiny pate began to sprout small drops of sweat under the lamp. As he pontificated, his head moved back and forth and soon she was quite mesmerised.

'So what do you think?' Dr Fornet said at length, opening his eyes.

Startled from her reverie, Violet nodded, but this didn't

Seeing George

appear to be the correct response, so she said, 'I'm sure I can try it.'

He nodded and closed his eyes again. After a minute or two of him not speaking, she stood and began to make her way toward the door.

'Don't forget to spend the necessary time with it,' Dr Fornet called out.

Violet shut his office door, feeling as though she were moving in a fog. She had no idea what Dr Fornet said and she really didn't care. She wandered down the corridor and into her room, where she kicked out the door catch and waited until the heavy wood swung shut. They didn't like the women to close their doors during the day.

Violet walked to the bed and lifted up the pillow. She doubled it over, then spread her legs and hoicked up her skirt. Staring out the window, she prodded the pillow up under her skirt, until the ends of it caught beneath her waistband. She smoothed her skirt down. Patted the mound. A real pregnant stomach would be heavier, of course, drag more on her back muscles and force her to walk a certain way.

She looked down.

The pillow mound was square and she couldn't quite alter it even by pulling the skirt material more tightly. It looked wrong. She pushed out the pillow and tossed it to the bed.

Violet chose a canvas walking shoe. Held it in the crook of her arm, close to her body, and tried to imagine a small face and delicate wisps of hair. A bit like her sister, Thelma, at birth.

Violet looked at her shoe. It didn't move, didn't cry. She dropped it and walked out the door.

Outside, a rash of daisy flowers covered the lawn. Violet pulled up a handful and plucked their yellow petals, letting them swirl to the grass. She walked further away from the building, further away from the flowerbeds, down the sloping lawn.

And then she found George.

He was standing beneath a line of Norfolk pine, looking very downcast despite the brilliant sun. She got such a fright she didn't notice the posy of wild flowers he was holding out toward her. But once she recovered herself she impulsively gave him a big hug.

'How did you get in?'

'I flew.'

She shot him a look of disbelief.

George leaned against the gruff bark of a pine. 'I'm quite light, Violet. Hollow bones like a bird. Besides, just because you haven't seen me fly doesn't mean it's not true.'

'But you can't just show up in here.' She could smell the lavender in the bouquet.

'I was worried they might have sorted your brain out.'

She frowned. 'Meaning what?'

'What are you doing in here? Why did you come here?'

'You know why, George.'

'Well, it hasn't worked.'

Seeing George

She stamped her feet. 'Stay out of it.'

He looked at her a moment — stunned — then threw back his head and laughed. Soon she was laughing too. It felt wonderful to laugh after the last twenty-four hours.

'You have to go.'

'No.' He reached out and grabbed her hand, smiling weakly. 'The Council has asked me never to see you again. They gave me until tonight to decide.'

She stared up at him, the head of her bouquet dropping toward the ground.

'That was their judgement; I won't even be allowed to see Peter anymore. I have to give you up, Violet, or they'll banish me for good.'

'Banish you?' The bees were humming as they settled into bobbing flower heads, the sun stroked her back, her hair. It seemed impossible that this could be happening on such a beautiful day. George couldn't go. She wouldn't let him go.

'I have to leave you or I have to leave them.'

'Stop saying it.'

'Don't let it end here, Violet.'

She continued looking at him, her eyes bright.

'We can make it different. Start somewhere new. Just the two of us.' He was looking down at her, openly, nakedly.

She shut her eyes. His hand felt so large over hers and the warm sun on her limbs made her feel dreamy. A plane droned high in the sky and small breezes licked about her neck and legs. Perhaps it would be simpler if she went somewhere else and started again.

When she was a child, she used to lie on the grass in the backyard and stare up at the sky that was blue and blue and blue. She had imagined everything under that sky. What it would be like to marry, to have children. It had felt limitless and infinite that sky — before her father died.

As she smiled up at the sun from behind closed eyes, Dr Fornet and Frank and Spatler & Smith and the women at the office became small black spots fading into that blue.

George tightened his grip on her hand and she swayed towards him. She could feel his muscles tense to support her, feel his tail coil along the ground, his eyes on her face. It was delightful to stand so still. To not be pulling her cardigan tighter, not be avoiding people's whispers, not worrying about her secrets from Frank. It was so easy here in the warm sun, in this quiet place.

'What should we do, Violet?'

'George —.' She was vaguely aware of him moving closer and she forced herself to open her eyes. The light flared in and he was just a black silhouette. She blinked and her eyes watered.

When he saw her squinting, blinded, he moved to block out the direct sun. Then she could see him again, but the breeze seemed a little colder. Even George's hand felt harsh against her skin.

She looked down, the grass a green blur. 'Please. Please don't ask me.'

'Violet —.'

Seeing George

Her heart made a large lump in her throat as she began to shake her head. 'He needs me,' she said.

George closed his eyes, and they stood as an unlikely statue for a long while.

· 29 ·

Only after Frank and Charlotte had left, did Violet notice the little yellow handmade card propped up on her stack of books. It was creased from being inside the young girl's pocket and had three texta-ed rainbows on the front with an emphasis on the red stripes. Inside it, her niece had drawn a big 'Thank you' and a picture of the brooch.

Violet dipped the card toward her face, shielding her eyes. So George had never been able to appreciate football or cricket. So he mostly spat out beer in his repeated attempts to drink the brewed alcohol. He had nevertheless talked with Frank about geography and the importance of magnetic fields. Spent hours arguing about whether fossils were fake or not. He'd been more than just Violet's confidante: he'd probably been the only real male friend Frank had had in the past twenty or so years. And if a child could

Seeing George

appreciate a gift, surely Frank was capable of appreciating what George had been for him? What was wrong with the man?

The back door slapped shut and she waited, card over her eyes, for her husband to come up to her bedroom. His boots travelled around the kitchen, into the lounge room and back again. Then nothing. Anger and frustration swelled her ribcage and Violet shoved the bedclothes away.

Frank didn't look up as she padded into the kitchen. The guts of the clock were strewn over a piece of newspaper in front of him and his large hands fiddled with the tiny gears.

'What's wrong with it?'

'Hands are sticking.'

'Well, do you have to pull the whole blinking thing to pieces at this hour?'

Frank blew dust from inside the clock, then flicked about the oscillating wheel with a tiny brush. He'd tried to explain it all to her once, but she hadn't the patience. She pulled at a chair until its legs scraped away from under the table, allowing her to sit.

'George thinks you can't see him anymore.'

Violet held her tongue.

'That what you told him, love?'

She reached out to sit Charlotte's card next to the exposed clockworks and Frank unclipped the gear train for the chime, letting it drop onto the newspaper. Then he used a fingertip to nudge it into parallel with some other stray apparatus.

'Not much use him coming around, is it?' he continued.

'Given that your friendship was based on him being a dragon. He said it was all right, you no longer seeing him that way, didn't he?' He paused to drip some dirty-coloured oil into the mechanism. 'Can never tell what's too much oil or not enough.'

Violet smacked her palm against the table top. 'How can you be so stupid, Frank? Of course I still see him as a dragon. I was just trying to figure out something that would satisfy you.'

He glanced at her briefly, then concentrated on realigning the gears. 'I guess that's your decision then.'

'My decision? If it's my decision I'll have you know that I won't stop seeing him.'

'I think you have to.'

'I don't have to do anything. I'm not six years old.' Her mouth felt dry and her heart raced. 'Damn it, Frank, George doesn't have anyone else.'

'That's my point.'

'Don't patronise me. That's what you hate, what you've always hated. I can't believe it's come to this and I never thought I'd say it, but you're a jealous, cruel old man and I'm sorry I love you.'

Frank fitted the clock face over the top of the golden twists of metal, then looked at her.

'Violet, I won't last long after you die. Wouldn't want to. That's what marriage is. But you've said dragons are around a long time and he won't let you go. Can't let you go. Hasn't fifty-odd years proved that?'

Seeing George

'So?'

'So say goodbye to him and give him the chance to love someone else.'

Violet felt like she'd been slapped in the chest. She dropped her head and blinked hard, breathed hard. Couldn't think. Couldn't form a single thought as everything she'd been feeling, all the pent-up emotion, came to a standstill.

She wanted to tell her husband not to pretend he was doing this for George's sake. He wasn't. He couldn't be. But different words burst from her mouth: 'I'm going to die. I'm going to die, Frank.'

And George would be left behind. And if she didn't say goodbye before she died, if she didn't insist upon it, George would never say goodbye to her. Never let her go. She had it all backwards. It was she and George who refused to see, not Frank. And she'd muddled it further with the dress-ups. Pretending to be younger and still healthy. Her eyes filmed.

'I've been so careless.'

'No, you haven't, love. Not yet.'

Frank's hands were useless on the newspaper now, but his voice was strong and full of compassion. She looked up. Saw him across the table from her, blurry at first, emerging through her tears, his blue eyes shining.

She trembled. Wanted to cover the pinking spot on her head, wanted to hide her shaking hands, wanted to be the beautiful young woman she had once been for her husband. But that was the grace of their marriage: that they'd accepted each other as was.

She pulled another crumpled tissue from her pocket, mopping under her chin where most of her tears were gathering. 'I knew you cared about George.'

Her husband rolled his eyes. 'I'll have a hard enough time taking care of myself without worrying about him too, is all.'

'Oh, Frank.' Violet put a hand to her chest, her heart didn't have to pound so much now. 'Those horrid things I said. Why didn't you just tell me?'

He looked at her and grinned.

'I would have listened.'

Frank began laughing.

'I would.' But she couldn't help smiling too. Then her tears fell again. 'I'm a stupid old lady.'

'You are my lovely wife.'

He stood and bent over the table to kiss her gently on the lips. Then he grabbed the clock and turned to drag it down the wall until it caught on the nail. She watched his large, capable hands and the way his greying hair stubbornly refused to lie smooth. Looked at his mouth. Damned mouth that barely spoke, and then when it did –. She was startled into laughing as the newly sprung clock chimed.

Frank set to adjusting it now that the trial had worked, and Violet eased her chair back from the table. The day wasn't quite over yet.

· 30 ·

Violet sat on her bed, hands knitted together in her lap. She'd not gone to dinner when the bell sounded. Hadn't eaten for a whole day now and had no desire to: is this what it was like for Gracie?

Her hands raked through her knotted hair in an attempt to tidy herself. But in the next minute she dropped her head. She kept losing the most important things. Her father, the chance to have children, George.

It was taking too much energy to sit up so she let herself sink onto the bed, shielding her eyes from the fluorescent lights.

'Violet?'

She startled and, looking towards the door, had to blink rapidly to bring him into focus. 'What are you doing?'

'What are *you* doing?' Frank took off his hat and strode to her suitcase, hurling it up onto the dresser and popping the locks.

Violet struggled to sit up, to look composed. She watched as her husband pulled out the dresser drawers, and emptied the blouses and slips into the suitcase.

'Frank, I can't just –.'

'Yes, you can, love. We've made a mistake. Same damn mistake we've been making ever since we got married.'

'Excuse me.' It was Mrs Staynor, all white uniform in the doorway.

Violet shuffled off the bed and stood uncertainly. But Frank kept on; swept up the two pair of shoes and dropped them on top of the clothes. His neck muscles tensed, but otherwise he betrayed no sign that he knew the nurse was there.

Mrs Staynor put a hand to her chest. 'We don't encourage this kind of leave-taking, Mr Rolden. We find it does the patient no good and unsettles everyone else.'

Violet tried to lay a restraining hand on Frank's arm, but he continued his determined packing of all her belongings. He even stripped back the bed linen and checked under the pillow. Violet looked blankly toward the nurse, but the large figure had disappeared.

'George came to see me.'

Frank stopped and held out his large brown hands. 'Are you ready?'

She bowed her head and sniffed, trying to stop her nose from running. He freed a hand to tilt up her chin, wiped her nose with his sleeve and repeated the question. She nodded, overwhelmed by his presence.

Seeing George

'Can I say goodbye to someone?'

Frank ushered her out the door and stood by while she went into Kathleen's room. She had heard the other women talking about her friend's return to open ward as they walked to dinner. But she hadn't the energy to go and visit her earlier.

When she opened the door she saw Kathleen lying stiffly in bed, her face lined and tired.

'I only missed two tablets. Only two,' she murmured when she saw Violet.

Violet came up closer and crouched down beside Kathleen, smoothing some stray red hair across her forehead. 'I'm going home,' Violet whispered.

Kathleen's eyes fluttered open and she smiled at the ceiling before her lids fell again. 'I hear voices,' she said, 'and they aren't my voices.'

Violet didn't know how to respond.

'No one else can hear the voices,' Kathleen said, opening her eyes again. 'It's not like George.'

Violet looked into Kathleen's eyes, then she took her friend's hand and squeezed it. 'Thank you,' she said.

Frank's jaw was clenched when Violet emerged from the room and he took her hand, pulling her toward reception. But his haste panicked Violet. She wrenched her hand from his and collapsed against the wall.

'I don't want to go yet.'

Her husband jiggled the suitcase handle, but spoke very calmly. 'We can do this.'

'I see a dragon, Frank, and I don't want to give him up.'
'I know.'

She looked down at his boots. At the suspended suitcase. At his lovely hands.

'We have to handle it together, Vi. That's what marriage is.'

'Violet?' Dr Fornet strode through the large corridor doors, looking naked without his white coat. Mrs Staynor was only a few steps behind.

Frank swung his back to the advancing pair, facing Violet. 'Me running away to Adelaide as soon as we had our first major blow, you coming here with our second, well, that was all wrong. We're supposed to stand side by side and face what comes. We promised that.'

Violet smoothed her skirt.

Drawing level with them, Dr Fornet rubbed a hand over his bald head. 'Why don't we move down to my office and talk.'

Violet shook her head.

'We need to calm down,' the doctor said.

'I saw George today.'

Dr Fornet spread his hands and looked at Frank. 'Well, there you are then, you see? The chap is nowhere about, yet Violet saw him. Isn't that proof —.'

'He came into the hospital to see me.'

'That's against protocol.'

Violet shifted her weight from one leg to the other, impatient.

Seeing George

'I don't know what you're expecting if you won't stick to the treatment regime,' Dr Fornet continued.

Frank, still acknowledging only Violet, said, 'I'll get to know George if I have to.'

She looked away. 'He's gone, I think.'

'He's gone nowhere. I might not know much about him, but I know that. Just tell me about us.'

She looked up at him and let the tears come. 'We can't have children.'

He nodded, smiling sadly at her.

Mrs Staynor reached out to touch her arm. 'Please Mrs Rolden, if you'll just see out the week.'

'You only need to know one thing, Vi.' Frank held out his free hand. 'I love you more than George does.'

She opened her mouth to deny what he was implying, when Dr Fornet tried to reach for the suitcase and Frank swung it away from him, causing the tall man to lurch forward, almost fall. Violet suddenly grabbed her husband's free hand, and ran with him past the reception desk toward the early evening light.

· 31 ·

As she made her way towards the phone, Violet wiped away the drying tears on her cheeks. She didn't want to stop seeing George. It hurt in the middle of her stomach. But Frank was right: telling him why would only make him refuse. She leaned against the wall to keep her balance, her fingers shaking as she pressed the familiar numbers.

'Hello, George speaking.'

'I thought you might have given up sounding so formal.'

A long pause. A pause filled with unspoken emotion. 'I don't like giving things up, Violet.'

'I wrote about us, George.'

'Beg your pardon?'

'I knew I couldn't rely on you to get any writing done.' She tried to sound snippy. 'So I kept diaries. And I'm sending them to you. I've told my niece she can read them

Seeing George

one day, but I want them to belong to you.'

His voice was very sober. 'I might enjoy that.'

Violet looked down at the carpet runner. Her back ached. 'She could even visit you.'

'Who?'

'Charlotte. My niece.'

There was more silence on the other end of the line.

'She can walk in the park with you, George.'

'I don't want a substitute.'

'No, she's not —.' Violet pressed a shaking hand to her mouth for a moment. 'She's my niece. I love her and I would like someone to tell her about me, that's all. She's a lot like me, but she's only a child and her memory won't be much, so when the time comes —.'

'Violet —.'

She raised her voice, 'When the time comes you could help her to see me. She might not understand about death, George, she might not understand and you could help her.'

There was a muffled sound and then he said, 'Thank you.'

Violet nodded to herself and the tears came hot on her cheeks, but she kept her voice steady. 'I'd best get out of this draught.' Then she hesitated, not wanting to say the words sticking in the back of her throat.

In the end, he spoke them for her. 'Goodbye, Violet.'

She tried to answer, but he hung up the phone straight away — perhaps so he wouldn't have to hear her. She cradled the receiver and said the words anyway.

'Goodbye, George.'

When she put down the phone she rested a moment against the hallway table, not quite sure how she felt. Seasick. She brushed a hand over her stomach. He'd be all right. Just take him a bit to adjust. Lovely dragon. Maybe he would go to Ireland now.

From the kitchen a glowing beacon of reflected light shone against the hallway wall. She set her chin and followed it back to Frank.

He'd left the kettle on and it was just getting rowdy. She sat, propping her head up with her hand. The flywire door banged when her husband returned from the yard and after using his elbow to turn off the gas, he washed his hands at the sink, although it barely reduced Gretel's meaty smell as the dog had slobbered all over his boots and trouser cuffs.

'I thought I heard a cricket just now,' he said. 'Getting late in the season for a cricket.'

Violet tried to reply and couldn't. Had to let her breath catch up, so just watched instead. Frank was wiping his wet hands against his trousers and poking around in the back of the pantry to get at the tin of shortbreads.

Unwrapping the plastic seal, he pushed the tin toward her so she could arrange a couple of biscuits on a side plate. The tea had brewed and he poured out two cups, sitting one in front of his wife.

Then he sat and they held hands across the kitchen table, Violet's small fingers resting in his large, callused

Seeing George

palms. They were content to be still for a while, listening to each other's breath and the echoing tick of the newly fixed clock. It was only sheer exhaustion that roused them.

'You going to drink your tea?'

Frank shook his head. 'I'm as tired as a tired thing.'

'Hop into bed then.'

He smiled. But neither of them wanted to break the quiet pleasure just yet. Violet pulled at a thread on her husband's shirt cuff, and under the table Frank stretched his long legs.

'Poor little cricket,' she said absently, as though just remembering. 'Out there madly rubbing his legs together. All he wants is someone to hear his music.'

'Someone will, love.'

Violet placed a hand on her husband's cheek. And they stayed sitting at the small table, waiting for the clock to tell them the late hour.

Epilogue

I wrapped the diaries in paper. They are a present, whether she recognises it or not. When I open the door, I meet the little one on the porch. She is facing the other way, isn't sure about being here – even though her mother's arm around her tries for social etiquette. That's all right. I don't know whether I want her here either.

Her hair is blond. Swings in sheets. She has a book tucked under her arm. In her back pocket is a ballpoint pen. I can see her ankles. She is short and smells like polished cedar floorboards, like dandelion tea.

I'm not sure why she's here and she's not sure why she's here and when she finally turns to look at me her expression is a stab of memory.

Acknowledgements

There are a number of people who made this book a joy to write. Thank you to David and Jasmin Topchian and their 'scholarship fund' for keeping me in bread and socks. Thank you to my mother, Diana Austin, for not minding that I didn't pay rent. Thank you to Matthew Stipanov and Clive Mitchell – my fellow partners in the Six Week Writing Challenge. Thank you to Imelda's Kitchen Table Writing Group for reading the entire work in serial form. Thank you to Sally Rippin who is sheer inspiration. Thank you to my brother, Daniel Austin, for his honesty and editing. Thank you to my editor, Nadine Davidoff, for believing that this book 'should be out there' and then making sure it was by giving me such precise direction. Thank you to all family and friends who championed me. And thank you most of all to the lovely Adam Simon, for giving me the freedom and encouragement to write when neither of us were sure such a thing was a good idea.